Boeing
Aircraft
Cutaways

Boeing
Aircraft
Cutaways

The History of Boeing Aircraft Company

Mike Badrocke & Bill Gunston

OSPREY
AVIATION

Contents

First published in Great Britain in 1998 by Osprey Publishing, Elms Court, Chapel Way, Botley, Oxford OX2 9LP

Main text by Bill Gunston
Captions provided by Dennis Baldry
Editor: Shaun Barrington
Design Manager: Mike Moule
Page layout: Mark Holt
Index: Janet Dudley

ISBN 1 85532 785 6

Printed in Hong Kong

98 99 00 01 02 10 9 8 7 6 5 4 3 2 1

Picture credits: photographs from the archives of Michael O'Leary. With grateful thanks to Philip Jarrett and Hugh Cowin for additional images. Colour section photography by Robbie Shaw, Mike Vines and John Ailes.

For a catalogue of all books published by Osprey Aviation please write to:
The Marketing Manager
Osprey Publishing Ltd, P.O. Box 140, Wellingborough, Northants NN8 4ZA, United Kingdom

Front of jacket, above left: **B-52D on flight-test near Wichita in the mid-1960s wearing SE Asia camouflage.**

Front of jacket, lower left: **Virgin Atlantic Airways' 747-238B** *Boston Belle* **(G-VJFK) was formerly operated by Qantas.**

Rear of jacket, top left: **Converted from a C-4, this 1917-vintage C-11 seaplane trainer was built for a Mr Hammondton of Bremerton, Washington.**

Rear of jacket, bottom left: **American Airlines' 707-123B pictured in 1961 with immaculate flight attendants.**

Rear of jacket, bottom right: **Double-bubble: fitting out the interior of a C-97 Stratofreighter.**

Half title page: **A 1966 portrait of William E. Boeing with the Model 1A, taken during celebrations to mark the company's 50th anniversary.**

Title page: **Hound Dog-armed B-52F, the final Stratofortress delivered from the Seattle production line.**

Opposite: **Apparently influenced by Gen. Billy Mitchell, in 1921 Army engineer I. M. Laddon created the Boeing GA-X 'armoured attack triplane' at McCook (Wright) Field in Dayton, Ohio. Also known as the GA-1, ten were built before the Army realized that the extra burden of carrying armour plate on the engine nacelles and lower fuselage merely made the aircraft a slightly better protected sitting duck.**

INTRODUCTION

William E. "Bill" Boeing was born in Detroit on 1 October 1881. He was the son of a timber merchant, and after graduating from Yale became one himself, but in Seattle, chief city of the lumber state of Washington. After a ride in a Curtiss seaplane in July 1914 he studied aircraft, and decided that he was unimpressed by the types on offer. In 1915 he said to his friend Cdr George Conrad Westervelt, USN, "I think we could build a better one".

Boeing learned to fly, whilst constructing a large building on offshore piling at the foot of Roanoke St, on the east shore of Lake Union in central Seattle. The building had three bays, one of which was a hangar where Boeing kept a Martin seaplane which he had bought in order to study the best contemporary aero technology. The rest of the space was fitted out as a workshop. Here Boeing assembled a team of 21, who built two examples of their first product, a seaplane called the B&W.

Westervelt (the "W") had the twin pontoons (floats) built in the Navy shipyard on Puget Sound, but was posted to the East Coast just as the first B&W was about to fly. Now on his own, Boeing decided to go into serious business as a planemaker. On 15 July 1916 the Pacific Aero Products Co was incorporated, with Boeing as President, his cousin E. N. Gott as Vice-President and J. C. Foley as Secretary. Two weeks later, on the 29th, their firstborn made a successful maiden flight. Though its linen covering was made taut by transparent dope, it was named *Bluebird*.

The first few aircraft were very like *Bluebird*, thoroughly practical machines marred only by unreliable engines. They were made in ones and twos, but in April 1917 the US entered the War and the Navy ordered a batch of 50. On 26 April Boeing changed the company's name to the Boeing Airplane Co. It expanded into the E W Heath Shipyard on the Duwamish River, south of Seattle, occupying a building called (because of its colour) the Red Barn. Here, before the Armistice of November 1918, Boeing completed 25 Curtiss HS-2L flying boats, of an original order for 50.

Boeing began with seaplanes. This elegant B&W of 1916 is about to slip gently into the water.

Wholesale cancellations followed the Armistice, so Boeing built everything from speedboats to furniture. Then in early 1920 the Army sought bids for 200 Thomas-Morse Scouts (single-seat fighters). These had been designed in 1918 by an established planemaker of Ithaca, New York, but it was standard practice for the Army and Navy to put the work out to tender and place the bulk order with the lowest bidder. While Thomas-Morse received a contract for 50, Boeing's bid of $1,448,000 won the main contract for 200 of the improved MB-3A version. Though geographically a long way from the other American aircraft firms, in 1920-25 the Seattle company also received contracts for the remanufacture of 354 DH-4 aircraft. The first modification was to interchange the pilot's cockpit and fuel tank, and the second was to replace the wooden-framed fuselage by a completely new one made of welded steel tube.

This work ensured the survival of Boeing as a planemaker, and also enabled it to move up into the field of high-performance landplanes. For 15 years, from 1921, Boeing was one of the world's major producers of fighters, for the Army, Navy and foreign customers. Closely related aircraft were used for observation, bombing, training and, especially, for carrying mail. Virtually all were landplanes, taken for testing either

Trailblazer. A bespectacled William E. Boeing, pictured on 3 March 1919.

to Sand Point Naval Air Station, about ten miles away, or to the Army's Camp Lewis, which was 50 miles away. This inconvenience was rectified by the building in 1928 of Boeing Field, which was also the airport for King County.

On 7 July 1925 Boeing flew the first new type with a Model number, 40 (numbers 1 to 39 were then assigned to the previous designs). The Model 40 was a Liberty-engined mailplane, and from it stemmed a succession of mailplanes that not only made Boeing leader in this field but also got it into the air-carrier business (see the Boeing 40 story).

By 1928 Boeing had delivered 268 aircraft, and grown to have a payroll of 800. The industry expected the Boeing air-mail route (Chicago to San Francisco) quickly to fail, because of the company's astonishingly low bid. Instead it prospered, Boeing explaining that by using Pratt & Whitney engines he was carrying mail instead of radiators and water. He began taking over other airlines, and began talks – initially with Frederick B. Rentschler of Pratt & Whitney – about industrial mergers.

The result was a huge conglomerate called United Aircraft and Transport Corporation. In 1928 this embraced Boeing and its subsidiary Hamilton Metalplane, Boeing Air Transport

The Model 5 seaplane trainer was produced in series for the Navy (designated C-650 through C-699).

In January 1934 the P-26A 'Peashooter' became the first monoplane pursuit ship to serve with the USAAC. Its all-metal construction was another first.

Pictured on 11 February 1952, the battle-hardened crew of *Max Effort*, a B-29 of the 19th BG, record 100,000 tons of bombs dropped in Korea. Superforts flew 21,000 sorties.

and its own subsidiary Pacific Air Transport, and the Boeing School of Aeronautics, Pratt & Whitney Aircraft and Chance Vought Aircraft. In 1929 it added Sikorsky, Stearman, Hamilton Aero (a propeller firm, which then merged with Standard Steel Propeller to form Hamilton Standard) and the airlines of Varney and National Air Transport. In 1930 the air carriers were all merged, to form United Air Lines. Outside this vast group, because it was part-Canadian, was the 1929 Boeing Aircraft of Canada.

On 8 February 1933 Boeing flew the first Model 247, the world's first modern all-metal stressed-skin multi-engined transport monoplane with retractable landing gear. Six months later it formed Boeing Aircraft Co as its manufacturing subsidiary.

In 1934 Bill Boeing, Chairman of the UATC board, was awarded the Daniel Guggenheim medal "for pioneering and

achievement in aircraft manufacturing and transportation". He was then told that by doing this he was breaking the law. The 1934 Air Mail Act made it illegal for any one company or conglomerate both to make and also operate aircraft. Accordingly, the airlines were hived off, United Aircraft Corporation was formed to manage the East Coast manufacturing firms, and Boeing went its own way, together with its Kansas subsidiary Stearman. Boeing himself retired to his yacht, but returned in World War 2 as an advisor, and on 14 May 1954 was delighted to attend the rollout of a jet transport, the Model 367-80, but better known as the prototype 707.

Later in 1934 Boeing took the first of what were to be several crucial decisions which risked more than the net worth of the company by building the prototype of the Model 299, a four-engined bomber which a newsman called the Flying Fortress. This first flew

on 28 July 1935. From then on, Boeing has been synonymous with large aircraft, which at first included flying boats (boat-type seaplanes). Major products have included the B-17, B-29/B-50, C-97/Stratocruiser, B-47, B-52 and, above all, the 367-80, from which stemmed the KC-135, which in turn led not only to many other C-135s but also the 707, 727, 737, 747, 757, 767 and 777.

On the last day of 1947 Boeing Aircraft merged into its parent, the Boeing Airplane Co. In the 1950s Boeing diversified

The arms race was in full swing when in October 1954 Boeing rolled out the 1,000th Stratojet from Wichita. This is a B-47E, the main production model, of which more than 1,400 were built. Unlike its successor the B-47 never dropped a bomb in anger, but during the 1962 Cuban missile crisis SAC's order of battle listed approximately 1,800 Stratojets, a force which was hugely more powerful than the Soviet bomber fleet.

into gas-turbine engines, ballistic missiles, hydrofoil ships and spacecraft, so in May 1961 it changed its name to The Boeing Company.

The huge global success of the big jets has made Boeing rich. In 1960 it purchased the Philadelphia helicopter firm Vertol, today called Boeing Helicopters. In 1996, for $3.1 billion, it purchased the former North American Aviation, part of the huge Rockwell Aerospace and Defense, returning it to its previous name as Boeing North American. In August 1997 it spent about $16 billion adding the even bigger McDonnell Douglas.

It wanted this company principally for its defence and space business, but the MD-11 is considered to have prospects as a freighter and the MD-95 is being aggressively continued as the Boeing 717 (see note below). The takeover has also made the F/A-18 Hornet family and the T-45 Hawk Boeing products. Over the years Boeing never lost sight of fighters – once its chief product – and, together with the Hornet, the X-32 Joint Strike Fighter could lead to Boeing becoming once again a major player in this field.

Painted in company livery, the 'Dash 80' poses for a photocall near Mt. Rainier. When the new jetliner was announced Boeing called it the Model 707 and the rest is bigger than history.

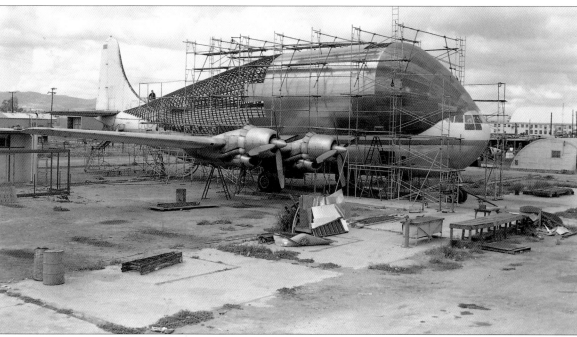

Several Stratoliners and Stratofreighters gained a new lease of life with Aero Spacelines, which from 1962 used its 'Guppy' conversions to ferry Saturn rocket components for NASA's Apollo programme.

INTRODUCTION

Clipper Golden Eagle, a 747-100F freighter, is proclaimed as the 200th Boeing jetliner for PanAm. By the late 1970s its fleet included 45 'Jumbos'. The 747 was designed for cargo.

Today, though huge orders are stretching Boeing Commercial Airplane Group to the limit, the company as a whole is in fact slimming down from a recent peak of over 200,000 employees worldwide. Further major acquisitions are unlikely, but we certainly have not seen the last of global linkages to assist not only marketing but also manufacture. Except for the Boeing 717, the following pages do not include previous Rockwell or McDonnell Douglas aircraft, but do feature the Osprey tilt-rotor aircraft, produced jointly with Bell, and the Comanche helicopter, produced jointly with Sikorsky.

Model numbers

As noted, in 1925 it occurred to Boeing to create a logical system of Model numbers. The main type then being designed was called Model 40, because research showed that it could be preceded by 39 others. The numbers continued into the 400s, some numbers being used for numerous versions, such as 299 for all B-17s, 367 for all

C-97s, 450 for all B-47s and 464 for all B-52s. During the 400 series in the 1950s Boeing began to create products other than aircraft, and the decision was taken to reserve 500-599 for gas-turbine engines and 600-699 for missiles. Thus, aircraft numbers began again at 700. By the time the long succession of studies for a jet transport – all given the number 367 with a suffix numeral – had resulted in a prototype being built, the true numbers had reached 706. Accordingly, the first type of jet transport was the 707. The next, the production tanker, happened to be the 717. The next was the 720, but the global impact of the 707 was suddenly appreciated as an enormous marketing advantage, far more important than a name. Thus, Boeing deliberately called each subsequent commercial jet the 727, 737, 747, 757, 767 and 777, and the MD-95 is now being marketed as the 717, even though this number still appears on many thousands of publications supporting the KC-135.

Note: Gallons are Imperial (1 Imp gal = 1.2 US gal) unless otherwise stated.

In 1965 Boeing was close to launching the 747 with double passenger decks - the configuration today favoured by arch-rival Airbus Industrie for its giant A3XX.

EARLY MODELS

ON THE SKIDS

Much later given the designation Model 1, Boeing's first product was a two-bay biplane whose only drawback was the unreliability of its 125hp Hall-Scott A-5 six-cylinder water-cooled engine. The structure was mainly spruce, with wire bracing and covering of doped linen fabric. Features included two floats with a small protective float under the tail, and dual controls in tandem cockpits. Two were built, and in 1918 both were sold to New Zealand, where – nobody having the slightest idea they might be historically important – they were eventually scrapped. In 1966 Boeing built a replica with a modern Avco Lycoming engine, called Model 1A.

The Models 2 and 3 had 100hp Hall-Scott engines, wings with considerable stagger and dihedral, a small fin ahead of the rudder, and elevators alone without a tailplane (horizontal stabilizer). The Model 4, originally known as the EA, was a landplane, two of which

The B&W was a collaborative effort. Undoubtedly a sound design, its performance was hampered by a temperamental powerplant.

Taken in August 1918, this view of a Model 2 emphasises its pronounced wing stagger.

DATA FOR MODEL 1:

Span	52ft 0in (15.85m)
Length overall	31ft 2in (9.47m)
Wing area	580 sq ft (53.9m²)
Weight empty	2,100lb (953kg)
Maximum loaded	2,800lb (1,270kg)
Cruising speed	67mph (108km/h)
Range	320 miles (515km)

The Model 3 (designated C-5 and C-6 by the Navy) inherited the wing stagger and prominent radiators of its predecessor. Mr Boeing's Martin is behind.

Painted and ready, the build quality of this Navy Model 5 trainer seaplane is consistent with the Red Barn protecting it.

were built for for the Army. Powered by a 100hp Curtiss V-8, they had side-by-side dual controls, and with a maximum speed of 67mph were the slowest Boeings ever built. The Model 5 was the first series production Boeing, 50 of these 100hp Hall-Scott trainer seaplanes being delivered. The Model 6, originally called the B-1, was a small flying boat of 1919, powered by a 200hp Hall-Scott L-6 (in effect half a Liberty 12) which was later replaced by a 400hp Liberty. It seated a pilot in the bow and two passengers side-by-side just behind him. It still exists, in the Seattle Museum of History and Industry (not the same as the Museum of Flight). The Model 7 was a lighter version with a 130hp Hall-Scott, with all three seats in a single three-cornered cockpit.

The Model 8 of 1920 was a landplane powered by a 200hp Hall-Scott, the wing and horizontal tail being almost identical to those of the Model 7. It set a fashion that became virtually standard through the 1920s in seating the pilot immediately behind side-by-side passengers (or, in mailplanes, the mailbags).

Through the 1920s Boeing built or rebuilt many aircraft designed elsewhere, notably at the Naval Aircraft Factory or by the Army at McCook Field.

BIPLANE PURSUITS

WASP SUCCESS

Mr Boeing never lost his "We can build a better airplane" outlook. Having suffered from the wooden construction of the MB-3A, his firm studied alternative methods and in 1921 even sent engineers to the principal fighter manufacturers in Europe. Making an airframe of aluminium alloys still appeared too risky, and the conclusion was that for the time being the best answer was a steel-tube fuselage and vertical tail, all made by arc welding in accurate jigs, and wooden wings with a box spar having mahogany webs and spruce flanges, the struts all being seamless steel tubes of streamline section.

In 1922 Boeing went ahead using their own money on the prototype Model 15, to be powered by a 300hp Wright-Hispano, as fitted to the MB-3A. The Army agreed to furnish the engine, and the armament of twin 0.30in guns ahead of the windscreen, with breeches accessible to the pilot.

In 1928 the Army accepted 16 PW-9Ds with aerodynamically balanced rudders (introduced on the Navy FB-3), improved brakes and engine radiator installation.

Before construction began, the 435hp Curtiss D-12 engine became available, and this was installed with the water-cooling radiator beneath the engine in a short duct. The Army was so impressed by what became known as the "tunnel radiator" that it asked Curtiss to adopt it, as a result of which the two firms battled for fighter contracts throughout the biplane era.

The first Model 15, originally known only by its Army designation XPW-9 (experimental pursuit, water-cooled, 9th type), made its first flight on 2 June 1923. It led to a long succession of Army PW-9 models and Navy fighters designated FB-1 to FB-6. Browning-gun armament comprised two 0.30in or, much

Equipped with lights on the lower wingtips, in 1923 this MB-3A (left) served with the 43rd Aero Sqn at Kelly Field, Texas.

The pugnacious P-12 as delivered in 1929. Subsequent models came without the streamlined fairings behind the nine cylinders, most having Townend-ring cowls to increase thrust.

more often, one 0.30in and one heavy 0.50in, and there was usually provision for two 122lb (55kg) or five 25lb (11.3kg) bombs. While the Army stuck to the D-12 engine, the Navy FB-3 and FB-5 had massive 510 or 520hp Packard engines and the FB-4 had a 450hp Wright aircooled radial.

The Wright engine proved unsatisfactory, and in early 1926 the Navy had it replaced by the product of a new company, the Pratt & Whitney R-1340 Wasp. Though initially rated at only 400 hp, it drove the fighter at the same speed as before, with a saving in weight of 278lb (126kg) and about 15 per cent in fuel burn, giving roughly 15 per cent longer range. Boeing later received Navy orders for 32 F2B-1 and 73 F3B-1 fighters powered by the Wasp, the F3B introducing an all-metal tail with a skin of corrugated aluminium.

Boeing carefully assembled numerous detail improvements conceived during experience

DATA FOR THE PW-9:

Span	**32ft 0in (9.75m)**
Length overall	**23ft 5in (7.14m)**
Wing area	**260 sq ft (24.15m²)**
Weight empty	**1,936lb (878kg)**
Gross weight	**3,120lb (1,415kg)**
Maximum speed	**159mph (256km/h)**
Initial climb	**1,445ft (440m)/min**
Range	**390 miles (628km)**

DATA FOR THE P-12F:

Span	**30ft 0in (9.14m)**
Length	**20ft 5in (6.22m)**
Wing area	**236.3 sq ft (21.95m²).**
Weight empty	**2,035lb (923kg)**
Gross weight	**2,726lb (1,236.5kg).**
Maximum speed	**195mph (314km/h)** *at 10,000ft (3,050m)*
Initial climb	**1,784ft (544m)/min**
Range	**300 miles (483km)**

with these Army and Navy pursuits, and combined them all in the Navy-owned Model 83, first flown on 25 June 1928. Structurally it broke little new ground, though the fuselage was shorter, rather hump-backed (giving the pilot a better view) and made of steel tube ahead of the cockpit and square-section aluminium-alloy tubing behind. The wings were untapered, and the corrugated-skin tail was neater, and the horizontal tail much larger.

The timing was perfect, and before biplanes began to look passé in the mid-1930s, Boeing delivered 586 of the improved types, the Army versions being designated P-12 to XP-12L and the Navy variants F4B to F4B-4A. Several were civil-registered, including a special two-seater built for Howard Hughes. Almost all had Wasp engines, of 450 or, more often, 500hp. Some of the engines were geared and/or supercharged, and the later models had a Townend-ring cowl. In 1930 Boeing built two parasol-monoplane prototypes, the Model 202 (XP-15) for the Army and Model 205 (XF5B-1) for the Navy. The totally different P-26 is described later.

Boeing F4B-4

1 Antenna mounting post
2 Upper fabric-covered wing panel
3 Starboard aileron
4 Interplane struts
5 Fabric-covered lower wing panel
6 Starboard lower navigation light
7 Tie-down shackle
8 Two-bladed fixed pitch metal propeller
9 Starboard mainwheel
10 Wheel brake, cable-operated
11 Split axle
12 Axle mounting V-struts
13 Faired shock absorber strut
14 Starboard underwing bomb rack
15 Townend ring engine cowling
16 Engine oil sump
17 Face plate fairing
18 Propeller hub
19 Cooling air vents, closed
20 Pratt & Whitney R-1340-16 nine-cylinder radial engine

21 Bayonet-type exhaust stubs, most aircraft later fitted with exhaust collector ring
22 Carburettor
23 Exhaust stub to carburettor heater
24 Mainwheel shock absorber strut attachment
25 Oil tank
26 Carburettor air intake
27 Engine hand-cranking adaptor

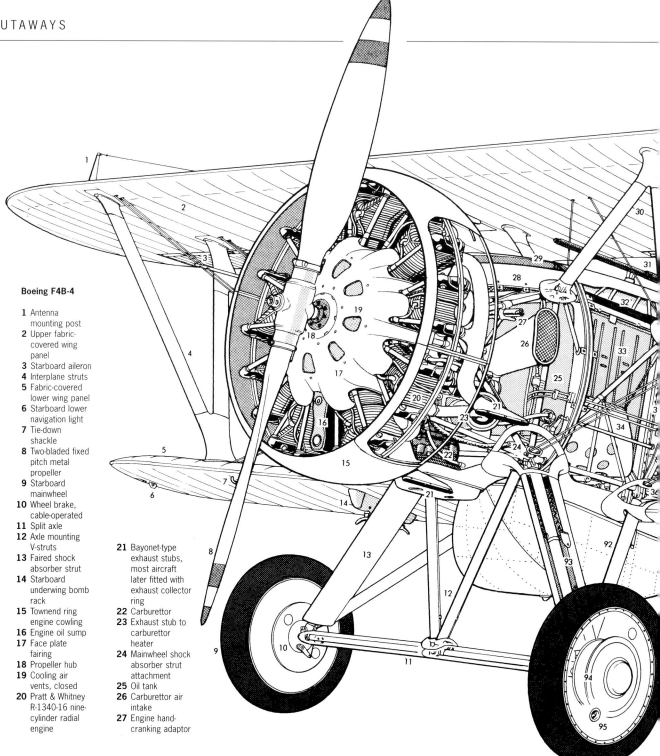

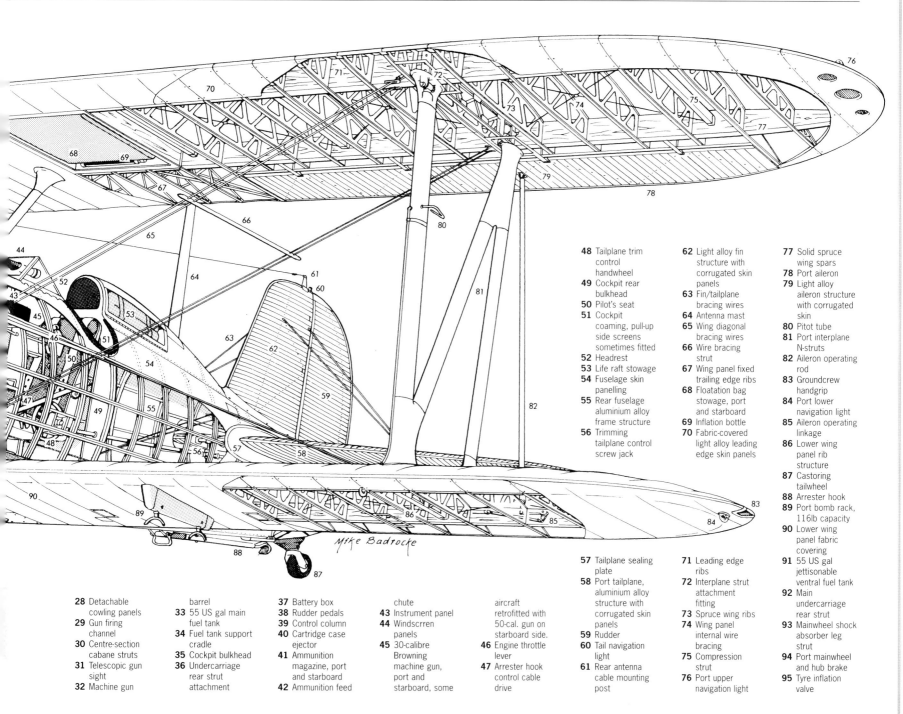

48 Tailplane trim control handwheel
49 Cockpit rear bulkhead
50 Pilot's seat
51 Cockpit coaming, pull-up side screens sometimes fitted
52 Headrest
53 Life raft stowage
54 Fuselage skin panelling
55 Rear fuselage aluminium alloy frame structure
56 Trimming tailplane control screw jack

62 Light alloy fin structure with corrugated skin panels
63 Fin/tailplane bracing wires
64 Antenna mast
65 Wing diagonal bracing wires
66 Wire bracing strut
67 Wing panel fixed trailing edge ribs
68 Floatation bag stowage, port and starboard
69 Inflation bottle
70 Fabric-covered light alloy leading edge skin panels

77 Solid spruce wing spars
78 Port aileron
79 Light alloy aileron structure with corrugated skin
80 Pitot tube
81 Port interplane N-struts
82 Aileron operating rod
83 Groundcrew handgrip
84 Port lower navigation light
85 Aileron operating linkage
86 Lower wing panel rib structure
87 Castoring tailwheel
88 Arrester hook
89 Port bomb rack, 116lb capacity
90 Lower wing panel fabric covering
91 55 US gal jettisonable ventral fuel tank
92 Main undercarriage rear strut
93 Mainwheel shock absorber leg strut
94 Port mainwheel and hub brake
95 Tyre inflation valve

57 Tailplane sealing plate
58 Port tailplane, aluminium alloy structure with corrugated skin panels
59 Rudder
60 Tail navigation light
61 Rear antenna cable mounting post

71 Leading edge ribs
72 Interplane strut attachment fitting
73 Spruce wing ribs
74 Wing panel internal wire bracing
75 Compression strut
76 Port upper navigation light

28 Detachable cowling panels
29 Gun firing channel
30 Centre-section cabane struts
31 Telescopic gun sight
32 Machine gun

barrel
33 55 US gal main fuel tank
34 Fuel tank support cradle
35 Cockpit bulkhead
36 Undercarriage rear strut attachment

37 Battery box
38 Rudder pedals
39 Control column
40 Cartridge case ejector
41 Ammunition magazine, port and starboard
42 Ammunition feed

chute
43 Instrument panel
44 Windscrren panels
45 30-calibre Browning machine gun, port and starboard, some

aircraft retrofitted with 50-cal. gun on starboard side.
46 Engine throttle lever
47 Arrester hook control cable drive

Mike Badrocke

A CALCULATED GAMBLE

In 1925 the US Post Office held a competition to find a replacement for the DH-4 as its standard mailplane. Boeing submitted the Model 40, first flown on 7 July 1925. Powered by a 400hp Liberty (the same as the DH-4) in an improved cowling with a tunnel radiator, it was made mainly of wood with fabric covering. The exception was that the front and rear parts of the fuselage were welded steel tube, and the main part of the fuselage (including the front steel-tube structure) was covered by thin plywood. This was the first Boeing to have a Type Number, its predecessors being given numbers retroactively.

The Post Office bought the prototype, but did not place a production order. In 1926 it was announced that the air-mail routes were to be priva-tized, and Boeing decided to produce the improved Model 40A. This had a more sensible fuselage structure entirely of steel tube, lengthened to accommodate a two-seat pas-senger cabin between the pilot and the forward (main) mail compartment. Mail capacity without any passengers was 1,200lb (544kg). Overall length came out by chance at exactly the same figure as before, because instead of the clumsy Liberty the engine was one of the new Wasps.

Eastbound from San Francisco, a Model 40A mailplane gains altitude over the Rockies en route to New York.

DATA FOR 40B-4:

Span	44ft 2.25in (13.47m)
Length	33ft 2.25in (10.116m)
Wing area	547 sq ft (50.82m^2)
Weight empty	3,722lb (1,688kg)
Gross weight	6,075lb (2,756kg)
Cruising speed	125mph (201km/h)
Service ceiling	16,100ft (4,907m)
Range	535 miles (861km)

Port
g the 40A,
r $1.50 a
housand
ts for each
after. This
e
red by the
id the bid
was $2.24
d miles)
demanded
m Boeing
would
ract. In six
1927
del 40As,
re on the
ago, Iowa
maha,
nne, Rock
ity and San
made
rt.
as sold to
an engine
fly the new
ly at 525hp.
fitted to
ere redesig-
oeing
d 38 Model
seating for
ey could
7kg) of
0H-4, were
nada.

Model 40B-4

1 Hamilton two-bladed fixed pitch propeller
2 Pratt & Whitney Hornet, nine-cylinder radial engine
3 Faired exhaust collector ring
4 Top cowling panels
5 Main compartment access hatch
6 Hatch securing straps
7 Mail/cargo compartment
8 Engine oil tank
9 Cowling air flap, ground adjustable
10 Engine accessory equipment
11 Engine bearer struts
12 Exhaust pipe to ventral cabin heater muff
13 Upper wing panel spruce rib structure
14 Ply-covered leading edge
15 Aileron balance cable pulleys
16 Mahogany wing tip ribs
17 Spruce wing tip edge member
18 Port upper aileron
19 Aerofoil section steel tube interplane struts
20 Diagonal wire bracing
21 Retractable landing light
22 Port navigation light
23 Port lower aileron

24 Cable control horns
25 Aileron hinge spar
26 Aileron interconnecting cables
27 Lower wing panel rib structure
28 Heavy gauge compression ribs
29 Wing panel internal diagonal wire bracing
30 Port mainwheel
31 Oleo-hydraulic shock absorber leg assembly
32 Optional wing root 40 US gal fuel tank, port only
33 Fuel fillers

34 Leading edge cabin fresh air intake duct
35 Inboard interplane struts
36 Fold-out step, mail compartment loading
37 Fuel pump
38 100 US gal fuselage fuel tank
39 Forward passenger door
40 Forward two-seat passenger compartment

41 Centre section cabane struts
42 Spindled spruce wing spars
43 Wing panel end rib
44 Central spar joints, offset to port
45 Trailing edge ribs
46 40-US gal fuel tank, starboard only
47 Fuel vent
48 Fuel filler cap
49 Starboard upper wing panel rib structure
50 Wing fabric covering
51 Starboard upper aileron

52 Starboard navigation light
53 Interplane struts
54 Starboard fabric-covered lower wing panel
55 Streamlined diagonal bracing wires
56 Canted inboard interplane struts
57 Aluminium alloy top decking
58 Cabin insulation
59 Cabin wall trim panelling
60 Rear passenger door
61 Two-seat rear passenger compartment
62 Plywood covered wing root walkway
63 Cockpit floor panel

64 Pilot's boarding steps
65 Rudder pedal bar
66 Tailplane trim handwheel
67 Engine throttle and ignition control levers
68 Control column
69 Instrument panel
70 Windscreen panels
71 Headrest
72 Padded cockpit coaming
73 Pilot's seat
74 Control cable pulleys
75 Pilot's stowage compartment
76 Ventral flare chute
77 Radio transmitter and receiver
78 Plywood covered cockpit bulkhead
79 Hinged stowage compartment access panel
80 Antenna mast
81 Extended headrest fairing

82 Fuselage top longeron
83 Welded steel tube fuselage primary structure
84 Bottom longeron
85 Spruce stringers
86 Diagonal wire bracing
87 Fuselage fabric covering
88 Port trimming tailplane
89 Tailplane spruce spar and rib structure
90 Fin/tailplane diagonal bracing wire
91 Welded steel tube elevator structure
92 Tailplane ventral bracing strut
93 Steerable tailskid, interconnected with rudder
94 Tail tie-down fitting
95 Tailskid elastic cord shock absorber
96 Trimming tailplane incidence screw jack, cable operated
97 Welded steel tube fin structure
98 Antenna cables
99 Rudder horn balance
100 Starboard fabric-covered trimming tailplane
101 Tail navigation light
102 Starboard fabric-covered elevator
103 Welded steel tube rudder structure, fabric-covered

Mike Badrocke/98

PASSENGERS – AND A ROOF

When Boeing began operating the SFO-Chicago mail route it was expected that passengers would be carried only on rare occasions. In fact, once it could be seen that the buyer of a ticket was likely to arrive, even the four-seat 40B-4s usually had all seats filled. This was despite the fact that passengers had to squeeze through a tiny door and sit in a constricted and uncomfortable box. Boeing Air Transport therefore judged that it would not be a mistake to test the economics of using much larger aircraft. Accordingly, the associated aircraft company produced the prototype Model 80, first flown on 4 August 1928.

Powered by three Wasp engines, this was to some degree a scaled-up Model 40, but with wings boldly made mainly from welded steel tube, like the fuselage. The cockpit was moved to the nose, accommodating two pilots side-by-side, with large windows all round and (intensely disliked

Model 80A-1

1 Centre Hamilton two-bladed propeller
2 Propeller hub fixing
3 Centre engine cowling
4 Cooling air intakes
5 Pratt & Whitney Hornet nine-cylinder radial engine
6 Exhaust collector ring
7 Exhaust collector tail fairing
8 Engine bearer struts
9 Oil tank
10 Cooling air gills
11 Engine bay bulkhead
12 Nose section skin panelling
13 Windscreen panels
14 Direct vision opening window panel
15 Engine throttle levers
16 Instrument panel
17 Centre control pedestal
18 Rudder pedals
19 Cockpit floor level
20 Underfloor control runs
21 Cockpit heater muff
22 Centre engine exhaust pipe
23 Passenger cabin heater muff
24 Baggage compartment door
25 Underfloor baggage compartment
26 Fire extinguisher

27 First aid kit
28 Pilot's seat
29 Control column
30 Cockpit side windows
31 Co-pilot's seat
32 Cockpit eyebrow windows
33 Glazed cockpit roof hatch
34 Cockpit rear bulkhead
35 Passenger cabin doorway
36 Forward passenger cabin
37 Wing spar attachment drag strut
38 Three-abreast passenger seating; 18-passenger layout
39 Inter-cabin bulkhead
40 Overhead lighting
41 Cabin wall trim panelling
42 Wing spar centre-section carry-through
43 Leading edge fairing panels
44 Centre (reserve) fuel tank
45 Fuel filler caps
46 Starboard main fuel tank; total fuel capacity 400 US gal (1,514 litres)
47 Antenna lead-in
48 Outer wing panel attachment rib
49 Leading edge nose ribs
50 Starboard engine nacelle
51 Starboard Pratt & Whitney Hornet engine
52 Hamilton two-bladed propeller
53 Interplane struts

54 Diagonal wire bracing
55 Starboard lower wing panel
56 Starboard navigation light
57 Upper wing outboard panel
58 Inter-spar compression struts
59 Wing panel internal wire bracing
60 Wing tip fairing
61 Starboard aileron
62 Aileron push-pull control rods
63 Corrugated aluminium aileron skin panelling
64 Fixed portion of trailing edge
65 Wire trailing edge
66 Fabric covered wing/fuselage fairing
67 Passenger cabin roof lining
68 Overhead hat rack
69 Cabin window panels
70 Rear passenger seat row
71 Individual fresh air scoops
72 Cabin air outlet ducts
73 Cabin rear bulkhead
74 Wash basin
75 Toilet compartment door
76 Cold water tank
77 Water filler cap
78 Hot water tank
79 Starboard side toilet compartment
80 Antenna mast
81 Fuselage top longeron

82 Horizontal spacers
83 Dorsal fabric covering
84 Control cable fairleads
85 Tailplane spar centre-section carry-through
86 Adjustable tailplane trim control
87 Fin/tailplane support structure
88 Tailfin construction
89 Starboard tailplane
90 Tailplane corrugated aluminium skin panelling
91 Auxiliary fin bracing struts
92 HF antenna cable
93 Starboard auxiliary fin
94 Elevator horn balance
95 Fabric covered auxiliary rudder
96 Fabric covered elevator
97 Corrugated aluminium fin skin panelling
98 Rudder horn balance
99 Fabric covered rudder construction
100 Tail navigation light
101 Tailplane bracing cables
102 Rudder tab
103 Auxiliary rudder construction
104 Port elevator construction
105 Elevator horn balance
106 Port tailplane construction

107 Fixed tailwheel
108 Tailwheel castoring mounting
109 Shock absorber strut
110 Fuselage tail fairing
111 Fin and tailplane support frame
112 Sloping fin attachment frame
113 Fuselage fabric covering

114 Diagonal wire bracing
115 Vertical spacers
116 Ventral fabric covered stringers
117 Fuselage lower longeron

118 Wardrobe compartment
119 Drinking water fountain
120 Passenger entry door
121 Entry vestibule
122 Hand fire extinguisher
123 Cabin heater sidewall air duct
124 Port aileron
125 Aileron hinge rib
126 Rear spar
127 Trailing edge ribs
128 Port elevator construction
129 Wing tip fairing construction
130 Lattice rib construction
131 Inter-spar compression struts

132 Front spar
133 Leading edge nose ribs
134 Inter-rib stiffeners
135 Port interplane struts
136 Lower wing panel fabric covering
137 Port navigation light
138 Retractable landing/taxiing lamp
139 Lamp housing
140 Diagonal bracing wires
141 Port mainwheel
142 Wheel disc cover
143 Main undercarriage shock absorber leg struts
144 Mudguard

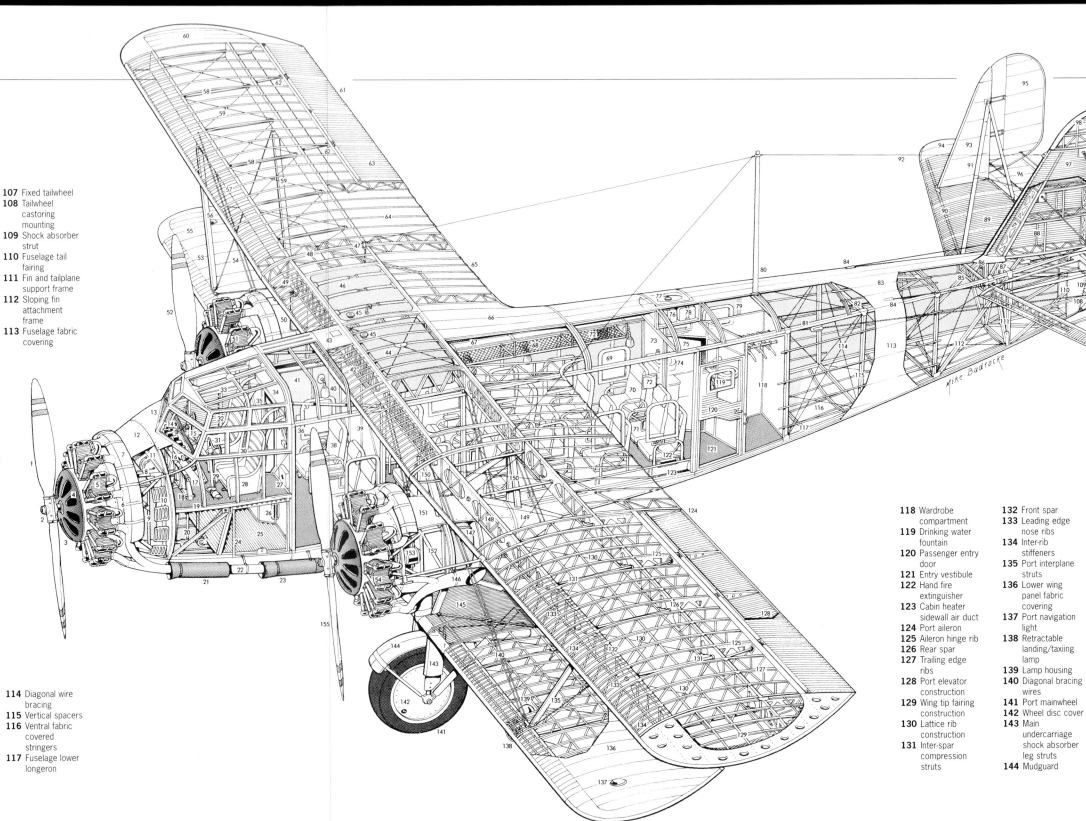

by pilots used to open cockpits) a roof over their heads. The main cabin was by previous standards luxurious. There were 12 seats of soft leather arranged two on the left and one on the right, each row beside a large window with curtains. Above were electric lights, and racks for hats and light luggage. For the first time the passengers had the services of a stewardess, and even hot and cold running water in the washroom.

Boeing built four Model 80s, followed by ten 80As. The latter replaced the 410hp Wasps by 525hp Hornets, enabling the fuselage to be lengthened to accommodate two extra rows of seats, for a total of 18.

Fuel capacity was also increased, and the wing was made from bolted square-section light-alloy tubing. Some 80As had cowled engines and various newer propellers. Ten were converted to 80A-1 standard by adding small auxiliary fins and rudders above the tailplanes. One, with 575hp Hornets, was modified as the 80B with no roof over the cockpit, in order to please the pilots. One 80A was salvaged from an Alaskan dump and is in the Seattle Museum of Flight.

A Model 80A-1 trimotor of United Air Lines thunders over Lake Michigan as it departs Chicago for California – a 22hr journey.

DATA FOR 80A:

Span	80ft 0in (24.38m)
Length	56ft 6in (17.22m)
Wing area	1,220 sq ft (113.3m²)
Weight empty	10,582lb (4,800kg)
Gross weight	17,500lb (7,938kg)
Cruising speed	125mph (201km/h)
Service ceiling	14,000ft (4,267m)
Range	460 miles (740km)

THOROUGHLY MODERN MONO

MONOMAIL

According to legend, after the 1928 Air Races Clair Egtvedt, Boeing v-p and general manager, was sharing an LA hotel room with Eddie Hubbard, v-p operations of Boeing Air Transport. Discussing future aircraft design, Hubbard said "Why don't we skin the whole fuselage in metal ? We have to use metal skin behind the engine, and to protect the fabric we have to line the whole mail compartment with metal as well." He then sketched the front view of his proposed mailplane. He drew just a large circle, with low cantilever wings on each side. Landing gears were inside the wing.

The problems were considerable. With a smooth (instead of corrugated) metal skin there had to be much more internal structure, or the skin had to be thicker and heavier. Hardly anyone had made metal cantilever wings (and some of those had broken in flight), and most cantilever wings had been above the

In 1930 the Model 200 Monomail exuded modernity. Of all-metal construction, its design set the pattern for future Boeings. The colours were green, grey and bright orange.

fuselage. The idea of a retractable landing gear was also almost unheard-of. Despite this, Boeing himself was excited, and authorised construction of a large new building with a big area allotted to Engineering.

It didn't help when in December 1928 illnesses killed Hubbard and took Egtvedt away from his desk for months. After prolonged study,

chief engineer A.N.'Monty' Monteith began serious drawing, and the Model 200, the Monomail, at last flew on 6 May 1930. His team had

earlier designed the XP-9 pursuit, with similar construction, but this had a braced wing and did not fly until November 1930. Only two Monomails were built, but both were successfully used by Boeing Air Transport, and this design was a vital stepping stone to all the Boeing aircraft that came after it.

In configuration it followed Hubbard's doodle of 1928, being an almost perfectly streamlined example of what is today accepted as how an aeroplane should be designed (though in 1930 it looked almost like science fiction). The only odd feature to modern eyes is that, to please the pilot, the single-place cockpit was completely open. The fuselage had a structure of light-alloy frames and stringers, skinned with duralumin sheet held by flush rivets. This made possible a smooth circular cross-section, and over 2,000lb (907kg) of mail could be carried in the 220 cu ft (6.2m³) compartment amidships. The metal tail also had smooth skins, without corrugations. As in the Model 80A, the wing was based on bolted square-section dural tubing, but made in the form of Warren (zigzag) trusses and with corrugated underskins between the spars, the whole then being covered by smooth outer skins.

On the nose was a 575hp B-series Hornet, surrounded by a short-chord Townend-ring cowl. The simple main landing gears could be cranked backwards until they were stowed inside the wing. A small part of each wheel projected, with a fairing behind it, so that a wheels-up landing should damage nothing but the propeller. In fact the two-blade Hamilton metal propeller was the main problem. Set in fine pitch the takeoff was excellent, but inflight performance was poor. In coarse pitch the Monomail went considerably faster, provided that, after a very long run, it could actually get airborne.

On 18 August 1930 Boeing flew the Model 221. This had a fuselage 8in (203mm) longer, and could seat six passengers between the engine and the cargo. Later, both aircraft were converted into Model 221As, with a longer fuselage accommodating an eight-seat cabin (plus 750lb, 340kg, mail), and with simple fixed landing gear.

Both Monomails were operated by Boeing Air Transport. On 27 March 1931 this carrier was one of four pioneer airlines (the others being Pacific Air Transport, National Air Transport and Varney Air Lanes), which grouped together to form United Air Lines. This photograph shows the six-passenger Model 221.

DATA FOR MODEL 200:

Span	59ft 1.5in (18.02m)
Length	41ft 2.5in (12.56m)
Wing area	535 sq ft (49.7m²)
Weight empty	4,758lb (2,158kg)
Gross weight	8,000lb (3,629kg)
Cruising speed (fine pitch)	135mph (217km/h)
Service ceiling	14,000ft (4,267m)
Range	530 miles (853km)

B-9

BEATEN BY MARTIN

In 1930 the Army Air Corps discussed with Boeing whether the advanced stressed-skin construction of the Monomail could be applied to the design of a bomber. The company agreed to undertake such an exercise at its own expense, and began the design of the Models 214 and 215. These differed mainly in that the 214 was powered by two 600hp Curtiss GIV-1510C liquid-cooled engines, while the 215 had ring-cowled Hornets of the same power.

The thick and broad cantilever wing comprised a rectangular centre section and slightly tapered outer panels with dihedral. The narrow semi-monocoque stressed-skin fuselage had an open ring in the nose for twin 0.30in guns, the gunner being able when required to lie in the bottom of the

Paced by a 'Peashooter' (which is actually closer to the camera), one of the five service-test Y1B-9As exercises its Hornet radials.

nose to aim the bombs (typically two of 1,100lb, 499kg) carried in an internal fuselage bay between the wing spars. Inside the nose was a tiny cabin for the radio operator. Next came tandem open cockpits for the pilot and copilot, with instruments which included the newly invented artificial horizon, turn/slip and directional gyro. Behind the wing was an open cockpit for a second gunner, again with twin 0.30in. The smooth-skinned tail featured a rudder moved by a trailing-edge servo tab, and the main landing gears could be winched up so that part of each wheel was housed in a recess.

The Hornet-engined 215 flew as a civil aircraft (X-10633) on 13 April 1931, and proved so satisfactory that on 14 August the Army purchased both aircraft, calling the 215 the YB-9. The Model 214 was more difficult, the vee-12 engines being cooled by Prestone glycol-based fluid circulated through a radiator under the cowling. Like the 215, this machine had two-

In stark contrast to the Army's lumbering fleet of biplane bombers, the Model 215 (YB-9) had remarkably uncluttered lines.

blade fixed-pitch propellers, but fitted with large spinners faired into the cowlings. By the time it flew, on 5 November

1931, both aircraft were in full Army markings, the 214 being designated Y1B-9 with serial 32-302 (the 215 being 32-301).

To Boeing's great disappointment, Martin later produced an even faster bomber which won the expected production contracts as the B-10. However, between July 1932 and March 1933 Boeing did go on to deliver five service-test Y1B-9A bombers, with Boeing Model number 246. These had supercharged 600hp Hornets driving three-blade fixed-pitch propellers, metal-skinned control surfaces, and carried four 600lb (272kg) bombs. Later they received redesigned fabric-covered rudders with inset tabs almost identical to those of the later Model 247.

DATA FOR THE MODEL 246/Y1B-9A:

Span	**76ft 0in (23.16m)**
Length	**51ft 5in (15.67m)**
Wing area	**959 sq ft (89.1m²)**
Weight empty	**8,599lb (3,900kg)**
Gross weight	**13,919lb (6,317kg)**
Maximum speed	**186mph (299km/h)**
Cruising speed	**158mph (254km/h)**
Service ceiling	**19,700ft (6,000m)**
Range	**1,150 miles (1,851km)**

247

EXECUTIVE STRESSED

After 1930 the USA and Germany led the world in the revolution in aircraft design made possible by the switch to stressed-skin construction using aluminium alloys. Boeing was in the forefront, but until 1932 failed to reap any major reward. Late in that year this situation began to change. Boeing's link with the huge United Air Lines naturally led to the design of a modern twin-engined transport based on the new type of airframe. The 247 was similar to the B-9 in size, but the wing was new, with straight taper and dihedral from the roots, though structurally made as a centre section and outer panels.

The fuselage had side-by-side seats for the pilot and copilot in an enclosed cockpit with shallow forward-sloping windscreens. The rather cramped cabin had the door on the right and five seats on each side, each beside a window, some passengers having to use inbuilt steps to climb over the two wing spars. There was provision for a stewardess, and at the rear were a tiny galley and washroom. Up to 400lb (181kg) of baggage and mail could be loaded into the nose, and a second compartment in the rear fuselage with a hatch on the left.

The engines were supercharged Wasp S1D1s rated at 550hp at 5,000ft (1,524m), in Townend-ring cowls on small-diameter nacelles like those of the bombers, and driving similar three-blade fixed-pitch propellers. The main landing gears were also similar to those of the bombers, but the retraction screwjacks were driven by electric motors. Several further innovations included deicing by pneumatically inflated rubber boots on the leading

NC-13354, a Model 247 of Western Air Express, waits on the ramp at Great Falls airport, Montana, in the mid-1930s.

edges, and neat inset trim tabs on the metal-skinned rudder, elevators and left aileron.

So sure was Boeing of success that it went straight into production, against orders from United partner-airlines that totalled 70. The first Model 247 began very success-ful testing on 8 February 1933. Each aircraft came off the line unpainted but looking shiny grey from the anodized skin. United Air Lines actually received 59 Model 247s, and Boeing also built two for the German airline Luft Hansa. The No 30 aircraft was completed as the 247A, painted silver and powered by 625hp Pratt & Whitney Twin Wasp Junior engines; it had a long career as the executive transport for United Aircraft Corporation.

At aircraft No 63, production switched to the Model 247D, 13 of this

Passengers travelled in considerable comfort, with individual seating and stewardess service.

type being built. They differed in having Wasp S1H1-G engines, rated at 500hp at 8,000ft (2,438m), with reduction gears driving larger three-blade Hamilton Standard propellers which could be set to either fine or coarse pitch. They were installed in long-chord NACA cowls on full-diameter nacelles. Fuel capacity was increased from 173gal (787 litres) to 227gal (1,033 litres). Appearance was improved by fitting normal backward-sloping windscreens, and the rudder and the elevators were skinned in fabric.

These changes transformed what had been an acceptable transport into an outstanding one. Whereas the 247 could fly 485 miles (780km) at 155mph (249km/h), the 247D had the performance given on page 32. Despite the increased weight,

The 247 helped to make United Air Lines a major player in American air transport. NC-13361 displays conventional windscreens.

Boeing 247D

1 Starboard elevator
2 Elevator tab
3 Tailplane construction
4 Tailcone
5 Tail navigation light
6 Rudder tab
7 Tab hinge control rod
8 Rudder construction
9 Rudder hinges
10 Sternpost
11 Tailfin construction
12 Rudder hinge control
13 Tailwheel shock absorber strut
14 Tailwheel mounting struts
15 Castoring tailwheel
16 Rear fuselage skin plating
17 Fin/tailplane fixing double frame
18 Port tailplane
19 Fuselage frame and stringer construction
20 Tailplane control cables

21 Access door to rear fuselage
22 Rear bulkhead
23 Port baggage compartment door
24 Baggage compartment
25 Water tank
26 Wash basin
27 Toilet compartment
28 Passenger entry door
29 Door latch
30 Trailing edge wing root fillet
31 Toilet compartment door
32 First aid box
33 Rear antenna masts
34 Curtained passenger windows
35 Passenger compartment floor level
36 Starboard window panels
37 Centre/rear fuselage joint frame
38 Starboard wing fuel tank, capacity 132 US gal (500 litres)

39 Fuel filler cap
40 Main undercarriage wheel housing
41 Stub wing girder construction rib
42 Outer wing panel rear spar joint
43 Rear spar girder construction

44 Trailing edge ribs
45 Starboard aileron
46 Wing tip construction
47 Starboard upper and lower navigation lights
48 Wing stringers
49 Leading edge nose ribs
50 Front spar

51 Lattice rib construction
52 Starboard landing/taxiing lamp
53 Landing lamp glare shield
54 Outer wing panel front spar joint
55 Main undercarriage leg pivot point

56 Retraction strut
57 Main undercarriage leg struts
58 Wheel hub cover
59 Tyre valve access
60 Starboard mainwheel
61 Cabin heater intake

62 Exhaust pipe shroud
63 Exhaust collector ring
64 Pratt & Whitney Wasp S1H1-G supercharged radial engine
65 Propeller reduction gearbox
66 Three-bladed

propeller
67 Propeller hub pitch change mechanism
68 Detachable engine cowlings
69 Oil cooler intake
70 Engine bearer struts
71 Engine oil tank
72 Fireproof bulkhead

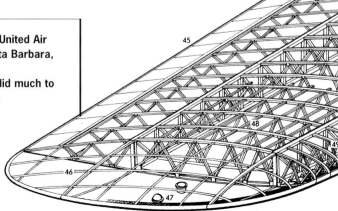

VIPs deplane from a United Air Lines' service at Santa Barbara, California. Sleek and sophisticated, 247s did much to make air travel more fashionable.

M. Badrocke

73 Oil cooler
74 Engine cowling support struts
75 Oil cooler outlet louvres
76 Centre/forward fuselage joint frame

77 Passenger seats
78 Fuselage main longeron
79 Cabin soundproofing and trim panels
80 Cabin heater air duct

81 Overhead luggage racks
82 Aerial cables
83 Port aileron trim tab
84 Aileron hinge control
85 Port aileron

95 Co-pilot's seat
96 Control column
97 Pilot's seat
98 Forward raked windscreen panels (early model); rearward sloping screens on later 247D
99 Instrument panel
100 Rudder pedals
101 Cockpit floor level
102 Cockpit front bulkhead
103 Battery
104 Radio transmitter and receiver
105 Electrical equipment rack
106 Flare launchers

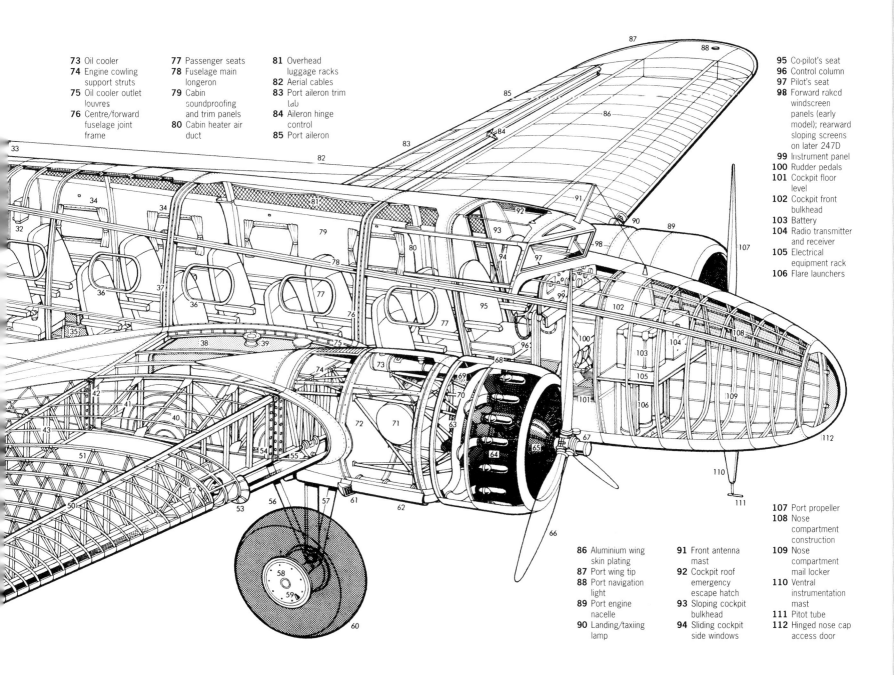

86 Aluminium wing skin plating
87 Port wing tip
88 Port navigation light
89 Port engine nacelle
90 Landing/taxiing lamp

91 Front antenna mast
92 Cockpit roof emergency escape hatch
93 Sloping cockpit bulkhead
94 Sliding cockpit side windows

107 Port propeller
108 Nose compartment construction
109 Nose compartment mail locker
110 Ventral instrumentation mast
111 Pitot tube
112 Hinged nose cap access door

247

the 247D was the first twin-engined transport that could unfailingly maintain height at full load with one engine inoperative. Nearly all the 247s were later brought up to this standard. One was modified as an armed VIP machine for a Chinese warlord.

The 247s and 247Ds had successful careers. The eighth 247D was diverted from United to Col Roscoe Turner and Clyde Pangborn, who fitted long-range tanks and in October 1934 flew it to third place (second in the Transport Handicap section) in the race from Mildenhall, England, to Melbourne; it then served with United. In 1942 United's aircraft were impressed as Army C-73s or passed to the Royal Canadian Air Force. One

Boeing 247 c/n 1726 was used by United, brought up to 247D standard (but still with original windscreens), passed to the RCAF and then served with the RAF as DZ203.

RCAF machine flew to England, where it was camouflaged and became DZ203 of the RAF, serving as an avionics testbed. In October 1944 this aircraft was fitted with a Minneapolis-Honeywell autopilot linked to an ILS receiver, and it then made the world's first fully automatic landing.

One 247D was sold by United in 1936 to Union Electric as an executive aircraft. Three years later it was sold to the Civil Aeronautics Authority, and today it is in the US National Air & Space Museum.

DATA FOR 247D:

Span	**74ft 0in (22.56m)**
Length	**51ft 7in (15.72m)**
Wing area	**836 sq ft (77.66m²)**
Weight empty	**9,144lb (4,148kg)**
Gross weight	**13,650lb (6,192kg)**
Cruising speed	**189mph (304km/h)** *at 12,000ft (3,658m)*
Range	**745 miles (1,199km)**

Lloyd Stearman's move to Lockheed predated the first Stearman Model 70, which appeared in December 1933. The most numerous Stearman was the PT-17 primary trainer, 2,942 of which were delivered to the US Army and 827 to the US Navy. Most had 220hp Lycomings; the 450hp R-985 Wasp Junior in the leading aircraft (right) and UK-registered G-BNIW (below) were fitted for postwar crop-dusting work. Thousands of Empire pilots also gained their wings on this big, rugged aeroplane.

NAVIGATION TURRET

BRIDGE

CATWALK

PAA

MENS ROOM

Kenneth W. Thompson

One of the classic American flying boats (with the Sikorsky S-42 and Martin 130), the 314 had ample room for the passengers and crew.

The magnificent 314 belonged to the golden age of the flying boat, when passengers enjoyed the kind of luxury found on transatlantic liners.

THIS DE LUXE COMPARTMENT HAS A BOOKCASE AND COCKTAIL TABLE

THE FLIGHT ENGINEER WATCHES HIS CONTROLS FROM THIS SWIVEL CHAIR

HOWARD KETCHAM INC.

THE LADIES' WASHROOM HAS LEATHER-COVERED STOOLS FOR PRIMPING

THE GALLEY, FINISHED IN DURALUMIN, HOLDS TWO STEWARDS

ATLANTIC CLIPPER HAS MODERN INTERIORS

TRANSATLANTIC LOWER BERTH

As befits anything so modern as a transatlantic passenger plane, the Atlantic Clipper will have modern furniture, designed under direction of Pan American engineers. In furnishing, the engineers' main concern was with weight and soundproofing. Weight is kept down by using duralumin furniture, light-weight fabrics, window-panes made of a plastic lighter than glass. For sound-proofing, walls are covered with fabric which has to be porous so that sound waves will pass through instead of being reflected. It must also be strong and elastic because it is fastened to the walls by snaps and removed for cleaning. Mohair with its loose weave was chosen for this purpose. The involved matter of selecting colors was done largely by Howard Ketcham, New York color expert. Clip-per colors had to be bright to reflect light and make the plane seem spacious and airy. On the other hand, they could not be too bright because the glare above the clouds would then be uncomfortable. Colors should not tire the eyes by being too gay and varied but they should not tire them by being too monotonous. The colors finally chosen for major use are "skyline" green, "Miami sand" beige and a shade called "Pan American blue." The Clipper's seven compartments will seat 60 and sleep 40 passengers. Others can nap in the lounge which seats 15 and is also the reading and dining room. Meals, which are prepared before take-off and kept warm in the plane's galley, are served here in shifts. For a cross-section picture in color of the Atlantic Clipper, turn the page.

B-17G *Sally B* in the role of the immortal *Memphis Belle*, B-17F 41-24485 of the 324th BS, 91st BG. (Photo: John Ailes)

Formerly of Paris-based l'Institute Geographique Nationale, Sally B has starred at UK airshows since 1975.

B-29 *Sentimental Journey* is preserved at the Pima County Museum in Arizona. The last flying Superfortress, USAAF 44-62070/N529B *Fifi,* is operated by the Confederate Air Force.

B-47E put out to grass at Barksdale AFB, LA. The small 'skylight' windows in the nose for the bombardier/navigator are visible just below the pilot's anti-glare panel. The six GE J47 engines are intact.

If the order to scramble came all eight Pratt & Whitney J57 engines on this B-52G could be started simultaneously.

Travelling at about 160mph (257km/h), a B-52G of Barksdale's 2nd BW prepares for touchdown.

'Big Belly' B-52Ds went to war from Guam carrying conventional bomb loads of 68,520lb (31,145kg).

Stratotanker refuels B-52G Stratofortress. Boeing's High-Speed Boom is another design classic.

Even the most senior KC-135 commander is unlikely to have served longer than this R, which will probably remain active beyond 2020. The first Stratotanker flew in 1956.

Electronic eavesdropper, one of the two Combat Sent aircraft. *Bark like a Dawg*, RC-135U 64-14849, was photographed during a deployment to RAF Mildenhall, Suffolk, in 1988.

PEASHOOTER

In September 1931, though Boeing was making a good living producing pursuits for both the Army and Navy, its designers were convinced that eventually even this class of aircraft would have to give up the fabric-covered biplane and switch to the stressed-skin monoplane. However, it was difficult with a thick-winged long-span monoplane to equal the speed, climb, ceiling and, especially, the agility of the compact biplane. After many discussions with the generally unenthusiastic Air Corps, Boeing decided to go ahead with company money on a compromise design: a fighter with both ancient and modern features.

The traditional features included an open cockpit (pilots demanded it), wire-braced wing and fixed landing gear (to reduce weight and cost, simplify the structure and provide anchors for the underwing bracing wires). Apart from the fact that the new pursuit was a monoplane, new features included a semi-monocoque stressed-skin fuselage, unbraced tail skinned with smooth metal and the use of a tailwheel, with powerful brakes on the mainwheels. A total of 89gal (405 litres) of fuel was housed under the cockpit and in two wing tanks. On the nose was a supercharged Wasp rated at 522hp at 10,000ft (3,048m) in a ring cowl, driving a simple fixed-pitch two-blade Hamilton propeller. There was the usual option of two 0.30in or one 0.30in and one 0.5in guns, and two 122lb (55kg) bombs or five practice bombs. Instead of

A P-26B (the definitive Air Corps version) shows off its split flaps, introduced to lower the landing speed from an alarming 73mph (117km/h). Retrofits included two-way radio.

being above the fuselage, the guns were just below mid-level, with five engine cylinders above and four below. Equipment included gyro instruments, radio and a liquid-oxygen vaporiser.

The Army supplied the engine, instruments and armament, and Boeing built two Model 248 prototypes and a static-test specimen.

DATA FOR FINAL P-26B STANDARD:

Span	27ft 11in (8.52m)
Length	23ft 9in (7.24m)
Wing area	149.5 sq ft (13.88m²)
Weight empty	2,302lb (1,044kg)
Gross weight	3,060lb (1,388kg)
Maximum speed	235mph (378km/h)
Service ceiling	27,000ft (8,230m)
Range	635 miles (1,022km)

Designated XP-986, the first aircraft flew on 20 March 1932. It seemed a good compromise, with just enough traditional features not to be dismissed as too radical. After much thought, the Army bought 111 with designation P-26A, powered by the 600hp R-1340-27. The first did not fly until 10 January 1934, but Boeing managed to deliver the whole order in six months. The P-26As were followed by two P-26Bs with the R-1340-33 with an injection-type carburettor and split flaps under the wings, and then 23 P-26Cs with minor fuel-system changes.

All 136 were later brought to P-26B standard. Popularly called "the Peashooter", these snarling monoplanes soon appeared obsolescent, and many were passed on to Panama and the Philippines. In the latter theatre one scored a combat victory in December 1941. Boeing offered the Model 281 for export, selling one to Spain and 11 to China. Five were sold by Panama to Guatemala, where one survived to 1955. One is in the NASM, while another is airworthy with Planes of Fame at Chino.

Boeing P-26A

1 Starboard navigation light, above and below
2 Wing skin panelling
3 Steel leading edge member
4 Pitot head
5 Landing wires
6 Two-bladed fixed pitch propeller
7 Engine cowling ring
8 Starter dog
9 Gun camera, mounted above starboard wing root
10 100lb HE bomb
11 30lb bomb
12 Type A-3 light bomb rack
13 Sway braces
14 Bomb release linkage, cable operated
15 Starboard mainwheel
16 Hinged axle link
17 Wheel spat fairing
18 Engine oil sump
19 Gun muzzle aperture
20 Engine faceplate
21 Cooling air holes
22 Reduction gear casing
23 Pratt & Whitney R-1340-27 nine-cylinder engine
24 Engine mounting ring frame
25 Engine accessory equipment bay
26 Exhaust stubs
27 Starboard wing fuel tank
28 Tubular gunsight
29 Sight support mounting
30 Oil filler

31 Engine oil tank, 7gal (30 litres)
32 Oil tank retaining strap
33 Carburettor air intake
34 Engine bearer struts
35 Cooling air louvres
36 Engine primer access panel
37 Rudder pedal hinge point in pilot's footwell
38 Carburettor intake/exhaust heat exchanger
39 Machine gun barrel in blast tube
40 Oil cooler
41 Main undercarriage bracing wires
42 Faired wire clamp
43 Wing root fillet fairing
44 Stub wing spar
45 Ammunition feed and cartridge case return chutes

46 Ammunition loading door, 500 rpg in underfloor magazines
47 Pilot's footboards
48 Browning M-2 0.3in (7.62mm) machine gun (2) alternative M-1921 0.5in (12.70mm) with 200 rounds on starboard side

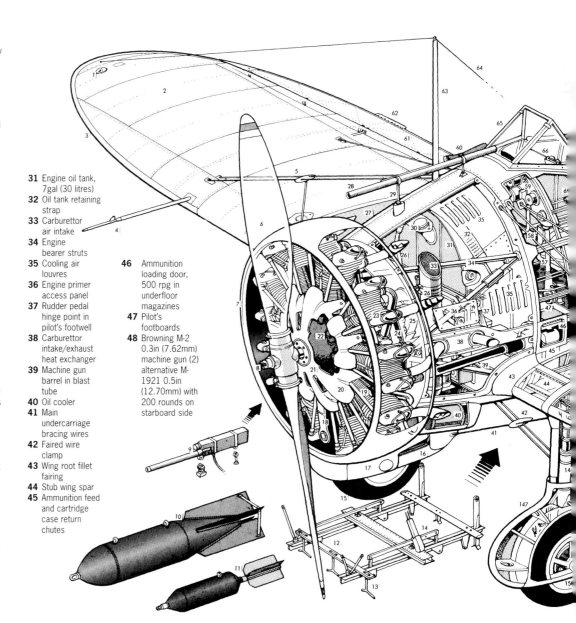

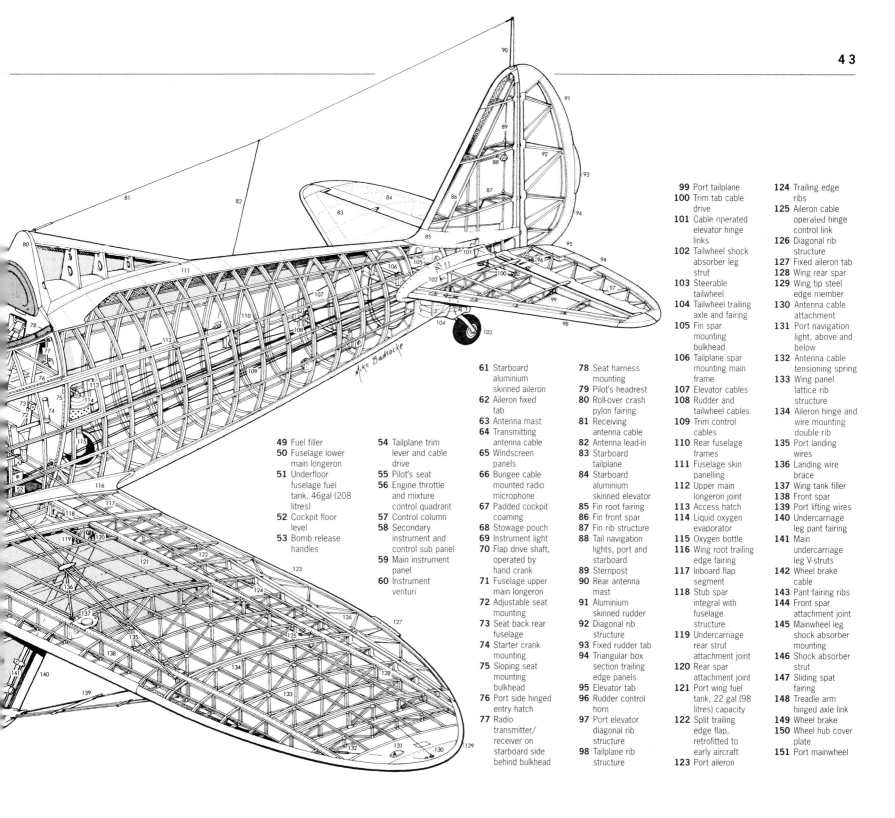

P-26

49 Fuel filler
50 Fuselage lower main longeron
51 Underfloor fuselage fuel tank, 46gal (208 litres)
52 Cockpit floor level
53 Bomb release handles
54 Tailplane trim lever and cable drive
55 Pilot's seat
56 Engine throttle and mixture control quadrant
57 Control column
58 Secondary instrument and control sub panel
59 Main instrument panel
60 Instrument venturi
61 Starboard aluminium skinned aileron
62 Aileron fixed tab
63 Antenna mast
64 Transmitting antenna cable
65 Windscreen panels
66 Bungee cable mounted radio microphone
67 Padded cockpit coaming
68 Stowage pouch
69 Instrument light
70 Flap drive shaft, operated by hand crank
71 Fuselage upper main longeron
72 Adjustable seat mounting
73 Seat back rear fuselage
74 Starter crank mounting
75 Sloping seat mounting bulkhead
76 Port side hinged entry hatch
77 Radio transmitter/receiver on starboard side behind bulkhead
78 Seat harness mounting
79 Pilot's headrest
80 Roll-over crash pylon fairing
81 Receiving antenna cable
82 Antenna lead-in
83 Starboard tailplane
84 Starboard aluminium skinned elevator
85 Fin root fairing
86 Fin front spar
87 Fin rib structure
88 Tail navigation lights, port and starboard
89 Sternpost
90 Rear antenna mast
91 Aluminium skinned rudder
92 Diagonal rib structure
93 Fixed rudder tab
94 Triangular box section trailing edge panels
95 Elevator tab
96 Rudder control horn
97 Port elevator diagonal rib structure
98 Tailplane rib structure
99 Port tailplane
100 Trim tab cable drive
101 Cable operated elevator hinge links
102 Tailwheel shock absorber leg strut
103 Steerable tailwheel
104 Tailwheel trailing axle and fairing
105 Fin spar mounting bulkhead
106 Tailplane spar mounting main frame
107 Elevator cables
108 Rudder and tailwheel cables
109 Trim control cables
110 Rear fuselage frames
111 Fuselage skin panelling
112 Upper main longeron joint
113 Access hatch
114 Liquid oxygen evaporator
115 Oxygen bottle
116 Wing root trailing edge fairing
117 Inboard flap segment
118 Stub spar integral with fuselage structure
119 Undercarriage rear strut attachment joint
120 Rear spar attachment joint
121 Port wing fuel tank, 22 gal (98 litres) capacity
122 Split trailing edge flap, retrofitted to early aircraft
123 Port aileron
124 Trailing edge ribs
125 Aileron cable operated hinge control link
126 Diagonal rib structure
127 Fixed aileron tab
128 Wing rear spar
129 Wing tip steel edge member
130 Antenna cable attachment
131 Port navigation light, above and below
132 Antenna cable tensioning spring
133 Wing panel lattice rib structure
134 Aileron hinge and wire mounting double rib
135 Port landing wires
136 Landing wire brace
137 Wing tank filler
138 Front spar
139 Port lifting wires
140 Undercarriage leg pant fairing
141 Main undercarriage leg V-struts
142 Wheel brake cable
143 Pant fairing ribs
144 Front spar attachment joint
145 Mainwheel leg shock absorber mounting
146 Shock absorber strut
147 Sliding spat fairing
148 Treadle arm hinged axle link
149 Wheel brake
150 Wheel hub cover plate
151 Port mainwheel

Mike Badrocke

PURSUITS, AND THE FIRST BIG BIRD

Boeing's first monoplane was the XP-9, or Model 96, an uninspired pursuit with a supercharged version of the old Curtiss vee-12 engine. The braced wings were recessed into the top of the semi-monocoque stressed-skin fuselage, the pilot sat in an open cockpit at the back, and there was a 0.5in gun on each side. Contracted for in May 1928, the XP-9 did not fly until 18 November 1930. It was notable as one of the first aircraft to feature the new form of fuselage construction.

In 1933-34 Boeing built three Army YP-29s and a Navy XF7B-1. These were basically far more promising pursuits, with completely modern stressed-skin structure, low-mounted cantilever wings with flaps, retractable landing gear, a controllable-pitch propeller and an enclosed cockpit. In each case a ring-cowled supercharged Wasp gave a speed of 230 to 250mph (370-402km/h). Sadly, the customers, especially the pilots, were not ready. These prototypes had to be rebuilt with open cockpits, and even then were thought to land too fast. Basically, pilots were used to biplanes.

Pilots disliked the XP-9, especially the poor view forward and below. Fixed gear held max speed to 213mph (342km/h).

A YP-29 warming up at Wright Field in June 1935. It was thoroughly modern, which made it virtually unsaleable, but it was ideal as a testbed for fuels.

Throughout 1935 Capt Frank Klein at Wright Field used a YP-29 for the first tests of 100-octane gasoline. The Army already had accurate figures for this aircraft on the best existing fuel (92 octane), and the new anti-knock fuel (actually about 98 octane) increased speed by 11 per cent, reduced takeoff run by 30 per cent and increased rate of climb by 40 per cent. The new fuel became standard for all Army combat aircraft on 1 January 1938, ahead of all other countries.

In a totally different sphere, in April 1934 design began on the Model 294. This monster was built on Army contract as the XBLR-1 (experimental bomber, long-range). Nearly three-quarters of the airframe weight was the huge equi-tapered wing, with a span of 149ft (45.4m), with electrically driven flaps, retraction bays for

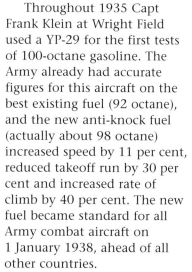

twin-wheel main gears and more fuel capacity than any previous aircraft. The relatively small circular-section fuselage provided sleeping bunks for the crew of 10, together with wing walkways for servicing the four 2,000hp Allison V-3420 double-vee engines. A capacious central bay accommodated four 2,000lb (907kg) bombs, and six guns provided defence in all directions.

The problem was that the engines were not ready, even though the first flight was repeatedly delayed. At last the giant, by this time called the XB-15, got into the air on 15 October 1937, grossly underpowered by four 1,000hp Pratt & Whitney R-1830-11 Twin Wasps. With these its performance was poor. It could,however, lift heavy loads (on 30 July 1939 it set a world record by lifting a payload of 71,167lb, 32,281kg, to 8,200ft, 2,500m), and it spent World War 2 as the XC-105 freighter.

Aluminium overcast. In 1937 the XB-15 experimental long-range bomber was the largest and heaviest aeroplane built in the USA up to that time.

B-17 FLYING FORTRESS

FOUR-ENGINED SUCCESS

In May 1934 Boeing, for the first time, found itself in the position of having to take a huge financial risk. Moreover, it had to do this at a time when not much money was coming in. Martin had got the Army orders for bombers. Boeing's established civil transport had been halted in its tracks by the DC-2. There appeared to be no further orders for pursuits. Most of the engineering staff were tied up on the gigantic Model 294, and in calendar year 1935 Boeing made a loss of $334,000. Yet the company was determined to compete for an Air Corps requirement, just received, for a multi-engined bomber to attack hostile fleets.

Multi-engined had always meant twin-engined, but Egtvedt, Monteith and young Ed Wells had been studying a transport with four engines spaced along the wing (as in the 294). Previous four-engined bombers had been ponderous and slow. They calculated that they could, for the first time, use four engines not to carry a heavier bombload but to fly further, faster and higher. Having established that a four-engined submission would not be disqualified, they went ahead on the Model 299. It had to be ready by August 1935. The civil-registered X-13372 flew on 28 July of that year

Powered by four 750hp Pratt & Whitney Hornets, driving Hamilton Standard variable-pitch three-blade propellers, the shiny new bomber looked, said a local reporter, like "a flying fortress". It had a crew of eight, four of them aiming defensive guns in five locations: the nose, above and below the rear fuselage and in blisters on each side. Amidships was the bay for eight 600lb (272kg) bombs. On 20 August this battleship of the sky was ferried to Wright Field. Egtvedt was there to meet it, and test pilot Les Tower asked "Where's everyone else?" Egtvedt said "They're expecting you in three hours' time." The new bomber had covered the 2,300 miles in nine hours.

On 30 October 1935 the 299 was destroyed when an Army pilot took off without realizing that the control locks

The first B-17B flew on 27 June 1939. Supercharger problems stretched deliveries, the Air Corps receiving its 39th and final B in March 1940.

Much more of a Flying Fortress, the B-17E needed a crew of ten. Seattle built every E; production ended on 28 May 1942 at No 1,023.

had not been released. With no competitor in the final judging, the production award went to the Douglas DB-1, as the B-18. But the Army was so impressed by the giant Boeing it reserved the previous number – 17 – for it, and began with an order in January 1936 for a service-test batch of 13. These, designated Y1B-17, were built in the new Plant 2 and delivered in early 1937. They differed from the prototype mainly in having Wright R-1820 Cyclone engines. As at that time the Army found it difficult to fund even a single new bomber, nobody would have believed that over the next seven years the B-17 would require nearly 70,000 Cyclones!

The first production version, the B-17B, introduced turbosupercharged R-1820-51 engines, as well as a rudder and flaps of increased area, a modified nose and hydraulic (instead of pneumatic) wheel brakes. The B-17C, flown in July 1940, had R-1820-65 engines, which with turbos gave 1,200hp for takeoff and a remarkable 1,000hp at 25,000ft (7,620m). As it was much lighter than later versions, this was the fastest, able to outrun most fighters at 323mph (520km/h). Other changes included better defensive fire-power, armour and self-sealing tanks. The idea was that a tight formation could offer such defensive fire as to make life difficult for hostile fighters, whilst cruising above the reach of most AA guns. This theory came unstuck in 1941 when No 90 Sqn, RAF Bomber Command, used the B-17C as the Fortress I in daylight.

Boeing put the RAF's salutary experience to immediate use. Distinguished by its much bigger fin, which improved bombing accuracy using the secret Norden bombsight, the B-17E introduced twin 0.5in guns in the extreme tail and twin-0.5in powered turrets above and below the fuselage. The ventral turret was sighted

B-17 FLYING FORTRESS

from a remote blister, but from the 113th B-17E it was replaced by a "ball turret" occupied by a small gunner. Next came the B-17F, distinguished by a longer frameless nosecap of moulded Plexiglas. Powered by R-1820-97 engines, still of 1,200hp for takeoff, the F had provision for external bomb racks for a maximum load of 8,000lb (3,629kg), though this would seldom be carried.

By 1943 Boeing, Douglas-Tulsa and Vega-Burbank (a Lockheed subsidiary) were all mass-producing the B-17G. Whereas the D, E and F had

been painted olive-drab, the G reverted to shiny metal, because there was little point in camouflage when 1,000 aircraft in formation were leaving contrails! The G introduced a

RAF Fortress Is were the first B-17s to see action. AM528 was one of 20 B-17Cs diverted to Britain, equipping No 90 Sqn in No 2 Group.

DATA FOR THE B-17G:

Span	103ft 9in (31.6m)
Length	74ft 9in (22.8m)
Wing area	1,420 sq ft (131.92m²)
Weight empty	36,135lb (16,391kg)
Maximum takeoff weight	65,500lb (29,711kg)
Maximum speed	287mph (462km/h)
Cruising speed	150mph (241km/h)
Service ceiling	31,700ft (9,662m)
Range	2,000 miles (3,219km)
	with (6,000lb, 2,722kg, bombload)

twin-0.5in chin turret, and had staggered 0.5in cheek guns in the nose, staggered waist guns and a new tail turret. Maximum bombload was 9,600lb (4,355kg). The only adverse feature was that, whereas the gross weight of the prototype had been 32,432lb (14,711kg), the B-17G was twice as heavy (see data) and this, together with the drag of the turrets, seriously affected performance.

Altogether 12,731 B-17s were built, including 2,995 by Douglas and 2,750 by Vega. Among dozens of rebuilds and conversions, one of the first was the YB-40 escort fighter

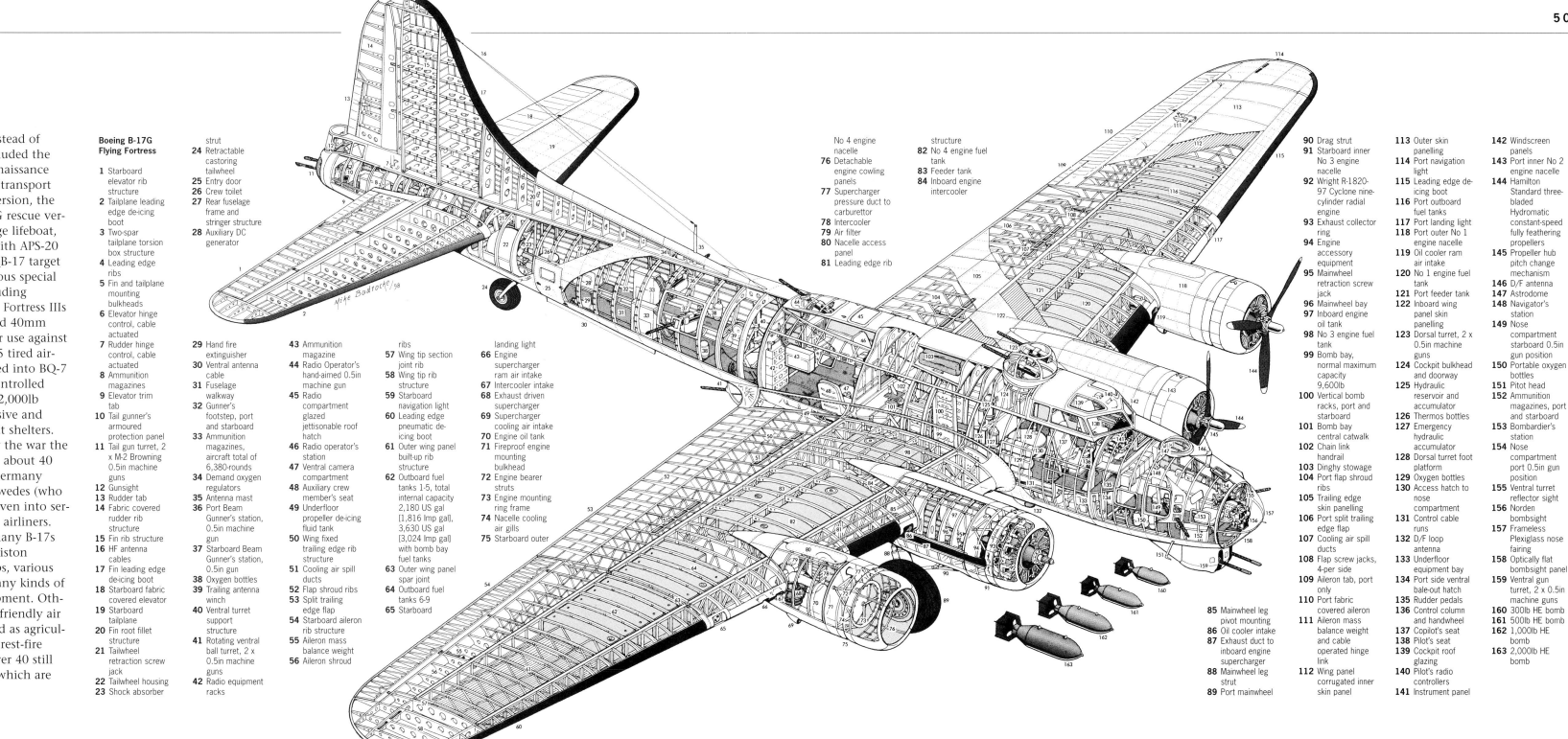

stead of
uded the
naissance
transport
ersion, the
G rescue ver-
ge lifeboat,
ith APS-20
B-17 target
us special
ding
Fortress IIIs
d 40mm
r use against
5 tired air-
d into BQ-7
ntrolled
2,000lb
ive and
t shelters.
the war the
about 40
ermany
wedes (who
ven into ser-
airliners.
any B-17s
iston
s, various
any kinds of
ment. Oth-
friendly air
d as agricul-
rest-fire
er 40 still
which are

**Boeing B-17G
Flying Fortress**

1 Starboard
   elevator rib
   structure
2 Tailplane leading
   edge de-icing
   boot
3 Two-spar
   tailplane torsion
   box structure
4 Leading edge
   ribs
5 Fin and tailplane
   mounting
   bulkheads
6 Elevator hinge
   control, cable
   actuated
7 Rudder hinge
   control, cable
   actuated
8 Ammunition
   magazines
9 Elevator trim
   tab
10 Tail gunner's
   armoured
   protection panel
11 Tail gun turret, 2
   x M-2 Browning
   0.5in machine
   guns
12 Gunsight
13 Rudder tab
14 Fabric covered
   rudder rib
   structure
15 Fin rib structure
16 HF antenna
   cables
17 Fin leading edge
   de-icing boot
18 Starboard fabric
   covered elevator
19 Starboard
   tailplane
20 Fin root fillet
   structure
21 Tailwheel
   retraction screw
   jack
22 Tailwheel housing
23 Shock absorber

24 Retractable
   castoring
   tailwheel
25 Entry door
26 Crew toilet
27 Rear fuselage
   frame and
   stringer structure
28 Auxiliary DC
   generator

29 Hand fire
   extinguisher
30 Ventral antenna
   cable
31 Fuselage
   walkway
32 Gunner's
   footstep, port
   and starboard
33 Ammunition
   magazines,
   aircraft total of
   6,380-rounds
34 Demand oxygen
   regulators
35 Antenna mast
36 Port Beam
   Gunner's station,
   0.5in machine
   gun
37 Starboard Beam
   Gunner's station,
   0.5in gun
38 Oxygen bottles
39 Trailing antenna
   winch
40 Ventral turret
   support
   structure
41 Rotating ventral
   ball turret, 2 x
   0.5in machine
   guns
42 Radio equipment
   racks

43 Ammunition
   magazine
44 Radio Operator's
   hand-aimed 0.5in
   machine gun
45 Radio
   compartment
   glazed
   jettisonable roof
   hatch
46 Radio operator's
   station
47 Ventral camera
   compartment
48 Auxiliary crew
   member's seat
49 Underfloor
   propeller de-icing
   fluid tank
50 Wing fixed
   trailing edge rib
   structure
51 Cooling air spill
   ducts
52 Flap shroud ribs
53 Split trailing
   edge flap
54 Starboard aileron
   rib structure
55 Aileron mass
   balance weight
56 Aileron shroud

57 Wing tip section
   joint rib
58 Wing tip rib
   structure
59 Starboard
   navigation light
60 Leading edge
   pneumatic de-
   icing boot
61 Outer wing panel
   built-up rib
   structure
62 Outboard fuel
   tanks 1-5, total
   internal capacity
   2,180 US gal
   [1,816 Imp gal],
   3,630 US gal
   [3,024 Imp gal]
   with bomb bay
   fuel tanks
63 Outer wing panel
   spar joint
64 Outboard fuel
   tanks 6-9
65 Starboard

ribs
66 Engine
   supercharger
   ram air intake
67 Intercooler intake
68 Exhaust driven
   supercharger
69 Supercharger
   cooling air intake
70 Engine oil tank
71 Fireproof engine
   mounting
   bulkhead
72 Engine bearer
   struts
73 Engine mounting
   ring frame
74 Nacelle cooling
   air gills
75 Starboard outer

landing light
66 Engine
   supercharger
   ram air intake
67 Intercooler intake

No 4 engine
   nacelle
76 Detachable
   engine cowling
   panels
77 Supercharger
   pressure duct to
   carburettor
78 Intercooler
79 Air filter
80 Nacelle access
   panel
81 Leading edge rib

structure
82 No 4 engine fuel
   tank
83 Feeder tank
84 Inboard engine
   intercooler

85 Mainwheel leg
   pivot mounting
86 Oil cooler intake
87 Exhaust duct to
   inboard engine
   supercharger
88 Mainwheel leg
   strut
89 Port mainwheel

90 Drag strut
91 Starboard inner
   No 3 engine
   nacelle
92 Wright R-1820-
   97 Cyclone nine-
   cylinder radial
   engine
93 Exhaust collector
   ring
94 Engine
   accessory
   equipment
95 Mainwheel
   retraction screw
   jack
96 Mainwheel bay
97 Inboard engine
   oil tank
98 No 3 engine fuel
   tank
99 Bomb bay,
   normal maximum
   capacity
   9,600lb
100 Vertical bomb
   racks, port and
   starboard
101 Bomb bay
   central catwalk
102 Chain link
   handrail
103 Dinghy stowage
104 Port flap shroud
   ribs
105 Trailing edge
   skin panelling
106 Port split trailing
   edge flap
107 Cooling air spill
   ducts
108 Flap screw jacks,
   4-per side
109 Aileron tab, port
   only
110 Port fabric
   covered aileron
111 Aileron mass
   balance weight
   and cable
   operated hinge
   link
112 Wing panel
   corrugated inner
   skin panel

113 Outer skin
   panelling
114 Port navigation
   light
115 Leading edge de-
   icing boot
116 Port outboard
   fuel tanks
117 Port landing light
118 Port outer No 1
   engine nacelle
119 Oil cooler ram
   air intake
120 No 1 engine fuel
   tank
121 Port feeder tank
122 Inboard wing
   panel skin
   panelling
123 Dorsal turret, 2 x
   0.5in machine
   guns
124 Cockpit bulkhead
   and doorway
125 Hydraulic
   reservoir and
   accumulator
126 Thermos bottles
127 Emergency
   hydraulic
   accumulator
128 Dorsal turret foot
   platform
129 Oxygen bottles
130 Access hatch to
   nose
   compartment
131 Control cable
   runs
132 D/F loop
   antenna
133 Underfloor
   equipment bay
134 Port side ventral
   bale-out hatch
135 Rudder pedals
136 Control column
   and handwheel
137 Copilot's seat
138 Pilot's seat
139 Cockpit roof
   glazing
140 Pilot's radio
   controllers
141 Instrument panel

142 Windscreen
   panels
143 Port inner No 2
   engine nacelle
144 Hamilton
   Standard three-
   bladed
   Hydromatic
   constant-speed
   fully feathering
   propellers
145 Propeller hub
   pitch change
   mechanism
146 D/F antenna
147 Astrodome
148 Navigator's
   station
149 Nose
   compartment
   starboard 0.5in
   gun position
150 Portable oxygen
   bottles
151 Pitot head
152 Ammunition
   magazines, port
   and starboard
153 Bombardier's
   station
154 Nose
   compartment
   port 0.5in gun
   position
155 Ventral turret
   reflector sight
156 Norden
   bombsight
157 Frameless
   Plexiglass nose
   fairing
158 Optically flat
   bombsight panel
159 Ventral gun
   turret, 2 x 0.5in
   machine guns
160 300lb HE bomb
161 500lb HE bomb
162 1,000lb HE
   bomb
163 2,000lb HE
   bomb

PRESSURIZATION

From 1934 Egtvedt, Monteith and later Ed Wells had studied how to build a four-engined commercial transport. By 1935 these sketches had hardened into the Model 300, virtually a passenger derivative of the 299. In 1936 the prime targets, United and American, decided to help Douglas build the DC-4. Undaunted, Boeing kept the interest of PanAm and TWA, the former even assisting financially. The key feature was to develop the 300 into the 307 with a fuselage which, for the first time in a production aircraft, was pressurized by blowers driven off the inboard engines.

The body, huge in comparison with existing transports, was of almost perfect streamline form with a diameter of 12ft (3.66m). The two-pilot cockpit was in the extreme nose, the row of windows fitting the unbroken exterior profile. Behind was a station for a new crew-member, a flight engineer. The main cabin had compartments for 33

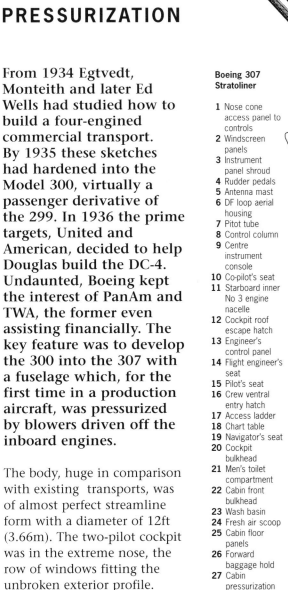

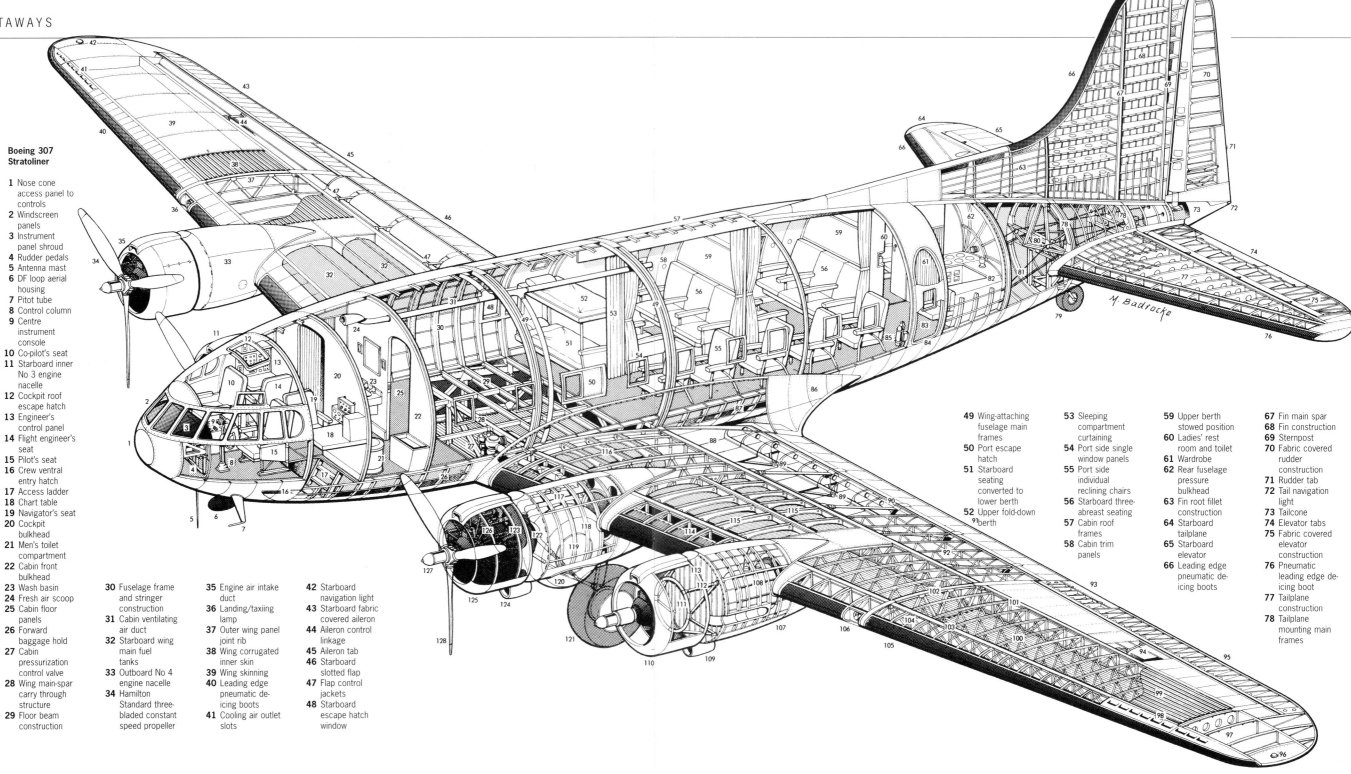

M. Badrocke

Boeing 307 Stratoliner

1 Nose cone access panel to controls
2 Windscreen panels
3 Instrument panel shroud
4 Rudder pedals
5 Antenna mast
6 DF loop aerial housing
7 Pitot tube
8 Control column
9 Centre instrument console
10 Co-pilot's seat
11 Starboard inner No 3 engine nacelle
12 Cockpit roof escape hatch
13 Engineer's control panel
14 Flight engineer's seat
15 Pilot's seat
16 Crew ventral entry hatch
17 Access ladder
18 Chart table
19 Navigator's seat
20 Cockpit bulkhead
21 Men's toilet compartment
22 Cabin front bulkhead
23 Wash basin
24 Fresh air scoop
25 Cabin floor panels
26 Forward baggage hold
27 Cabin pressurization control valve
28 Wing main-spar carry through structure
29 Floor beam construction

30 Fuselage frame and stringer construction
31 Cabin ventilating air duct
32 Starboard wing main fuel tanks
33 Outboard No 4 engine nacelle
34 Hamilton Standard three-bladed constant speed propeller
35 Engine air intake duct
36 Landing/taxiing lamp
37 Outer wing panel joint rib
38 Wing corrugated inner skin
39 Wing skinning
40 Leading edge pneumatic de-icing boots
41 Cooling air outlet slots

42 Starboard navigation light
43 Starboard fabric covered aileron
44 Aileron control linkage
45 Aileron tab
46 Starboard slotted flap
47 Flap control jackets
48 Starboard escape hatch window

49 Wing-attaching fuselage main frames
50 Port escape hatch
51 Starboard seating converted to lower berth
52 Upper fold-down berth

53 Sleeping compartment curtaining
54 Port side single window panels
55 Port side individual reclining chairs
56 Starboard three-abreast seating
57 Cabin roof frames
58 Cabin trim panels

59 Upper berth stowed position
60 Ladies' rest room and toilet
61 Wardrobe
62 Rear fuselage pressure bulkhead
63 Fin root fillet construction
64 Starboard tailplane
65 Starboard elevator
66 Leading edge pneumatic de-icing boot

67 Fin main spar
68 Fin construction
69 Sternpost
70 Fabric covered rudder construction
71 Rudder tab
72 Tail navigation light
73 Tailcone
74 Elevator tabs
75 Fabric covered elevator construction
76 Pneumatic leading edge de-icing boot
77 Tailplane construction
78 Tailplane mounting main frames

79 Retractable tailwheel
80 Tailwheel mounting structure
81 Tailplane cont cables
82 Galley
83 Steward's fol seat
84 Passenger en door
85 Fire extinguish
86 Trailing edge wing root fille
87 Rear baggage compartment
88 Slotted flap profile
89 External flap hinges
90 Flap torque shaft
91 Aluminium skinned flap construction
92 Flap shroud construction
93 Aileron tab
94 Aileron contro linkage
95 Port fabric covered ailer
96 Port navigatio light
97 Wing tip construction
98 Cooling air ou slots
99 Corrugated w inner skin
100 Lattice wing ribs
101 Rear wing spar
102 Outer wing pa joint rib
103 Front spar
104 Leading edge nose ribs
105 Leading edge pneumatic de icing boots
106 Port landing/ taxiing lamp

**'The Transcontinental Airline',
TWA shared the distinction of
introducing the world's first
pressurized airliner. A gleaming
NC-19907 flies into La Guardia,
New York City.**

passengers, which could be converted with nine in reclining seats and 16 in sleeper berths. Joints and doors were sealed, and the pressurization system was automatically controlled so that above 8,000ft (2,438m) internal pressure fell away more slowly than outside, until at 14,000ft (4,267m) the differential had reached its limit at the modest value of 2.5lb/sq in (0.176 kg/cm²).

The prototype 307 was otherwise based on the B-17C, though it had civil Cyclone G-102 engines, rated at 1,100hp for takeoff and 900hp at 17,300ft (5,273m), driving constant-speed feathering propellers. Maximum weight was 42,000lb (19,051kg). A row of fixed slots was provided at each wingtip. Registered NX-19901, the prototype flew on 31 December 1938. On 18 March 1939 it crashed while demonstrating asymmetric stalls to a KLM delegation, all 13 on board being killed. Boeing quickly fitted a much larger vertical tail resembling that of the later B-17E.

In 1940 four Stratoliners were delivered to PanAm and six to TWA. Howard Hughes wanted an upgraded 307 for a world flight. Told he would have to join the queue after TWA, he bought the airline and diverted its first aircraft (he fitted R-2600 engines and extra tanks, but never made the flight). From December 1941 TWA operated their aircraft as olive-drab C-75 transports temporarily sold to the US Government for use overseas. On return to TWA, in July 1944, they were rebuilt as the SA-307B-1 with 1,200hp engines in B-17G installations on B-17G wings, larger B-17G horizontal tails mounted further aft, with cabin compartments removed to allow 38 seats, pressurization deleted and a B-29 type electrical system. Later they were used by the French line Aigle Azur on the route to Indo-China.

DATA FOR 307B-1:

Span	107ft 3in (32.69m)
Length	74ft 4in (22.66m)
Wing area	1,486 sq ft (138.05m²)
Weight empty	31,120lb (14,116kg)
Maximum weight	54,000lb (24,494kg)
Cruising speed	184mph (296km/h)
Range	1,750 miles (2,816km)

314

A SALESMAN'S PITCH (AND YAW)

In February 1935 PanAm and Boeing discussed the possibility of building a flying boat with sufficient range to fly the North Atlantic. Boeing said that it was already overloaded; the annual accounts were in the red, and it was already working on the XB-15, B-17 and Model 307. New hire Wellwood Beall asked the new chief engineer Bob Minshall why a wing and tail of XB-15 type should not be used to help meet PanAm's request. Though he had been hired as a salesman, Beall himself did preliminary sketches. In April 1936 PanAm extended the deadline for submissions, and two months later it signed a $3 million contract for six Model 314s, with a further six on option.

A second key to success was availability of the 14-cylinder Wright GR-2600 engine, rated at 1,500hp, driving 13ft (3.96m) Hamilton Standard constant-speed feathering propellers. Tanks in the wings and stabilizing sponsons held 3,497gal (15,897 lit) of fuel. The enormous hull provided accommodation for a crew of 10, and for 74 passengers in up to nine compartments on slightly different levels, with sleeping accommodation for 40. Up to 10,000lb (4,536kg) of baggage and mail could be loaded into the bow and into compartments on the upper level behind the flight crew.

Far too large to be erected in the factory, the parts for NX18601 were assembled on the ramp, launched into the Duwamish river and towed to Seattle's seaport on Elliot Bay. Roll stability was inadequate, especially in a breeze, with wingtips entering the water, but on 7 June 1938 Eddie Allen made the first flight. He managed to land on Lake Washington, but reported that the only way he could make a gentle turn was by closing the throttles on one side. A new twin-fin tail was fitted, and eventually the answer was found to be to retain the twin fins and rudders and restore a centre-line fin, without a rudder.

Deliveries began in January 1939, and on 20 May 1939 PanAm began the first mail service across the North Atlantic,

with a scheduled passenger service on 28 June. They took up the option, the second six aircraft being designated 314A to reflect the use of 1,600hp 709C Cyclones driving 14ft (4.27m) propellers, fed with 4,503gal (20,471 lit) of newly available 100-octane fuel. The interior was rearranged for 77 day passengers. The 314s were similarly modified. In 1941 three of the 314As were purchased by BOAC, establishing a link with the British airline which has grown to make Boeing

PanAm's first 314A was named *Yankee Clipper* by Mrs Franklin D. Roosevelt.

almost its sole supplier. All 12 boats operated intensively in camouflage in World War 2. PanAm's remaining nine, retaining their *Clipper* names, briefly became Army C-98s before serving (as 'B-314s') with the Navy. Postwar, service with charter operators led to two forced landings, one in the Pacific, the other the Atlantic.

DATA FOR THE 314A:

Span	**152ft 0in (46.33m)**
Length	**106ft 0in (32.31m)**
Wing area	**2,867 sq ft (266.34m²)**
Weight empty	**48,400lb (21,954kg)**
Maximum takeoff weight	**84,000lb (38,102kg)**
Cruising speed	**188mph (303km/h)**
Range	**3,685 miles (5,930km)**

RENTON CO-PROJECT

In 1940 Boeing's future looked rosier, with the start of design of the Model 344 patrol flying boat for the Navy and the Model 345 strategic bomber for the Army. Both shared a very similar design of wing, with a new Boeing-117 aerofoil profile and the exceptional aspect ratio of 11.5, in order to meet unprecedented demands for long range. The flying boat was powered by basically the same 18-cylinder Wright R-3350 engine as the bomber, but by only two engines instead of four. Each R-3350-8 was rated at 2,300hp, and drove a propeller with three broad "paddle" blades and the exceptional diameter of 17ft (5.18m). Of course, instead of a slim pressurized tube the fuselage of the flying boat was deep and slab-sided, with accommodation for a crew of up to 10.

Wing cells could carry four torpedoes or 20 bombs of 1,000lb (454kg) each. Ball-type turrets in the nose and tail each

DATA FOR THE SEA RANGER:

Span	139ft 8.5in (42.48m)
Length	94ft 9in (28.88m)
Wing area	1,826 sq ft (196.4m²).
Weight empty	41,531lb (18,838.5kg)
Maximum takeoff weight	101,129lb (45,872kg).
Maximum speed	228mph (367km/h)
Patrol speed	127mph (204km/h)
Range	4,245 miles (6,831km)

housed twin 0.5in guns, and in the production PBB four more were to be mounted in the dorsal turret and waist positions. Tanks in the wings housed the remarkable capacity of 7,973gal (36,245lit), giving a calculated endurance of 72 hours. This resulted in a maximum weight almost double the "60,000lb" estimated by the technical press when the existence of the Sea Ranger was released in summer 1942. This weight required the use of JATO (jet-assisted takeoff) rockets to get off the water at full load.

The major sections of the XPBB-1 prototype, Navy number 3144, were made in Plant 1 and then sent by barge for assembly in the new Plant 2, which was built and owned by the Navy at Renton, on the south shore of Lake Washington. Here it was painted Sea Green and Light Grey, with national markings devoid of the central red disc, starting a successful flight test programme at Sand Point on 9 July 1942. On 23 February 1943 the prototype returned to Renton, which was already tooling up to build an initial 57 PBBs. The Navy then decided that its needs could be met by the old PBY, and the PBB contract was cancelled. Instead, Renton was assigned to the Army to build the B-29.

Soon to be dubbed the 'Lone Ranger', Boeing's final flying boat rides 'on the step'; the cockpit hatch appears to be open.

344 XPBB-1 SEA RANGER

AS COMPLEX AS IT GETS

Throughout the late 1930s Boeing argued with the Army that the B-17's turbosuperchargers ought to be partnered by a pressurized fuselage, as proposed in the Model 334. The Army had barely enough money to keep the B-17 programme active, but encouraged Boeing to keep the unpaid 334 studies going. The outbreak of World War 2 sharpened the Army's interest, and on 29 January 1940 it sent a Request for Proposals to five companies for a bomber which could fly very high, with pressurized crew compartments, and also achieve unprecedented distances and speeds. On 8 September 1940, Boeing received a contract for two (later three) Model 345 bombers, designated XB-29, plus a test specimen.

The B-29 far transcended the complexity of any previous aircraft, and opened up a totally new world of aviation technology. In such areas as thickness of wing skins, hydraulic and electrical power

and the number of separate machines on board, the new bomber exceeded current practice by from 80 to 2,000 per cent. The wing closely resembled that of the 344 flying boat, but on the leading edge were not two but four Wright R-3350 Duplex Cyclone engines. The white-hot exhaust was led back to escape through two General Electric B-11 turbos, one on each side of the nacelle, from which the compressed mixture was fed via a large intercooler to the gear-driven supercharger in a magnesium-alloy casing on the rear of the crankcase. Wright, GE and Boeing toiled for years to suppress the catastrophic backfires, magnesium fires and

Superfortress *Spirit of Lincoln* was trialled with Allison V-3420 liquid-cooled double engines.

other problems, and give each of the 18 cylinders the correct supply of mixture and adequate cooling.

With so complex an aircraft other difficulties were numerous, but the US industry was acquiring a reputation for trampling difficulties to death by sheer engineering strength. The wing, the strongest made at that time, abandoned truss construction in favour of spars and ribs with sheet webs. This made it possible to seal the inter-spar box to accommodate 7,896gal (35,895 litres) of fuel.

The fuselage was a smooth-skinned tube with a diameter of 112in (2.84m). The nose of multi-pane Plexiglas housed the bombardier in the centre, with the pilot and copilot immediately behind. The navigator sat behind the pilot, the engineer behind the copilot, and the radio operator behind the engineer. Next came an unpressurized section with front and rear bays for various bombloads, the heaviest being 40 of 500lb (227kg). Above these bays a crawl tunnel connected to the rear pressurized section housing three transparent domes over sighting stations controlling the two dorsal and two ventral turrets, each with twin 0.5in guns (in the B-29A, four in the forward dorsal). Isolated in a pressurized tail compartment was a fourth gunner with (usually) one 20mm and two 0.5in.

The four fuselage turrets were linked to the sighting stations by a complex electrical system so that, should any station be knocked out, another station could take over its turret(s). Each engine drove a generator serving a high-power system which among other things operated the twin-wheel landing gears and the large one-piece Fowler flaps which extended aft on steel tracks. These flaps were crucial in permitting a wing loading of 77.6lb/sq ft (380kg/m²), double that of the B-17. The cabin environmental system was energised by a compressor on each inboard engine. Leading edges were deiced by pulsating rubber boots, an automatic system maintained longitudinal trim by dropping bombs alternately from the front and rear bays, and between the bomb bays many aircraft had radar, such as APQ-13 (H₂X).

The first prototype, 41-002, was built in Plant 1 and assembled at Boeing Field. It had 2,200hp R-3350-13 engines driving 17ft 0in (5.18m) three-blade propellers, and was painted olive drab.

B-29-65-BW serving with the 3510th CCTW at Randolph AFB, Texas, 1953.

Allen made the first flight on 21 September 1942. He and his crew had many problems, notably including engine fires, and their luck finally ran out with the No 2 aircraft on 18 February 1943, when they catastrophically just failed to reach the airfield. By this time an unprecedented production programme was swinging into operation.

Plant 1 built only the three XBs. Boeing's enormous new factory adjacent to the former Stearman plant at Wichita, Kansas, built 14 service-test YB-29s, with R-3350-21s still driving the three-blade propeller. Wichita followed with 1,620 B-29s, powered by the R-3350-23, of unchanged power, driving the 16ft 7in (5.05m) four-blade Hydromatic propeller that became standard. A further 357 B-29s were produced by Bell at Marietta,

Georgia, and 204 by Martin at Omaha, Nebraska. Boeing's new Renton plant built 1,119 B-29As with the four-gun forward dorsal turret and a wing divided not into two but into five sections, increasing span by 12in (305mm). Finally, Bell built 311 B-29Bs, which were lightened and simplified by stripping out the complex defensive system, leaving just the gunner in the tail, with APG-15B radar fire control. Almost all the engine nacelles, as big as a fighter fuselage, were made by Fisher Body division of General Motors. On 10 June 1946 production ceased at 3,628, all except the first 20 being unpainted.

Though the B-29 was

DATA FOR B-29:	
Span	**141ft 3in (43.05m)**
Length	**99ft 0in (30.18m)**
Wing area	**1,739 sq ft (161.56m²)**
Weight empty	**74,500lb (33,795kg)**
Maximum takeoff weight	**135,000lb (61,240kg)**
Maximum speed	**357mph (575km/h)** *at 30,000ft (9,144m)*
Cruising speed	**290mph (467km/h)**
Range	**3,250 miles (5,230km)**
	with 10,000lb (4,536kg) bombload

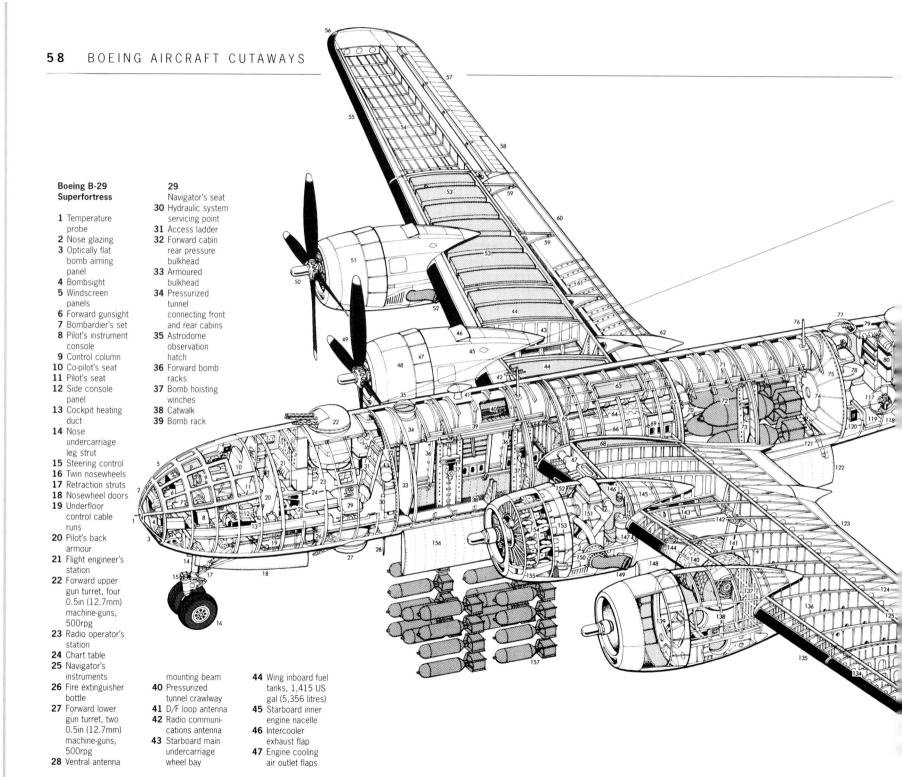

Boeing B-29 Superfortress

1 Temperature probe
2 Nose glazing
3 Optically flat bomb aiming panel
4 Bombsight
5 Windscreen panels
6 Forward gunsight
7 Bombardier's set
8 Pilot's instrument console
9 Control column
10 Co-pilot's seat
11 Pilot's seat
12 Side console panel
13 Cockpit heating duct
14 Nose undercarriage leg strut
15 Steering control
16 Twin nosewheels
17 Retraction struts
18 Nosewheel doors
19 Underfloor control cable runs
20 Pilot's back armour
21 Flight engineer's station
22 Forward upper gun turret, four 0.5in (12.7mm) machine-guns, 500rpg
23 Radio operator's station
24 Chart table
25 Navigator's instruments
26 Fire extinguisher bottle
27 Forward lower gun turret, two 0.5in (12.7mm) machine-guns, 500rpg
28 Ventral antenna

29 Navigator's seat
30 Hydraulic system servicing point
31 Access ladder
32 Forward cabin rear pressure bulkhead
33 Armoured bulkhead
34 Pressurized tunnel connecting front and rear cabins
35 Astrodome observation hatch
36 Forward bomb racks
37 Bomb hoisting winches
38 Catwalk
39 Bomb rack

40 mounting beam
40 Pressurized tunnel crawlway
41 D/F loop antenna
42 Radio communications antenna
43 Starboard main undercarriage wheel bay

44 Wing inboard fuel tanks, 1,415 US gal (5,356 litres)
45 Starboard inner engine nacelle
46 Intercooler exhaust flap
47 Engine cooling air outlet flaps

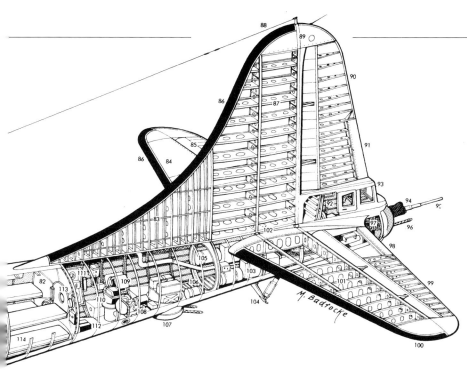

48 Engine cowling panels
49 Hamilton Standard 4-bladed 16ft 7in constant-speed propellers
50 Propeller hub pitch change mechanism
51 Starboard outer engine nacelle
52 Exhaust stub
53 Wing outboard fuel tanks, 1,320 US gal (4,991 litres) maximum internal fuel load 9,363 US gal including bomb bay ferry tanks
54 Wing bottom skin stringers

55 Leading edge de-icing boots
56 Starboard navigation light
57 Fabric-covered aileron
58 Aileron tab
59 Flap guide rails
60 Starboard Fowler-type flap
61 Flap rib construction
62 Inboard nacelle tail fairing
63 Life raft stowage
64 Wing panel centreline joint
65 Wing/fuselge attachment main frames
66 Pressurization ducting
67 Heat exchanger
68 Centre section fuel tank, 1,333 US gal (5,046 litres)
69 Cabin heater
70 Pressurization

control valve
71 Fuselage framing
72 Rear bomb bay, 4 x 2,000lb bombs shown
73 Bomb rack
74 Access door
75 Rear cabin front pressure bulkhead
76 Radio antenna mast
77 Upper gun turret sighting hatch
78 Upper gunner's seat
79 Remote gun controller
80 Radio and electronics racks
81 Upper gun turret, two 0.5in (12.7mm) machine-guns, 500rpg
82 Rear pressure bulkhead
83 Fin root fillet
84 Starboard tailplane
85 Starboard elevator
86 Leading edge

de-icing boots
87 Tailfin construction
88 HF antenna cable
89 Fin tip fairing
90 Fabric covered rudder construction
91 Rudder tab
92 Pressurized tail gunner's compartment
93 Armoured glass window panels
94 Tail gun camera
95 20mm cannon, 100-rounds
96 Twin 0.5in (12.7mm) machine-guns, 500rpg
97 Remotely controlled ball turret
98 Elevator tab
99 Port fabric covered elevator construction
100 Tailplane leading edge de-icing boot
101 Tailplane construction

102 Fin/tailplane attachment joints
103 Tail turret ammunition boxes
104 Retractable tail bumper
105 Oxygen bottles
106 APU fuel tank
107 Rear ventral turret, two 0.5in (12.7mm) machine-guns, 500rpg
108 Auxiliary power unit (APU)
109 Oblique camera
110 Vertical camera
111 Crew entry door
112 Batteries
113 Pressure bulkhead access door
114 Crew rest bunks
115 Toilet
116 Radio communications tuning units
117 Remote gunsight
118 Gun aiming blister
119 Gunner's seat, port and starboard
120 Voltage regulator
121 Bomb door hydraulic jacks
122 Rear bomb bay doors
123 Port Fowler flap
124 Flap shroud ribs
125 Rear spar
126 Outer wing panel joint
127 Aileron tab
128 Fabric covered aileron construction
129 Wing tip fairing
130 Port navigation light
131 Wing stringers

132 Outer wing panel ribs
133 Front spar
134 Leading edge nose ribs
135 Leading edge de-icing boots
136 Port wing fuel tank bays
137 Engine nacelle firewall
138 Nacelle construction
139 Engine mounting frame
140 Twin mainwheels
141 Main undercarriage leg strut
142 Mainwheel pivot mounting
143 Port mainwheel bay
144 Hydraulic retraction jack
145 Nacelle tail fairing
146 Self-sealing oil tank, 85 US gal (322 litres)
147 Hydraulic reservoir
148 Mainwheel doors
149 Exhaust stub
150 Exhaust driven turbo-supercharger
151 Intercooler
152 Engine cooling air exit flaps
153 Exhaust collector ring
154 Wright Cyclone R-3350-57A, 18-cylinder, two-row radial engine
155 Engine intake ducting
156 Forward bomb bay doors
157 20 x 500lb (227 kg) bombs, maximum bomb load 20,000lb (9,072kg)

superb to fly, at first crews found many difficulties, and notably failed to achieve anything like the design range. The first mission was against Bangkok rail yards on 5 June 1944, by which time the miles per gallon achieved by average crews had been doubled. By 1945, 20 USAAF groups from the Marianas were sending 500 bombers at a time to destroy Japanese industry. The war was abruptly ended – without the need for a costly invasion of Japan – by nuclear weapons dropped on 6 August 1945 by *Enola Gay* and on 9 August by *Bock's Car*. Three aircraft landed in Soviet territory, and the Tupolev design bureau copied them to produce the Tu-4.

Many B-29s continued in front-line USAF service through the Korean conflict, and 87 were lent to a grateful RAF who called them the Washington B.1. Numerous modified versions included the RB-29 for Elint (three were shot down north of Hokkaido), the F-13 for photo-reconnaissance, WB-13 for weather reconnaissance and KB-29 tankers. The Model 345 was also the starting point for the C-97, Stratocruiser and B-50.

POST-WAR UPDATE

345 B-50

In 1943 Boeing studied B-29s with more powerful engines, as a result of which two aircraft were converted. The first of the 13 YB-29s, 41-36954, was retrofitted with 2,600hp Allison V-3420 liquid-cooled engines – the massive unit based on a pair of V-1710 engines, which had been intended for the XB-15 – to become the XB-39 (photo, page 56). The other was a production B-29A-5, 42-93845, which was fitted with 3,000hp Pratt & Whitney R-4360-33 Wasp Major engines, to become the XB-44.

The R-4360, with four compact "corncob" rows of seven cylinders, gave particularly good results. Plans were made to switch production to the Model 345-2, the B-29D. This aircraft featured the 3,500hp R-4360-35, installed in very neat cowlings below which were large inlets for a single giant General Electric CH-7A turbosupercharger. The propeller was a four-blade Curtiss Electric, with a diameter of 17ft 2in (5.23m) with feathering and braking capability. Other changes included a lighter and stronger wing made mainly of the new 75ST alloy, a taller vertical tail

able to fold down to enter hangars, with a hydraulically boosted rudder, deicing by eight Stewart Warner combustion heaters (three in each outer nacelle and two in the fin), hydraulic nosewheel steering and electrothermal deicing of the nose windows.

In July 1945 the first block of 200 B-29D bombers was ordered from Renton, but after VJ-Day this was cut to 60. In order to keep it in the post-war programme the designation was changed to B-50A, and

Fresh from Seattle's Plant 1, this **B-50D** was photographed on 31 August 1949.

eventually 79 were built. The first, 46-002, made its first flight on 25 June 1947. Its designation remained B-50A-1-BN, even though the programme was actually transferred to Seattle's Plant 1, whose code was BO. This factory followed with 45 B-50Bs with a locally strengthened airframe to permit a gross weight increased from 168,708lb (76,526kg) to 170,000lb (77,112kg). The YB-50C with a stretched fuselage and 4,500hp R-4360-51 VDT (variable-discharge turbine) compound engines was cancelled, along with the intended

DATA FOR THE B-50D:

Span	**141ft 3in (43.05m)**
Length	**100ft 0in (30.48m)**
Wing area	**1,720 sq ft (159.8m²)**
Weight empty	**81,000lb (36,741kg)**
Maximum takeoff weight	**173,000lb (78,471kg)**
Maximum speed	**400mph (644km/h)**
Cruising speed	**277mph (446km/h)**
Range	**4,900 miles (7,886km)**
	with 28,000lb (12,701kg) bombload

B-54 production version. The final contracts for Boeing piston-engined bombers were for 222 of the Model 345-9-6 B-50D. This had the flat bomb-aiming panel set into a frameless nose of moulded Plexiglas and racks under the outer wings for 583gal (2,650-litre) tanks or 4,000lb (1,814kg) bombs. From No. 16 a receptacle was provided aft of the cockpit for Flying Boom refuelling.

Production of the Super-fortress was concluded by 24 Model 345-31-26 TB-50H crew trainers. Unarmed, these reached 418mph (673km/h) at 31,000ft (9,449m), the last being delivered on 11 March 1953. Among rebuilds and conversions the outstanding programmes were conversion by Hayes Industries of 112 B-50A/B bombers into KB-50J tankers, and all 24 TB-50H trainers into KB-50K tankers. Like KB-29 versions, these tanker variants had British-type hose-drum units in the extended tail and in under-wing pods just inboard of the tips. To get nearer to the speed and height of jet receiver aircraft, two General Electric J47 jet booster pods were added under the wings between the outer nacelles and the hose-drum pods. Other conversions resulted in 43 RB-50 reconnaissance air-craft and 36 WB-50Ds for weather reconnaissance. KB and WB aircraft served in Vietnam until 1968.

F-100Cs from the 322nd Fighter Day Group, Foster AFB, Texas, take a drink from a KB-50D.

STRATO-VARIOUS

367 C-97 STRATOFREIGHTER

Almost in parallel with the design of the 345 bomber the Boeing project engineers schemed a transport derivative. This had a huge pressurized fuselage with a cross-section resembling an inverted 8, the main floor being at the joint between the lower lobe with the same diameter as a B-29 fuselage and a longer upper lobe of greater (11ft, 3.35m) diameter. In January 1942 the Army Air Force ordered three Model 367 prototypes, designated XC-97. Bombers had priority, and the first XC-97 did not fly until 9 November 1944.

Powered by 2,325hp Wright R-3350-57A engines, the new transport had virtually the same wings, nacelles, tail and landing gear as the B-29, and the wing even passed through the lower lobe at the same point. The enormous new upper lobe gave the transport a whale-like appearance, and featured a nose flight deck resembling a much bigger version of that of the 307, with windows fitted into the exterior profile. At the rear the lower lobe ended in large left/right clamshell doors so that vehicles could be driven up ramps (not part of the aircraft), and other cargo could be loaded by an electrically powered hoist

running on rails along the 74ft (22.55m) length of the upper deck. This deck could accommodate three loaded 1.5-ton trucks, two 7.6ton (7,722kg) Locust light tanks, 83 casualties on litters (stretchers) or 134 seated troops with their weapons. In 1944 such capability was breathtaking.

In July 1945 the Army ordered six YC-97s, three YC-97As and a VIP YC-97B. The YC-97A, Model 367-4-6, eventually changed the basis of the design to the B-50, with 3,000hp R-4360-35A engines, 75ST alloy, thermal deicing and the tall folding fin. Four-blade Curtiss Electric reversing propellers were fitted, but with

diameter reduced to 16ft 8in (5.08m). This increased maximum payload from 41,400lb to 53,000lb (24,041kg). The C-97A, the first production Stratofreighter, introduced APS-42 weather radar in a chin radome, HamStan propellers of unchanged diameter and extra tanks in the outer wings; 27 were bought, later increased to 50, entering service on 15 October 1949. Next came 14 C-97Cs with a strengthened floor and changed radio and instrumentation, used on medevac service to Korea.

The next new-build model was the 367-4-29, KC-97E, the first Stratotanker. Powered by 3,500hp R-4360-35C engines,

The C-97A served with MATS from October 1949. Its upper hold provided a usable length of about 74ft (22.55m).

Introduced in 1953, the KC-97G was the main production version. Boosted by J47 turbojets, KC-97Ls survived with ANG units until the late 1970s.

60 were delivered with 5,995gal (27,255-litres) of transfer fuel in tanks on the upper deck and a new design of Boeing Flying Boom aimed by an operator lying in a rear-fuselage gondola. The main-deck tanks could be removed, and the boom installation replaced by clamshell doors. Next came 159 Model 367-76-29 KC-97F, powered by 3,800hp R-4360-59B engines. Finally came the huge total of 592 Model 367-76-66 KC-97G, with B-50D type underwing tanks and various modifica-tions to facilitate use as either a tanker or a transport.

The 888 aircraft of the C-97 family were all built at Seattle, Renton being closed in the post-war cutback. They had a long and successful career, and were modified into 14 sub-types, including two with 5,700ehp Pratt & Whitney T34 turboprops. In addition many were put through civilian con-

Aero Spacelines' Pregnant Guppies had the largest cargo compartment of any aircraft. Turboprop 377SGT-201s linked Airbus factories between 1971-1997.

versions as agricultural sprayers, forest-fire water bombers and swollen-body "Guppy" transports. The only foreign military user was Israel, which bought several ex-USAF aircraft as tankers, electronic-warfare platforms and as para-troop and cargo transports, some having a locally designed swing-tail loading modifica-tion. Boeing spent years trying to get USAF support for a jet derivative, and eventually built the 367-80.

DATA FOR THE KC-97G:

Span	141ft 3in (43.05m)
Length,	117ft 5in (35.8m) *including flight-refuelling boom*
Wing area	1,769 sq ft (164.34m²)
Weight empty	84,990lb (38,551kg)
Maximum takeoff weight	175,000lb (78,980kg)
Cruising speed	300mph (482km/h)
Range	4,300 miles (6,920km) *without using transfer fuel*

"BUILD THEM. WE'LL SELL THEM."

To an outsider it seemed obvious that Boeing should produce a commercial transport derived from the C-97, but the market for so large, complicated and expensive an aircraft appeared to be very limited. On 5 September 1945 Boeing was in bad shape. Wholesale cancellations of the huge wartime contracts had resulted in massive layoffs and plant closures, while wartime profits were followed by big tax bills. This was what faced William M. 'Bill' Allen, Boeing's lawyer, who on that day became the company's President, on Egtvedt's becoming Chairman.

Allen was to steer with a firm hand for nearly 30 years. Told on his first day as President that there was no way they could meet the upper limit on price of $1.25 million unless at least 50 Model 377s were sold, he replied "We're going to build 50 Stratocruisers. Now our job is to sell them". In all essentials the 377 resembled the YC-97B, with minor

Model 377 Stratocruiser

1 Windscreen panels
2 Instrument panel shroud
3 Back of instrument panel
4 Rudder pedals
5 Control column handwheel
6 Cockpit eyebrow windows
7 Overhead switch panel
8 Co-pilot's seat
9 Centre control console
10 Pilot's seat
11 Nosewheel steering wheel
12 Cockpit floor level
13 Underfloor control runs
14 Nose undercarriage pivot fixing
15 Nosewheel leg door
16 Twin nosewheels
17 Steering control jacks
18 Torque scissor links
19 Nosewheel rear strut
20 Retraction screw jack
21 Retraction motor
22 Folding observer's seat
23 Radio operator's station
24 Engineer's swivelling seat
25 Flight engineer's instrument
26 VOR antenna
27 Cockpit roof glazed hatch
28 Radio and electronics rack
29 Antenna lead-in

30 Crew toilet
31 Cabin bulkhead
32 Flight deck doorway
33 Navigator's seat
34 Chart table
35 Crew access ladder to lower deck
36 Nosewheel well
37 Fuselage nose section joint frame
38 D/F loop antennas
39 ADF sense antenna
40 Forward cargo hold
41 Baggage restraint nets
42 Starboard side baggage door
43 First class seating compartment, eight seats
44 Forward emergency exit window
45 Privacy curtaining
46 Fold-down double bunks, upper and lower
47 HF antenna mast
48 Ladies' cloakroom and

windows, port and starboard
62 Fuel filler cap
63 Inner wing panel fuel cells; total fuel capacity 7,790 US gal (29,450 litres)

toilet, starboard side
49 Main water tank
50 Drinking water tank
51 Toilet
52 Men's cloakroom
53 Wing inspection light
54 Wash basins
55 Drinking water dispenser
56 Magazine rack
57 Upper lobe section joint frame
58 Wing spar centre section carry-through
59 Centre section fuel cells
60 Fuselage centre section construction
61 Emergency exit

64 Starboard inner engine nacelle
65 Intercooler air flap
66 Ventral filtered air intake
67 Turbo-supercharger

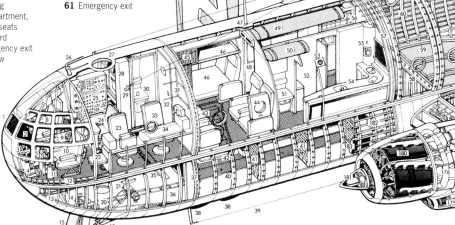

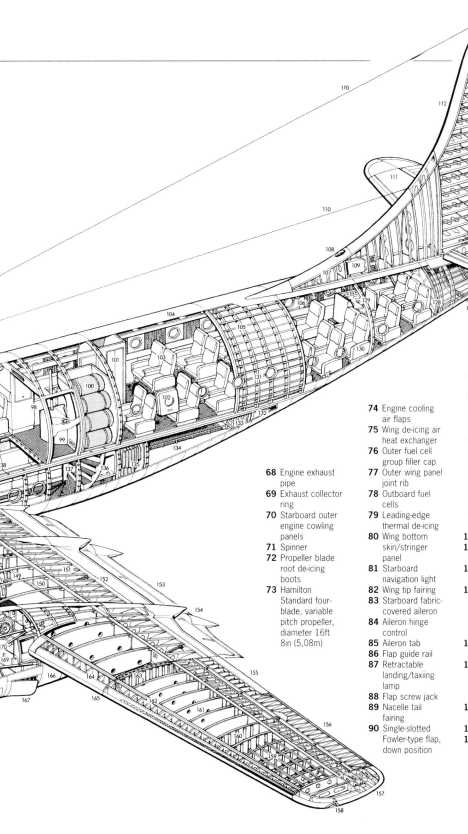

377 STRATOCRUISER

129 Flight attendant's control station
130 Rear cabin seating
131 Cabin window panels
132 Rear cargo/baggage hold
133 Baggage restraint netting
134 Luggage shelf
135 Wardrobe
136 Bar unit
137 Circular staircase
138 Lower deck lounge, 12-passenger capacity
139 Aileron servo motor
140 Central flap drive electric motor
141 Wing root attachment joint
142 Wing root rib
143 Inboard fuel cell bays
144 Water injection tank, capacity 30 US gal (114 litres)
145 Main gear bay
146 Retraction screw jack and electric motor
147 Twin mainwheels
148 Main gear leg strut
149 Undercarriage leg pivot fixing
150 Rear spar
151 Flap shroud ribs
152 Port single-slotted Fowler-type flap
153 Flap down position
154 Nacelle tail fairing
155 Aileron tab
156 Fabric-covered aileron construction

157 Wing tip fairing construction
158 Port navigation light
159 Wing stringers
160 Wing rib construction
161 Outboard fuel cell bays
162 Front spar
163 Outboard wing panel joint rib
164 Leading-edge nose ribs
165 Leading-edge thermal de-icing
166 Port outer engine nacelle
167 Intercooler air flap
168 Engine air intake
169 Nacelle firewall
170 Engine bearers
171 Engine mounting ring
172 Detachable cowling panels
173 Mainwheel doors
174 Intercooler
175 Oil cooler
176 Exhaust collector ring
177 Engine accessory equipment bay
178 Engine oil tank, capacity 36 US gal (136 litres)
179 Supercharger air ducting
180 Pratt & Whitney R-4630 Double Wasp, 28-cylinder four-row radial engine
181 Propeller hub pitch change mechanism
182 Fuselage lower lobe frame and stringer construction
183 Electrical system junction box

91 Flap rib construction
92 Upper position light
93 Curtained window panel
94 Cabin trim panelling
95 Main cabin flooring
96 Seat mounting rails
97 Overhead luggage rack
98 Galley
99 Passenger doorway
100 Life raft stowage
101 Rear toilet compartment
102 Emergency exit window
103 Main cabin tourist class seating, 52 seats (BOAC layout)
104 Fuselage skin plating
105 Rear fuselage frame and stringer construction
106 Rear emergency exit window
107 Fin root fillet
108 De-icing air scoop

109 De-icing air heat exchanger
110 VHF antenna cables
111 Starboard tailplane
112 Fin leading-edge thermal de-icing
113 Tailfin structure
114 De-icing air outlet louvres
115 Fabric-covered rudder construction
116 Rudder tab
117 Tab operating rod
118 Rudder hydraulic booster
119 Rudder torque shaft
120 Control surface servo motor
121 Tailcone
122 Tail navigation light
123 Elevator tab
124 Fabric-covered elevator construction
125 Tailplane construction
126 Tail bumper shock absorber
127 Retractable tail bumper
128 Rear pressure bulkhead

68 Engine exhaust pipe
69 Exhaust collector ring
70 Starboard outer engine cowling panels
71 Spinner
72 Propeller blade root de-icing boots
73 Hamilton Standard four-blade, variable pitch propeller, diameter 16ft 8in (5,08m)

74 Engine cooling air flaps
75 Wing de-icing air heat exchanger
76 Outer fuel cell group filler cap
77 Outer wing panel joint rib
78 Outboard fuel cells
79 Leading-edge thermal de-icing
80 Wing bottom skin/stringer panel
81 Starboard navigation light
82 Wing tip fairing
83 Starboard fabric-covered aileron
84 Aileron hinge control
85 Aileron tab
86 Flap guide rail
87 Retractable landing/taxiing lamp
88 Flap screw jack
89 Nacelle tail fairing
90 Single-slotted Fowler-type flap, down position

377 STRATOCRUISER

The 377 entered service with PanAm on 1 April 1949 (San Francisco-Honolulu).

changes. The engine was the 3,500hp R-4360-CB2, driving either Curtiss or HamStan four-blade propellers of 16ft 8in (5.08m) diameter. Provision was made for a flight crew comprising two pilots, navigator, radio operator and engineer. The upper deck could seat 55 to 100 passengers (at a time when anything over 60 was exceptional); alternatively it could be equipped with 28 upper and 28 lower sleeping berths, with separate men's and women's dressing rooms, plus five seats. At the rear was unprecedented galley and toilet space, while the feature that made the headlines was that behind the wing there

DATA FOR THE 377	
Span	141ft 3in (43.05m)
Length	110ft 4in (33.63m)
Wing area	1,769 sq ft (164.34m²)
Weight empty	(typical) 84,900lb (38,511kg)
Maximum takeoff weight	145,800lb (66,135kg) *originally*
	148,000lb (67,133kg) *later*
Cruising speed	300-340mph (483-547km/h)
Range	4,200 miles (6,759km)

The roomy main cabin: seats could be reclined or made up into double beds. This helped on 15-hour sectors.

could be a lower-deck bar, or 14 extra seats.

The eleventh off the C-97 line was completed as the 377-10-26, registered NX-90700, and flown on 8 July 1947. It was later sold to PanAm, who placed the first and largest order for 20, and at one time operated 27. All were later fitted with CH-10 turbos to increase engine power, and ten were given extra tankage for non-stop transatlantic service. Other customers were BOAC (six, later augmented by 11 more bought from other operators), AOA, SAS and two domestic operators, United and Northwest, both of whom specified square passenger windows.

Allen's courage just about paid off, total sales being 55. Many were later converted to carry cargo, five were modified by Israel Aircraft Industries for military service, and several became the different species of "Guppy" for transporting sections of spacecraft and wide-body airliners.

TOO LATE

In 1942 the US Navy foresaw the increasing need for a carrier-based multirole fighter with exceptional range. Though Boeing's last Navy fighter had been a biplane, the Navy nevertheless asked the company for a proposal, and the result was a contract of 4 May 1943 for three XF8B prototypes.

These were straightforward in configuration, but notable for their size and power. The engine was a 3,000hp Pratt & Whitney R-4360-10, driving an Aeroproducts six-blade contra-rotating propeller of 13ft 6in (4.1m) diameter. The outer wings folded upwards hydraulically, and the main landing gears retracted backwards, the axles rotating through 90° (subject of a Boeing patent which Curtiss used under licence on over 14,000 fighters). The pilot sat under a sliding bubble canopy to aim the six 0.5in guns (production aircraft would have had six 20mm) and, via an advanced optical system, aim the bombs. An internal bay could accommodate two bombs of 1,600lb (726kg)

or four of 500lb (227kg). Alternatively two torpedoes could be carried on underwing racks.

All three were delivered. The first, painted Midnight

More than twice as heavy as a Bearcat, the XF8B was a versatile single-seater. Hunched behind the pilot is a flight-test observer.

Blue, flew on 27 November 1944. The other two were unpainted. They proved to be outstanding aircraft, though the war's end terminated the programme. In any case, the Navy was concerned at the idea of a lone pilot flying 12-hour missions. In fact the F8B might have proved a valuable aircraft. The post-war belief that jets made such aircraft obsolete was soon shown to be nonsense by the less-powerful Douglas AD Skyraider, of which 3,180 were delivered in the 1950s.

DATA FOR F8XB:

Span	**54ft (16.46m)**
Length	**43ft 3in (13.18m)**
Wing area	**489 sq ft (45.43m²).**
Weight empty	**13,519lb (6,132kg)**
Maximum takeoff weight	**21,691lb (9,839kg)**
Maximum speed	**432mph (695km/h)** *at 26,900ft (8,200m)*
Cruising speed	**190mph (306km/h)**
Range	**2,800 miles (4,506km)**
	with 3,200lb (1,452kg) bombload

A SMALL OBSERVATION

Utterly unlike any other Boeing aircraft, this liaison and observation lightplane for the Army was built at Wichita, but received a mainstream Model number. Even stranger, design began soon after World War 2 had finished, in July 1946, and the first of two XL-15 prototypes flew on 13 July 1947.

The basic objective was the best possible all-round view for the pilot and back-seat observer. The airframe was simple light-alloy, and could rapidly be dismantled for towing behind a Jeep. Landing gear with a tall tailwheel could quickly be replaced by floats. Though the Lycoming O-290-7 engine provided only 125hp, STOL capability was achieved by enormous trailing-edge 'flaperons'. Above the outer wings small spoilers augmented lateral control at speeds down to 36mph (58km/h). Wichita also delivered ten YL-15s, but lacking money for production the Army was obliged to turn these over to the US Department of the Interior for use in Alaska.

The penultimate YL-15, 47-431, was one of several examples tested at Wright-Patterson AFB, Ohio. The Model 451's main intended role was spotting and directing artillery fire – exciting work from an unprotected gondola. The Scout could be towed as a glider up to 165mph.

DATA FOR YL-15:

Span	40ft 0in (12.19m)
Length	25ft 3in (7.70m)
Wing area	269 sq ft (24.99m²)
Weight empty	1,509lb (684kg)
Maximum takeoff weight	2,050lb (930kg)
Cruising speed	101mph (163km/h)
Takeoff/landing	over 50ft (15m) 590ft (180m)
Range	230 miles (370km)

"TOTAL DISINTEREST"

In 1944 Boeing began studying how to design a jet-propelled bomber. Early ideas included the Model 424, an aircraft of B-29 type with twin-jet pods attached directly under the wings. To obtain an aerodynamically clean wing the 432 put the engines in the fuselage. This led to the 448 with sweptback wings and tail, powered by four engines in the top of the humpbacked fuselage and two in the tail.

Despite protective firewalls the USAF thought the idea dangerous, and so Boeing switched to the 450, which featured highly efficient wings swept at 35° carrying the engines disposed across the span, in twin-engine inboard pods hung on pylons and single engines mounted directly under the wing near the tips. This arrangement was aerodynamically outstanding. The pylons suspending the inboard pods were a novel idea, and an unexpected bonus was that they caused upper-surface vortices preventing tip stall. Access to the engines was perfect, they were entirely out-

side the airframe (with the possibly lethal turbines of the inboard engines ahead of the leading edge). The engine masses damped out flutter or vibration of the slender wings.

Problems were numerous. There was little room in the wing for fuel, so the enormous fuel mass all had to be in the fuselage, along with the 20,000lb (9,072kg) bomb-load, resulting in severe wing bending loads. The only possible landing gear comprised twin-wheel main gears ahead of and behind the bomb bay, with small outrigger gears retracting into the inboard nacelles. As the pilot could not rotate on takeoff in the usual way, the attitude on the ground had to be nose-up, so that the aircraft would fly itself off once adequate speed had been gained. Loss of an outer engine would need extremely powerful correction by the rudder. The B-47 thus pioneered fully powered, irreversible flight controls, with artificial feel on the rudder proportional to q (dynamic pressure) as well as to pedal deflection. Instead of having a crew of ten, there would be just three: a pilot under a fighter-type canopy, a copilot

The futuristic 46-065 created shockwaves before it left the ground.

behind him with a clever sight to aim the twin 0.5in guns in the tail, and a navigator/bombardier in the nose. The wing loading would in later versions reach the seemingly incredible value of 155lb/sq ft (756kg/m²), double that of a B-29, four times that of a B-17!

When this wing loading was combined with the high-speed profile of the swept wing and the sluggish acceleration from early turbojets it appeared doubtful that the Model 450 could ever be operated from USAF runways, even with the use of 18 rocket motors of 1,000lb (454kg) thrust each to assist takeoff

and a large ribbon parachute to slow the landing. Moreover, however hard Boeing tried, the range was far short of what the USAF wanted. For this reason, the first Commander of the newly formed Strategic Air Command, George C.Kenney, was to express "total disinterest". Despite this, the 450 was so advanced in concept that in April 1946 two prototypes were ordered, designated XB-47.

The first was rolled out from Plant 2 on 12 September 1947, and created a global sensation. Nothing remotely like it had ever been seen before. After a wait for good weather, at Seattle and over the Cascade Mountains and at the test base at Moses Lake, Bob Robbins and copilot Scott Osler donned their new bonedome helmets and delivered the first Stratojet, 46-065, to Moses on 17 December 1947, 44th anniversary of the first flight of the Wright Brothers. Even though it·had early J35 engines of only 3,750lb (1,701kg) thrust, it was a delight to fly, though at low speeds it was impossible to handle the roll due to yaw. Eventually the XB, and all subsequent B-47s, had the first electronic yaw damper, based on inverse-frequency response. Robbins just selected what seemed to be the best yaw-damper gain. Another problem was transonic pitchup, which was largely cured by two rows of vortex generators along the outer wings.

Once these problems had been overcome, Boeing invited Gen K. B. Wolfe to fly the new prototype. Of course, he was utterly captivated, and the USAF soon found money for the first 50 B-47As (Model 450-10-9). Deploying the B-47

meant establishing bases in England, North Africa, Turkey, Taiwan and Japan, and increasing the tanker force. Boeing assigned production of the B-47 to the huge former B-29 plant at Wichita, which would otherwise have been closed.

Powered by General Electric J47-11 turbojets each rated at 5,200lb (2,359kg) thrust, the B-47A had an empty weight of 73,240lb (33,222kg) and maximum takeoff weight of 151,324lb (68,641kg). The bomb bay was tailored to house a Mk 6 thermonuclear weapon, or up to 22,000lb (9,979kg) of conventional bombs. In the tail were to be two 0.5in guns, aimed by the copilot or automatically by radar direction. The latter, initially the A-2 system, was beyond the state of the art in both vacuum-tube electronics and mechanical design. GE, Avco-Crosley and many other

firms toiled for years, and it was not until 23 May 1954 (when 800 B-47s were in service) that Boeing could announce that the tail guns could "knock down enemy interceptors at night or in fog".

The first B-47A, 49-1900, made its first flight on 25 June 1950. On the same day war broke out in Korea. This unleashed the fiscal floodgates, and Boeing never looked back. By this time nobody in the Pentagon or at Wright Field complained that the B-47 had too short a range. Indeed, despite the cost of the B-47, the need was thought to be so urgent that the wartime B-29 manufacturing pool was resurrected. The next version, the B-47B, Model 450-11-10, was made by Boeing (381), Douglas at Tulsa (10) and Lockheed (the former Bell plant) at Marietta (8). This version had higher gross weight, provision for a flight-refuelling receptacle to mate with Boeing's Flying Boom, a fully operative K-2 radar bombing system, four reconnaissance cameras and, from the 88th aircraft, J47-23 engines rated at 5,800lb (2,631kg); on the other hand, most initially had no tail guns.

The major production version was the B-47E, Model 450-157-35. This was externally identified by having an all-

metal nose housing a complicated optical periscope, simpler inlets for the inboard twin-jet pods, provision for 1,416gal (6,435-litre) underwing tanks, and operative tail armament in the form of a twin-20mm turret aimed by the A-5 system in early E-models, replaced later by the MD-4. Less obvious were the J47-25 engines, rated with water injection at 7,200lb (3,266kg), ejection seats for the crew, and the ability to take off with a jettisonable collar under the rear fuselage carrying 33 of the solid rocket motors. Boeing built 913 of the E-model, backed by 274 from Douglas and 385 by Lockheed. Almost all were painted with white anti-flash paint over the sides and undersurface to protect against nuclear radiation. Later updates gave rise to the designations B-47E-II and E-IV.

Wichita built 240 RB-47E reconnaissance aircraft (some ordered as B-47Es), with a longer and more conical nose housing a photographer/navigator. In the former bomb bay were 11 cameras supported by photoflash bombs and cartridges. Another 32 aircraft were completed as the RB-47H for passive electronic reconnaissance (Elint) missions. This version, distinguished by its bluff hemispherical nose radome, was cleared to a new

DATA FOR B-47E-II:

Span	116ft 0in (35.36m)
Length	109ft 10in (33.48m)
Wing area	1,428 sq ft (132.66m²)
Weight empty	80,756lb (36,630kg)
Maximum takeoff weight	198,180lb (89,893kg)
Maximum after inflight refuel	206,700lb (93,759kg)
Maximum speed	606mph (975km/h) *at 16,300ft (4,970m)*
Cruising speed	498mph (801km/h) *at 38,500ft (11,735m)*
Range	4,640 miles (7,468km) *with 10,000lb (4,536kg) bomb-load*

f 221,000lb
this
own in or
East.
amounted
while a
$230,000,
$2 mil-
Boeing
nal deliver-
57. At that
28 Medium
ith 45
plus 300 in
other roles.
g, SAC
35min.
vident that
uld have to
er the
Speed at
sly
wist caused
this was
orse, to
eapon from
an auto-
controlled
n Immel-
g at the 45°
arely, in an
oss), and
strengthen-
. The final
were 24
Weather
late 1969,
ving to 1970
s intelli-
ations.

Boeing B-47E-II Stratojet

1 In-flight refuelling receptacle, open
2 Bomb sight periscope aperture
3 Navigator's instruments
4 Bomb sight periscope
5 K-bombing system radar equipment
6 Nose compartment floor level
7 Ventral ejection hatch
8 Navigator/ bombardier's downward ejection seat
9 Nose compartment ditching hatch
10 Drift indicator
11 Radio and electronics equipment racks
12 Radar scanner
13 Ventral radome
14 K-4A navigation and bombing radar equipment
15 Pressurized crew compartment inner skin
16 Internal walkway
17 Flight deck floor level
18 Rudder pedals
19 Control column
20 Instrument panel shroud
21 Windscreen wiper
22 Windscreen panels
23 Jettisonable cockpit canopy cover
24 Cockpit sunblinds
25 Starboard side console panels
26 Pilot's ejection seat
27 Co-pilot's instrument panel

28 Sextant aperture
29 Antenna mast
30 Co-pilot's ejection seat
31 Tail gunsight and firing controls
32 Oxygen bottles
33 Swivelling seat mounting
34 Pressurized section internal entry door
35 Forward auxiliary fuel tank
36 Maintenance access hatch
37 Crew entry hatch
38 Retractable boarding ladder
39 Cockpit air conditioning plant
40 Forward main undercarriage hydraulic retraction jack
41 Nose compartment rear bulkhead
42 Forward mainwheel doors
43 Steerable twin wheel forward landing gear
44 Multi-plate disc brakes
45 Steering control unit
46 Main undercarriage leg pivot fixing
47 Bomb bay anti-buffet deflector door, open
48 Bomb door hydraulic jack
49 Hydraulic reservoir
50 Hydraulic equipment bay
51 Forward main fuel cell; total internal capacity 14,610 US gal (55,305 litres)
52 Wing spar attachment bulkhead
53 Spar/fuselage attachment joint

54 Wing panel root attachment bolted joint
55 Centre section fuel tank
56 Wing centre-section fuel tank carry through
57 Dorsal control and cable ducting
58 Starboard wing panel root joint
59 Starboard fuel injection water/alcohol tanks; total capacity 600 US gal (2,271 litres)
60 Fuel and air system piping
61 Starboard outrigger wheel
62 Inboard twin-engine nacelle
63 Detachable engine
64 Nacelle pylon
65 Inboard engine oil tanks, capacity 9.4 US gal (35.6 litres) each
66 Oil filler caps
67 Fuel piping to external tank
68 Starboard external fuel tank, capacity 1,780 US gal (6,738 litres)
69 Fuel tank pylon
70 Outboard engine fuel and air system ducting
71 Vortex generators
72 Outboard engine nacelle

73 Outboard engine oil tank, capacity 9.4 US gal (35.6 litres)
74 Starboard navigation light
75 Wing-tip fairing
76 Outboard aileron segment

77 Aileron hydraulic actuators
78 Nacelle tail fairing
79 Inboard aileron segment
80 Aileron tab
81 Outboard Fowler-type flap segment, down position
82 Inboard Fowler-type flap segment, down position
83 Flap rib construction
84 Flap guide rails
85 Screw jacks

86 Screw jack drive shaft
87 Central flap drive hydraulic motor
88 Aileron control linkages
89 Centre main fuel tanks
90 Close-pitched fuselage frame construction
91 Fuel and air system pipe ducting
92 Dorsal maintenance walkway

93 Maintenance access hatches
94 Electronics cooling air intake
95 Equipment air conditioning plant
96 Fin root fillet
97 Air intake to de-icer heater

98 Tailplane de-icing air ducting
99 Fin/tailplane attachment main frame
100 Tailplane spar root joint
101 Starboard tailplane
102 HF antenna cable
103 Starboard elevator
104 Fin leading edge
105 Fin rib construction
106 Fin tip antenna fairing

107 Tail navigation and position lights
108 Rudder rib construction
109 Rudder tab
110 Rudder hydraulic actuator
111 Tail-gun radar equipment
112 Gun direction radome
113 Two M24A1 20-mm cannon
114 Swivelling tail turret
115 Elevator tab
116 Ammunition feed chutes
117 Ammunition tanks, 350 rounds per gun
118 Port elevator
119 Elevator rib construction

120 Port tailplane construction
121 Elevator control linkage
122 Approach/ drogue parachute stowage
123 Ammunition loading door, open
124 Brake parachute housing
125 Rudder control linkages
126 Chaff/flare dispenser

127 Aft electronics equipment bay
128 Strike camera
129 Ventral access hatch
130 Aft. main fuel tanks
131 Aerojet 14AS1000 assisted take-off (ATO) bottles (33)
132 ATO bottle jettisonable mounting cradle
133 Aft main undercarriage leg pivot fixing
134 Twin wheel truck
135 Hydraulic retraction jack
136 Wheel bay
137 Aft mainwheel doors
138 Bomb bay fuel tank
139 Port inboard Fowler-type flap

140 Flap shroud ribs
141 Flap screw jacks
142 Flap down position
143 Outboard Fowler-type flap segment
144 Aileron tab
145 Inboard aileron segment
146 Outboard engine nacelle tail fairing
147 Aileron hydraulic actuators
148 Outboard aileron segment
149 Aileron rib construction
150 Wing-tip fairing
151 Port navigation light
152 Outboard engine oil tank
153 Outboard engine nacelle
154 Intake centre-body/starter-generator housing
155 General Electric J47-GE-25A turbojet engine
156 Engine flame cans
157 Nacelle pylon
158 Outer wing panel rib construction
159 Rear spar
160 Lower wing skin/stringer panel
161 Front spar
162 External fuel tank side brace
163 Port external fuel tank
164 Fuel tank rib construction
165 Tan pylon
166 Leading-edge hot air de-icing
167 Leading-edge nose ribs
168 Fuel system piping

169 Inner/outer wing skin panel joint rib
170 Nacelle tail fairing
171 Engine exhaust ducting
172 Outrigger wheel leg strut
173 Torque scissor links
174 Port outrigger wheel
175 Outrigger wheel doors
176 Engine nacelle construction
177 Ventral landing/taxiing lamp
178 Engine air intakes
179 Inboard General Electric J47 engine
180 Nacelle pylon construction
181 Pylon attachment joint
182 Inboard engine oil tanks
183 Inner wing panel rib construction
184 Leading-edge fuel and air system piping
185 Port wing water/alcohol injection tanks
186 Internal bomb bay
187 Bomb mounting racks
188 Bomb-door rib construction
189 Bomb-door, open
190 1,000lb (454kg) HE bombs; maximum bomb load 20,000lb (9,072kg)
191 2,000lb (907kg) HE bomb
192 4,000lb (1,815kg) HE bomb
193 Mk 28 (B-281N) free fall 20-megaton nuclear weapon

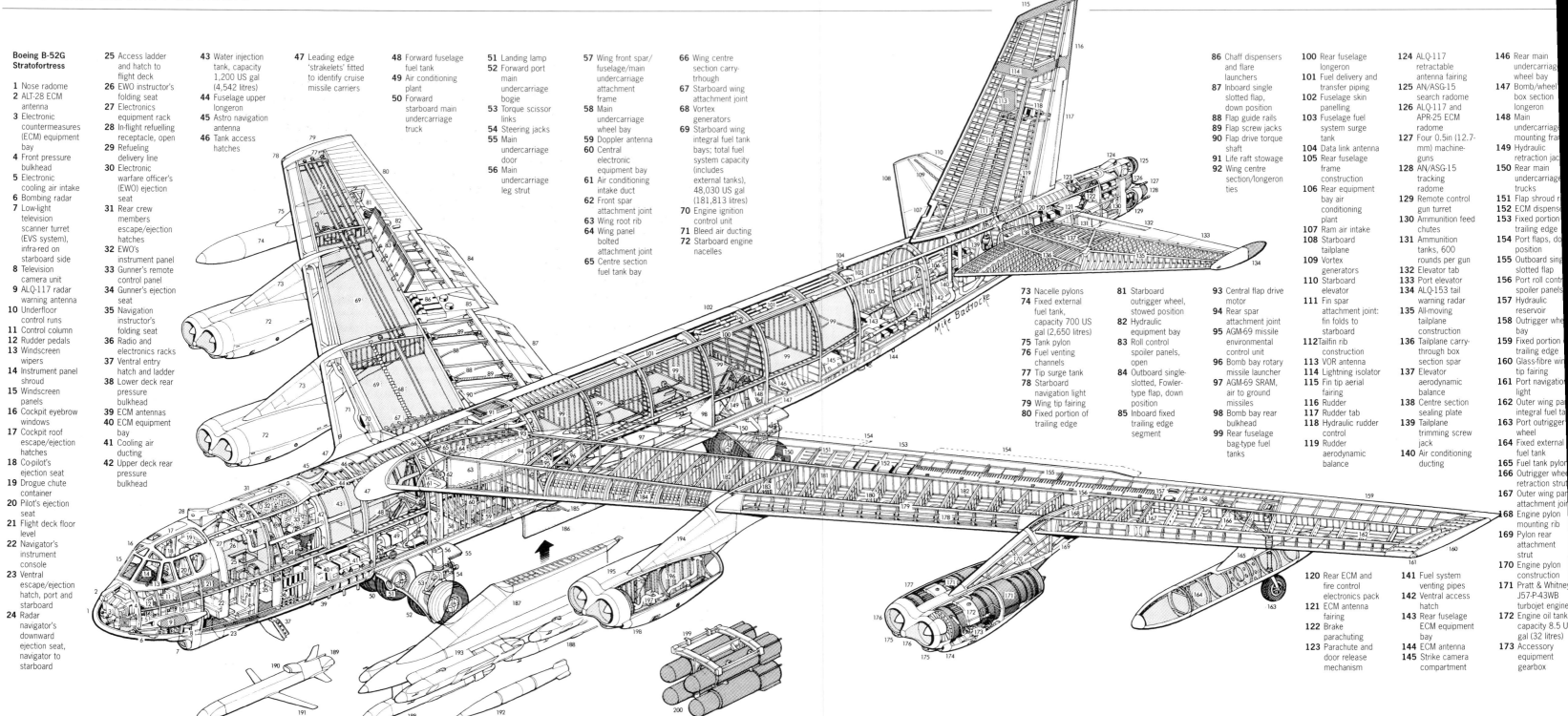

Boeing B-52G Stratofortress

1 Nose radome
2 ALT-28 ECM antenna
3 Electronic countermeasures (ECM) equipment bay
4 Front pressure bulkhead
5 Electronic cooling air intake
6 Bombing radar
7 Low-light television scanner turret (EVS system), infra-red on starboard side
8 Television camera unit
9 ALQ-117 radar warning antenna
10 Underfloor control runs
11 Control column
12 Rudder pedals
13 Windscreen wipers
14 Instrument panel shroud
15 Windscreen panels
16 Cockpit eyebrow windows
17 Cockpit roof escape/ejection hatches
18 Co-pilot's ejection seat
19 Drogue chute container
20 Pilot's ejection seat
21 Flight deck floor level
22 Navigator's instrument console
23 Ventral escape/ejection hatch, port and starboard
24 Radar navigator's downward ejection seat, navigator to starboard

25 Access ladder and hatch to flight deck
26 EWO instructor's folding seat
27 Electronics equipment rack
28 In-flight refuelling receptacle, open
29 Refueling delivery line
30 Electronic warfare officer's (EWO) ejection seat
31 Rear crew members escape/ejection hatches
32 EWO's instrument panel
33 Gunner's remote control panel
34 Gunner's ejection seat
35 Navigation instructor's folding seat
36 Radio and electronics racks
37 Ventral entry hatch and ladder
38 Lower deck rear pressure bulkhead
39 ECM antennas
40 ECM equipment bay
41 Cooling air ducting
42 Upper deck rear pressure bulkhead

43 Water injection tank, capacity 1,200 US gal (4,542 litres)
44 Fuselage upper longeron
45 Astro navigation antenna
46 Tank access hatches
47 Leading edge 'strakelets' fitted to identify cruise missile carriers

48 Forward fuselage fuel tank
49 Air conditioning plant
50 Forward starboard main undercarriage truck
51 Landing lamp
52 Forward port main undercarriage attachment frame
53 Torque scissor links
54 Steering jacks
55 Main undercarriage door
56 Main undercarriage leg strut

57 Wing front spar/fuselage/main undercarriage attachment frame
58 Main undercarriage wheel bay
59 Doppler antenna
60 Central electronic equipment bay
61 Air conditioning intake duct
62 Front spar attachment joint
63 Wing root rib
64 Wing panel bolted attachment joint
65 Centre section fuel tank bay

66 Wing centre section carry-through
67 Starboard wing attachment joint
68 Vortex generators
69 Starboard wing integral fuel tank bays; total fuel system capacity (includes external tanks), 48,030 US gal (181,813 litres)
70 Engine ignition control unit
71 Bleed air ducting
72 Starboard engine nacelles

73 Nacelle pylons
74 Fixed external fuel tank, capacity 700 US gal (2,650 litres)
75 Tank pylon
76 Fuel venting channels
77 Tip surge tank
78 Starboard navigation light
79 Wing tip fairing
80 Fixed portion of trailing edge

81 Starboard outrigger wheel, stowed position
82 Hydraulic equipment bay
83 Roll control spoiler panels, open
84 Outboard single-slotted, Fowler-type flap, down position
85 Inboard fixed trailing edge segment

86 Chaff dispensers and flare launchers
87 Inboard single slotted flap, down position
88 Flap guide rails
89 Flap screw jacks
90 Flap drive torque shaft
91 Life raft stowage
92 Wing centre section/longeron ties

93 Central flap drive motor
94 Rear spar attachment joint
95 AGM-69 missile environmental control unit
96 Bomb bay rotary missile launcher
97 AGM-69 SRAM, air to ground missiles
98 Bomb bay rear bulkhead
99 Rear fuselage bag-type fuel tanks

100 Rear fuselage longeron
101 Fuel delivery and transfer piping
102 Fuselage skin panelling
103 Fuselage fuel system surge tank
104 Data link antenna
105 Rear fuselage frame construction
106 Rear equipment bay air conditioning plant
107 Ram air intake
108 Starboard tailplane
109 Vortex generators
110 Starboard elevator
111 Fin spar attachment joint: fin folds to starboard
112 Tailfin rib construction
113 VOR antenna
114 Lightning isolator
115 Fin tip aerial fairing
116 Rudder
117 Rudder tab
118 Hydraulic rudder control
119 Rudder aerodynamic balance

120 Rear ECM and fire control electronics pack
121 ECM antenna fairing
122 Brake parachuting
123 Parachute and door release mechanism

124 ALQ-117 retractable antenna fairing
125 AN/ASG-15 search radome
126 ALQ-117 and APR-25 ECM radome
127 Four 0.5in (12.7-mm) machine-guns
128 AN/ASG-15 tracking radome
129 Remote control gun turret
130 Ammunition feed chutes
131 Ammunition tanks, 600 rounds per gun
132 Elevator tab
133 Port elevator
134 ALQ-153 tail warning radar
135 All-moving tailplane construction
136 Tailplane carry-through box section spar
137 Elevator aerodynamic balance
138 Centre section sealing plate
139 Tailplane trimming screw jack
140 Air conditioning ducting
141 Fuel system venting pipes
142 Ventral access hatch
143 Rear fuselage ECM equipment bay
144 ECM antenna
145 Strike camera compartment

146 Rear main undercarriage wheel bay
147 Bomb/wheel box section longeron
148 Main undercarriage mounting fra
149 Hydraulic retraction jack
150 Rear main undercarriage trucks
151 Flap shroud r
152 ECM dispense
153 Fixed portion trailing edge
154 Port flaps, do position
155 Outboard sing slotted flap
156 Port roll contr spoiler panels
157 Hydraulic reservoir
158 Outrigger whe bay
159 Fixed portion tip fairing
160 Glass-fibre wir tip fairing
161 Port navigatio light
162 Outer wing pa integral fuel ta
163 Port outrigger wheel
164 Fixed external fuel tank
165 Fuel tank pylor
166 Outrigger whee retraction stru
167 Outer wing par attachment joir
168 Engine pylon mounting rib
169 Pylon rear attachment strut
170 Engine pylon construction
171 Pratt & Whitney J57-P-43WB turbojet engine
172 Engine oil tank, capacity 8.5 US gal (32 litres)
173 Accessory equipment gearbox

HEAVIEST OF THE HEAVYWEIGHTS

Outwardly looking rather like a bigger B-47, this heavy bomber actually had a totally different gestation. In April 1945, with the monster Convair B-36 about to fly, the Army Air Force issued a requirement for a second-generation strategic bomber with much higher performance. At that time there appeared to be no chance of any jet bomber meeting the 5,000-mile (8,047km) radius of action suggested. In June 1946 Boeing's Model 462, resembling a bigger B-50 powered by six 5,500shp Wright T35 Typhoon turboprops (seemingly the only option), was accepted, and a study contract issued as the XB-52.

The first flight-cleared XT35 began flight testing slung under the nose of a B-17 in September 1947, but by this time it was becoming apparent that in the new field of gas turbines Wright Aeronautical were falling behind. The original Model 462 was deficient in range, and so Chief Engineer Ed Wells and his team followed with a succession of Model 464 studies with only four engines, but of 9,000shp each. The 464-16 carried 90,000lb (40,820kg) of bombs but had a poor range. The 464-17 met the 10,000-mile (16,093km) range demanded, but only with a single nuclear weapon; moreover, it could not exceed 400mph and weighed 480,000lb (217,728kg) at take-off. By March 1947 the 464-25 had a slightly swept wing, and a new landing gear with four two-wheel trucks in a row along the centreline. By August 1947 this had become the 464-29, with Pratt & Whitney XT57 turboprops of 12,000shp each and no defensive armament except in the tail.

In January 1948 Boeing's inability to come up with a really good answer, Northrop's impressive flying wings, the fact that Gen Kenney (Commander of SAC) doubted the viability of an intercontinental bomber, and the implacable opposition of the Navy, resulted in the XB-52 being cancelled. Unexpectedly, on 24 June 1948 the USSR began a blockade of Berlin, and the XB-52 was promptly resurrected. Wells had never stopped doo-

dling, and Boeing soon received a $29.4 million contract for a mock-up of the 464-35 and two prototypes, the first to be ready in early 1951. The Dash-35 made use of flight refuelling, and was thus smaller and faster than earlier projects, and had more obvious sweepback; but nobody liked the massive gearboxes and contra-rotating propellers.

On Thursday 21 October 1948 Wells, Schairer, Maynard Pennell, Harold Withington, Art Carlsen and George Blumenthal checked in to the Van Cleve hotel in Dayton, Ohio, with masses of paper describing the definitive 464-350-0. By cutting the range to 6,000 miles, this weighed a more manageable 280,000lb (127 tonnes), and could cruise at well over 400mph. Col Pete Warden hardly looked at what the Boeing team had brought. He said "We don't believe any turboprop can do the job. I'd like you to let me have an updated proposal for a jet that I can take to urgent discussions in the Pentagon." By chance they had with them all the graphs and figures from a Medium-Bomber Study based on the use of four of the

8,500lb-thrust Westinghouse J40 turbojets, which promised significantly better fuel economy. The team worked non-stop through the weekend, basically just doubling the Medium-Bomber Study to come up with a new Model 464-49 with a 35° swept wing under which were hung on pylons not four J40s but four pairs. The final report was typed by a public stenographer and assembled into a book, each page stamped SECRET, accompanied by a beautifully finished desk model made of balsa and dope from a Dayton hobby shop. It was all on Warden's desk at 8am, Monday.

A week later the turboprop was history, and Boeing began refining the 464-49 into the 464-67, for which a Phase II contract was signed in March 1949. The XB-52 first prototype became USAF No 49-230. The second, 49-231, was redesignated as the YB-52, because the money for it was taken from Logistics Command, which is not supposed to fund experimental (XB) aircraft.

In the actual aircraft the eight engines were not the J40, which proved to be a failure, but Pratt & Whitney YJ57-3 two-spool turbojets each rated at 8,700lb (3,946kg). Each twin-engine pod weighed nearly six tons, and as they were respectively 34ft 2in (10.4m) and 60ft (18.29m) from the centreline they exerted a powerful effect in damping flutter. This was especially important in a wing which at rest sagged 9ft (2.74m) when the fuel tanks were filled, and which on test was bent at the tips 10ft down and 22ft up!

No less than 32,362gal (147,120 litres) of fuel was housed in flexible bladders, seven between the spars of the enormous wing and six along the top of the fuselage. Integral tankage seemed too difficult because of the structure's flexibility. The four trucks were rearranged in side-by-side pairs, with hydraulic steering beyond ±20°. This enabled the B-52 to land in a crosswind with the four trucks all "crabbed" in the same direction, wheels aligned with the runway and wings level. To protect the outer pods small outrigger wheels were added near the wingtips. Instead of tilting the fuselage on the ground, it was made level and the wing was set at an angle of incidence of almost 8°.

Aerodynamically the main refinement was to sweep forward the line of maximum wing thickness at the root, as had just been done in the British V-bombers. This enabled the thickness/chord ratio of 8 per cent to be raised to 15 per cent at the root (remarkable for a jet), where each wing was bolted to the massive bridge structure in the fuselage. This saved weight and provided more room for fuel. On the trailing edge were four enormous Fowler flaperons, driven hydraulically to serve as both flaps and ailerons, augmented by three sections of spoiler above each wing.

The colossal tail was unique. The need for powerful yaw authority following loss of an outboard pod was to be met by a hydraulically powered fin. The crosswind landing gear was a better answer, so the fin was made fixed, but arranged to hinge down horizontal for entering a hangar. On the trailing edge was a rudder having only one-tenth of the fin chord, with hinge moments low enough to be handled by a spring tab on the trailing edge. The original idea of making the massive tailplane the primary control surface in pitch was abandoned, following doubts over hydraulic reliability. It became just a trimming surface, driven by a 200:1 gearbox from two hydraulic motors, one driving the irreversible jackscrew and the other the nut. On the trailing edge are elevators as narrow as the rudder, again driven by manual tabs. With adjustment of centre of gravity by pumping fuel it is possible to fly a B-52 on the elevators alone.

Not least of the bold decisions was that Boeing took on board the arguments of the AiResearch company, and used bleed-air turbines to drive the secondary power systems. Compressed air bled from the engines was ducted through lagged pipes which glowed at orange heat (400°C, 750°F) to drive small turbines arranged in many parts of the aircraft, which shrieked at over 60,000rpm, surrounded by flak curtains. These in turn were geared down to electric generators, hydraulic pumps, the cabin pressurization and conditioning system, water-injection pumps and other services. In contrast, no air was bled for ice protection, except of the engine inlets. The windscreens, pitots and feel sensors were heated electrically.

The prototypes were arranged for a pilot and copilot in tandem, under a fixed but jettisonable canopy with 12 Plexiglas panes. The tail armament had not yet been decided. Covered in cotton fabric, the XB was towed on the night of 29 November 1951 to the new Flight Test building on Boeing Field. Here it soon carried out systems and taxi testing, but did not fly for almost a year. This was principally because, despite prior testing on a B-47, the lateral control system took a long time to reach its final form.

Thus, the YB-52, which was rolled out on 15 March 1952, was the first to fly. The date was 15 April, and the crew, A. M. 'Tex' Johnston (B-52 project pilot and later the company's colourful Director of Flight Test) and Lt-Col Guy M. Townsend. Boeing issued a photograph of the takeoff after airbrushing out not only the landing gears but also the eight trails of black smoke.

From the start it was clear the giant was a superb flying machine, but the bold decision was taken to redesign the lateral control system. The four sections of flap were interlinked so that all moved in unison, as flaps only, under jackscrews geared to electric motors. The gap between the inboard and outboard flaps, blasted by the inboard pair of engines, was occupied by "feeler" ailerons, driven manually by trailing-edge servos to provide the pilot with a feel for roll input. The real lateral controls were six sections of spoiler above each wing. These could be opened symmetrically as airbrakes, or asymmetrically following engine failure. Nevertheless, the B-52 would always be tricky following failure of outboard engines, and any attempt to overshoot on asymmetric power at light weights was likely to result in uncontrolled roll and structural damage.

Thus, the heaviest aircraft built up to that time was controlled mainly by manually operated surfaces. This reflected the innate conservatism of the company, at a time when auxiliary power systems were prone to failure. Pilots soon got used to the B-52's odd qualities, even the fact that the exceptional wing incidence meant that on takeoff you went up like a lift even though the fuselage was pointing downwards!

From 5 August 1954 the prototypes were followed by three B-52A bombers with proper provisions for the crew of six on two decks. The obvious change was that the two pilots were now seated side-by-side, a change prompted by Generals LeMay and Griswold sitting in a British Valiant. The pilots and navigator had upward ejection seats and the bombardier and radar operator

The YB-52 spawned the biggest manufacturing programme in US history. (See pages 38/39.)

could fire their seats downward. The tail gunner, with four 0.5in guns aimed by Bosch Arma MD-5 radar, could sever his turret from the aircraft. The engine was the J57-9W, rated at 10,000lb (4,536kg) for takeoff with water supplied from a tank near the tail. Under each outer wing was an 833-gal (3,787-litre) auxiliary tank, and behind the cockpit was a Flying Boom receptacle.

The first full production aircraft was the 464-201-3, delivered as 23 B-52Bs and 27 RB-52Bs, the latter having provision for a pressurized compartment for two operators and four large cameras, or electronic countermeasures. The B was the first to have a radar bombing system, the MA-2 adding a ton and a million dollars (unit price was about $14.4 million). The tail gunner had twin 20mm guns,

above which loomed the impressive A-3A radar. Service began on 29 June 1955 with 93BW at Castle AFB, California. In service problems included the occasional destruction of tyres by trucks jamming in the 20° position, and cracking of the flaps near the jets caused by water-injection takeoffs. At the 10,000-hour point only two aircraft had been lost, but by late 1956 the total had risen to six, mainly because of hydraulic fires or disintegration of the screaming air turbines.

In the B-52C (464-201-6) the engine was the J57-19W or -29WA, rated with water injection at 12,100lb (5,489kg). The water was moved to a 125gal

(568-litre) tank in each wing root, and the underwing tanks were enlarged to no less than 2,500gal (11,365 litres) each. The maximum weight thus went up from the 390,000lb (176,904kg) of the prototypes to 450,000lb (204,120kg). Tail armament reverted to four 0.5in, but with new radar direction. The first of 35 of this version first flew on 9 March 1956, introducing anti-flash white paint on the undersides. Bombload, actually carried on training missions, was up to four B28, each with yield variable up to 1,450kt, from 1961 progressively replaced by the B43 of 1Mt and later the B61 (100-500kt) and B83 (1Mt). A normal maximum load of conventional bombs was 24,000lb (10,886kg).

The B-52D (464-201-7) introduced MD-9 radar fire control for the tail guns, and deleted provision for the recon capsule. Seattle made 101, and a further 69 were made at Wichita, following the mistaken proclamation that the Soviet Union was making strategic bombers at a higher rate. In 1965, during the Vietnam war, every B-52D was given the HDB (high-density bombing) modification, which enabled it to carry over 60,000lb (27,216kg) of conventional bombs: 84 of 500lb or

42 of 750lb internally, plus 24 of 750lb on long ejector racks carried on pylons under the inboard wings.

The B-52E, 464-259, introduced the IBM-integrated ASQ-38(V) navigation/bombing system, with Raytheon ASB-4 radar and GPL APN-89 doppler, among many other items. Seattle made 42 and Wichita 58, at such a high rate that unit price bottomed at only $6.08 million. The B-52F, 464-260, had visibly different engine installations. Each J57-43W, rated at 13,750lb (6,237kg), had compressor blading changed from titanium to steel, and each pod had its own injection water tank in the wing leading edge beside the pylon. Chin inlets on each pod served the oil coolers, and a third inlet supplied air to cool a 40kVA alternator mounted on a Sundstrand constant-speed drive inside a large blister. This at last replaced the system of bleed-air turbines. Seattle made 44 B-52Fs, and Wichita 45.

Eliminating the hot piping allowed the wing to be sealed to form integral tanks. This increased internal fuel to 38,827gal, which enabled the underwing tanks to be reduced in size to only 583gal, giving a total of 39,993gal (181,808 litres), an increase of 5,395gal. This was the main

difference in the B-52G, 464-253, and it increased high-altitude range from 7,370 miles to 8,406 (13,528km). The number of spoiler sections above each wing was increased from six to seven, which enabled the fin to be reduced in height by 8ft (2.44m) and the ailerons to be eliminated. The Flight Manual says that total loss of spoilers can to some degree be overcome by sideslipping with the rudder, but that a landing in this condition should not be attempted. The gunner was moved to the main crew compartment, using the new ASG-15 fire control with a TV link. Refinement of the airframe reduced structure weight by about five tons, despite an increase in takeoff weight to 488,000lb (221,357kg). Provision was made to carry two AGM-28 Hound Dog cruise missiles on pylons under the inboard wing, and also to

launch two ADM-20 Quails (tiny jet aircraft each able to simulate a B-52 on radars) from the forward bomb bay. All 193 of this model were made at Wichita, Seattle supplying the forward fuselage.

It had been expected that production would stop with the G, but invention of the ALBM (air-launched ballistic missile) resulted in Wichita producing 102 of the further upgraded B-52H (464-261). This was locally strengthened to enable it to operate at 310kt IAS (357mph, 574km/h) "under the radar", which in peacetime means 400ft. Range was greatly increased by fitting the Pratt & Whitney TF33-3 turbofan, based on the J57, rated at 17,000lb (7,711kg), which also enabled water to be eliminated. The tail defence was redesigned, with a single six-barrel 20mm gun directed by Emerson ASG-21 fire con-

trol. Less obvious was that the engine-driven alternators were uprated from 40 to 120kVA.

The first B-52H flew on 6 March 1961, with four dummy ALBMs, and the last – last of 744 B-52s – was rolled out on 22 June 1962. The GAM-87 Skybolt ALBM was cancelled, but the B-52G and H went on to carry eight AGM-69A SRAMs (short-range attack missiles) on an internal rotary dispenser, and a further 12 in tandem triples on long underwing racks. Later still both were equipped to carry 12 AGM-86B cruise missiles on the external racks, and in recent years the longer CSRL (common-stores rotary launcher) has enabled eight AGM-86C conventional cruise missiles to be carried internally. The most recent precision weapon to be added is AGM-142A Raptor, derived from Israel's Popeye.

There is no room even to list the 28 other kinds of munition carried today by the surviving B-52H force, nor the 43 items of avionics or the 19 upgrade programmes which have kept them effective. The author doubts that, even though the B-52H is to serve well beyond the Millennium, it will be retrofitted with four Allison (Rolls-Royce) 535 engines, despite the enormous advantages this would bring.

DATA FOR B-52H:

Span	185ft 0in (56.39m)
Length	160ft 11in (49.05m)
Wing area	4,080 sq ft (379m²)
tion	with SALT-treaty strakelets denoting Cruise-Missile Integra
Weight empty	195,500lb (88,679kg)
Maximum takeoff	505,000lb (229,068kg)
Maximum after inflight refuel	566,000lb (256,738kg)
Maximum speed (clean)	620mph (998km/h)
Low penetration speed	357mph (575km/h)
Maximum range	10,130 miles (16,303km) no inflight refuelling

DASH FOR CASH

In July 1949 de Havilland flew the prototype Comet jet transport. The public response of the US industry and airlines was to regard this as an uneconomic aberration, but the writing was on the wall. Before the year was out, the leading manufacturers of civil transports, Douglas and Lockheed, had lobbied Congress for Federal aid to help build a rival. After much argument, in 1950 this was thrown out.

Boeing, an also-ran in the civil field, had a more immediate problem. The KC-97 tanker was seriously flawed by the fact that, in order to be refuelled, USAF jets had to come down to half their altitude and slow to half their speed. Boeing did the obvious and continued its Model 367 studies into turboprops and eventually swept-wing jets, but all attempts to get military funding for a jet tanker/transport failed.

In the past Boeing had repeatedly produced commercial derivatives of bombers, but attempting to do this with the B-47 proved unfruitful, and with the B-52 it was never even tried. An accompanying sketch shows one of the studies based on the B-47, and one wonders how it was ever considered seriously (in East Germany Dr Brunolf Baade actually got a jet transport with this layout, derived from the Soviet Type 150 bomber, into production!). Instead, the Model 367 studies were continued, settling on 35° sweepback and four turbojets hung in pods below and ahead of the wing.

In 1950 there appeared to be a choice of three engines. Wright, supplier of engines for the B-17 and B-29, intended to import the British Olympus, an outstanding engine. Westinghouse was developing the J40. Pratt & Whitney was at last "coming out of the wood"

with the J57, and Boeing decided that, because of its high pressure ratio (and consequent fuel economy) and probable rapid accumulation of military flight time, this engine appeared to offer the best blend of performance and low risk.

Once an engine had been selected, it was possible to begin actual project design. In 1951 major elements were coming together in the Model 367-64, with two twin-engine pods which appeared to offer minimum drag.

At the end of 1951 it was decided for safety reasons to put each engine in a separate pod. Spacing these across the span was found to exert a beneficial effect in damping flutter and also in preventing spanwise airflow above the wing without the need for fences.

This reworking of the B-47, unsurprisingly, did not proceed to the technical drawing board.

By this time the Model number had reached 367-80, but as the design had diverged completely from the original 367 the decision was taken to allot a fresh number to the production aircraft. This number happened to be 707.

Bearing in mind the growth of the Cold War, and of a hot war in Korea, it is remarkable that Boeing continued to be rebuffed in its search for military funds, but it was privately assured that, should it fly a prototype, orders for a jet tanker/transport were almost certain to follow. In other words, the Air Force correctly calculated that Boeing would be prepared to risk its own money.

By 1952 matters were coming to a head. To the astonishment of many Americans, the Comet was to begin scheduled airline service on 2 May, and a month beforehand Bill Allen called a board meeting for 22 April to decide what to do. On 15 April the YB-52 made its first flight, and this made a positive decision easier. On the following day Beall reported that Pratt was prepared to offer a commercial J57 engine, to be designated JT3. Schairer said a single prototype could support development of both a military tanker/transport and a commercial airliner. Pennell said it would meet all expected customer demands, would halt the Comet in its tracks, and would generate ton-miles at three times the rate of the C-97. John Yeasting said it would provide data for pricing production versions, and accountant Jim Barton said the prototype could be built for $15 million. This and other inputs were in the boardroom for consideration on 22 April. Following Allen's recommendation, the board voted unanimously to risk $16 million.

Engineering design began on 20 May 1952. The wing followed one of the established profiles of the "23" family, with a straight leading edge and sweepback of 35° at the $\frac{1}{4}$ chord line. The structure was made more rigid than that of the bombers, and the whole space between the sheet-web spars was sealed to form an integral tank.

Like the bombers, in cruising flight lateral control was to be by spoilers, with feel provided by small feeler (or flipper) ailerons between the inboard and outboard flaps, as on the B-52. Each wing had inboard and outboard spoilers made in two sections, mounted immediately ahead of one of the sections of hydraulically operated double-slotted flap.

Thus, the spoilers were of the slot-lip type. With flaps down they guided the air to flow at high velocity through the narrow slot to flow over the flap. When opened, the slot vanished, and so did much of the lift, powerfully augmenting the roll authority of even a small spoiler deflection. With flaps extended, conventional outboard ailerons were unlocked, to provide even greater lateral control at low airspeeds. After touchdown, both spoilers could be fully opened as airbrakes, simultaneously destroying much of the wing lift to make the wheel brakes more effective. All four ailerons were operated manually by geared tabs, their hinge moments being reduced by internal leading-edge aerodynamic balance. The wing

Renton, 15 July 1954: the Model 367-80 makes its maiden flight.

leading edge was fixed. The fuselage was basically a stretched version of that of the C-97, with the same "double-bubble" cross section, but with the upper and lower lobes merged to eliminate the external crease. The structure and skin were strengthened to bear the stresses of much higher indicated airspeeds and a pressure differential of 8.6lb/sq in (0.605kg/cm²). What Boeing called the cab section was more compact than that of the C-97, and had a short nose section added in front for future installation of weather radar. Compared with the B-52 the cockpit had an

opaque roof, shallower windows with just two wide flat panes in front, a shallower front panel and larger central pedestal. There was a station for a navigator behind the pilot and for a flight engineer behind the copilot.

The tail introduced modest dihedral on the tailplane, which was pivoted and driven by an irreversible electrically powered ballscrew for trimming purposes. The elevators and rudder were, like the ailerons, operated purely manually by spring tabs, with the surface moment reduced by internal (compound-shelf) aerodynamic balance. Boeing considered this a remarkable achievement, though where the rudder was concerned they had to think again, as explained in the story of the KC-135 (page 82). One of the few completely new features for Boeing was the use of four-wheel bogies (trucks) on each main landing gear. These retracted inwards hydraulically into an underfloor bay in the fuselage, the jack travelling inwards on a walking beam. Each wheel had multi-disc brakes. The hydraulically steerable twin-wheel nose gear retracted forwards.

The 367-80 was fitted with four Pratt & Whitney JT3C-1 turbojets, initially flight cleared at 9,500lb (4,309kg) but later rated at 10,500lb (4,763kg). Each engine was installed in its own pod, with large access doors, and had a plain short jetpipe without reverser. Fuel was housed in three integral tanks in each wing and bladders in the centre section, the total capacity originally being 8,674gal (39,434 litres); later this was slightly increased.

Worried at landing this fast and heavy aircraft on contaminated runways, Boeing had considered fitting a braking parachute, but eventually decided that the Bendix antiskid brakes would be adequate. The 90ft (27.4m) upper-deck cabin had a large cargo door at each end on the left, and four very small windows on each side. It was furnished for cargo, but had seat rails for up to 130 passengers seated 3+3. Initially these rails anchored a few seats and test instrumentation. The aircraft was painted in a company colour scheme of copper-brown and yellow, and given the registration N70700 to reflect the fact that this aircraft was the prototype of the Model 707.

For the first time, there were thousands of guests and workforce at the ceremonial rollout on 14 May 1954. Exactly a week later, as Tex

DATA FOR THE 367-80 AS ORIGINALLY BUILT:

Span	**129ft 8in (39.37m)**
Length	**119ft 6in (36.42m)**
Wing area	**2,395sq ft (222.5m²)**
Weight empty	**92,120lb (41,786kg)**
Maximum takeoff weight	**190,000lb (86,184kg)**
Maximum speed	**582mph (937km/h)** *at 25,000ft (M0.838)*
Cruising speed	**550mph (885km/h)**
Service ceiling	**43,000ft (13,106m)**
Range	**3,530 miles (5,681km)**

Johnston neared completion of high-speed taxi and brake tests, the left main gear came up through the wing and the left pods scraped on the runway. The trunnion behind the main wing box had been made from a faulty forging, and its weakness had been exacerbated by a design fault. An embarrassing picture was networked worldwide, but the USAF was unperturbed by so temporary a problem. To Boeing's relief, it informed the company that it had given up the idea of using B-36s or B-47s as tankers, and asked for proposals for a production programme based on the military derivative of the 367-80.

The first flight of the 367-80, the second US jet transport if one includes the rather pointless Chase XC-123A, was made from Renton by Johnston and copilot Dix Loesch on the afternoon of 15 July 1954. From that time onwards Boe-

ing has never looked back. It has moved from third place in commercial transport production, trailing far behind Douglas and Lockheed, to become not just Number One but, except for a European rival, to enjoy something approaching a monopoly position.

At first the Dash-80 was used to carry out the normal certification flying, and also increasingly in its primary role of demonstrator. It was flown at an early date by USAF pilots, and later in 1954 a complete air-refuelling station was built under the rear fuselage, with an improved high-speed Flying Boom. To power the enlarged 707 Intercontinental Pratt produced the bigger JT4A engine, and one of these was then installed for testing in the port inner (No 2) position, calling for special piloting techniques. Major aerodynamic research was undertaken with wing gloves that dramati-

cally altered wing profile and area, and with various movable leading-edge devices.

In 1959 the enormous Bendix AMQ-15 weather-reconnaissance radar was installed in a swollen nose radome, with the main racking in the cabin cooled by a ram inlet above the fuselage. To support the Boeing 727 a JT8D engine was hung on the left side of the rear fuselage, with an upward-curved jetpipe to direct the jet above the tailplane, while slats and triple-slotted flaps increased lift coefficient. All four main engines were then replaced by Pratt & Whitney JT3D turbofans, each rated at 17,000lb (7,711kg), resulting in the designation 367-80B. In 1963, for NASA, the wing was rebuilt with wide-chord blown flaps which could be depressed to 90° with boundary-layer control by transonic bleed air from the engines. This required a larger tailplane to be fitted, with inverted Krueger flaps on its leading edge. One of the last test programmes was to evaluate a high-flotation landing gear with eight main wheels on each leg and four nosewheels. In 1972 the Dash-80 was retired to the National Air and Space Museum, which lent it to the Seattle Museum of Flight close to its birthplace.

367-80

717, KC-135 C-135

ONLY ONE CUSTOMER

Though Boeing assigned the Model number 707 to its production jet transport, the programme got under way at a time when the airlines were unreceptive. All their money was spent on Super Constellations and DC-6s and 7s. PanAm's Trippe said "Passengers are unlikely to be attracted to jets". TWA's Damon said "Civil jets? Not for another ten years". Conversion of fleets to turboprops – "about 1955", said Bob Gross of Lockheed – looked the better option. In the near term there appeared to be only one customer for Boeing's jet transport: the USAF, primarily for a jet tanker.

On 5 October 1954 the first order was placed, for 29 tankers designated KC-135A. Boeing assigned the new Model number 717 because, not only were the tanker and the civil airliner obviously different in their furnishings, but by late 1954 the 707 had begun to proliferate in a parallel programme into different versions all characterised by a wider fuselage. Subsequent 707

development made these aircraft resemble the original 367-80 prototype in configuration only. The KC-135A however, adhered as closely as possible to the prototype, to minimise cost and risk.

A fundamental feature was that, as it was guessed that the military aircraft would accrue flight-hours at one-tenth the rate of the 707, its structure could be designed to a safe-life figure, using 7178 alloy as the ruling material. This significantly reduced structure weight in comparison with that of the 707, whose airframe had to be made fail-safe, using traditional 2024 alloy.

Compared with the Dash-80 the KC-135A fuselage was made one frame longer and 12in (305mm) wider. Changing the fuselage cross-section is one of the most difficult and costly things a manufacturer can be faced with, and it was a severe setback when the USAF insisted that, in adhering to C-97 size, Boeing had made the Dash-80 too narrow (it was an even bigger blow when the 707 had to be made wider still, see later). The tanker's upper deck was left completely bare, with a strong cargo floor and

seat rails. On the left side was a single cargo door 114in (2.9m) wide ahead of the wing. On the right side were two escape hatches each with a small window; on the left was one of these, together with a single small window aft. As initially delivered, the KC-135A was cleared to carry on the upper deck 50,000lb (22,680kg) of cargo or 80 passengers in removable triple seats, but these loads were later upgraded to 83,000lb (37,649kg) or 160 passengers. The cockpit was equipped for pilot and copilot, with a navigator behind on the right. The flight-engineer station was replaced by racks of electronics and the entry stairway, which also served as an escape chute. At the rear of the flight deck was a well-equipped washroom. In the roof were two celestial observation windows. Weather radar

was installed in the nose, serving a small display on the right of the cockpit pedestal, visible only to the copilot. A long HF probe antenna projected ahead of the top of the fin.

The KC-135A went into production with Pratt & Whitney J57-31 turbojets each rated at 11,800lb (5,352kg). Some later had the J57-43WB, as fitted to many B-52 bombers, but by 1962 the standard engine, retrofitted throughout the USAF fleet, was the J57-59W, rated with water injection at 13,750lb (6,237kg). The KC-135A became notorious for its deafening noise and black smoke on takeoff. Sound waves caused rapid cracking on the flaps and underside of the rear fuselage, resulting in local reinforcement which included bonding 25 doubler strips right round the fuselage between the wing and tail. Remarkably, the customer did not request the addition of reversers.

Though the airframe was similar in size to the Dash-80, the fuel system capacity was considerably increased. Each wing bolted on at the root contained three integral tanks. In the wing centre box were six bladder cells, there were four bladders in the fuselage under the floor ahead of the wing box, five under the floor immediately behind the main-gear bays, and one filling the above-floor space under the fin behind the aft pressure bulkhead. All but 833gal (3,785 litres) could be transferred to receiver aircraft, but usually air refuelling was done from the fuselage tanks only.

All KC-135As were fitted with a fairing under the rear fuselage for a boom operator station equipped with three pallets with safety harness, communications and oxygen for an operator, instructor and student. Either a Standard or a High-Speed Boom could be fitted, extended telescopically by fuel pressure from 28ft (8.53m) to 47ft (14.33m), and "flown" by twin ruddervators to engage with the receiver receptacle.

Flow rate was initially 750gal/min, but in the 1980s new pumps raised this to 1,000gal (5,455 litres)/min. Nearly all tankers were fitted with a boom receptacle in the upper forward fuselage, with the added ability to receive fuel via their own boom.

The first KC-135A, 55-3118, flew on 31 August 1956, and the type became operational with the 93rd Air Refueling Squadron at Castle AFB in June 1957. By that time, thanks to a politically inspired panic, deliveries from Renton had

reached 15 per month, despite the rapidly growing 707 programme. The first 29 were Model 717-100A, the next 68 were 717-146 and production then continued with the 717-148 until the 732nd and last (64-14840) was delivered on 12 January 1965. Including derived versions, 820 Model 717s and 739s were built, costing (Boeing said) $1.66 billion, or $2 million each.

These 820 aircraft were delivered in seven versions, denoted by asterisks * in the following list:

DATA FOR KC-135A:

Span	**130ft 10in (39.88m)**
Length	**134ft 6in (40.99m)**
Wing area	**2,433 sq ft (226.03m²).**
Operating weight empty	**106,306lb (48,220kg)**
Maximum fuel	**189,702lb (86,049kg)**
Normal takeoff weight	**301,600lb (136,806kg)**
Maximum takeoff weight	**316,000lb (143,338kg)**
Typical cruising speed	**532mph (856km/h)** at 35,000ft (10,668m)
Mission radius	**1,150 miles (1,850km)**
	(offload 120,000lb, 54,432kg fuel)
	(offload 24,000lb, 10,886kg) 3,450 miles (5,552km).

DATA FOR KC-135R:

Dimensions unchanged.	
Operating weight empty	**119,231lb (54,083kg)**
Maximum fuel	**203,288lb (92,211kg)**
Maximum takeoff weight	**322,500lb (146,286kg)**
Mission radius	**1,725 miles (2,776km)**
	(offload 127,750lb, 57,947kg); at a radius of 2,875 miles (4,627km) fuel offload is increased over KC-135A by 150 per cent

KC-135A* Original tankers modified as previously described to withstand sonic fatigue damage. Trying to correct Dutch roll (a high-altitude uncommanded repeated combined rolling/yawing motion) led to severe trouble with dynamic sloshing of fuel, especially with almost empty tanks when the whole fuel mass can slosh about; this led to improvements to the flight controls and to the fuselage tanks. One of the first aircraft delivered suffered a hard-over rudder lock, and when an American Airlines 707 was lost from what was suspected to be the same cause the rudder was made fully powered, a mandatory fleet modification. In 1959 failure of the 707 to achieve British certification without modification (see later) resulted in increased fin area, and a similar taller fin was introduced to the KC-135 from the 583rd aircraft, earlier aircraft being modified by kits. To enable the KC-135 to refuel probe-equipped aircraft a standard 13ft (4m) kit was provided to mate the boom with a hose/drogue. There have been several structural rework programmes, and most KCs have been painted with low-drag grey aliphatic polyurethane. For aircraft re-engined with the F108, see KC-135R. Since 1980 many aircraft (see KC-135E) and derived versions have been retrofitted with components salvaged from retired commercial 707/720 aircraft, notably engines and horizontal tails (larger than the KC-135A tail). JT3D-3B engines have been retrofitted, complete with pod (with reverser, previously absent) and pylon, the engine redesignated TF33-102, rated at 18,000lb (8,165kg). The water system is removed. Most recent major upgrade has been to attach a Flight Refuelling Mk 32B hosereel pod under each outer wing. Today Pratt & Whitney is targeting c. 200 aircraft of the Air National Guard and Air Force Reserve still fitted with the J57 as candidates for the JT8D-219.

C-135A* Model 717-157, 3 transports with short fins ordered as KC-135A, a further 18 built without boom station, strong floor, 126 seats or 44 stretchers/54 casualty seats.

EC-135A Tanker conversions (11+) as post [nuclear] attack comm. relay platforms.

JC-135A, JKC-135A Special test conversions, often bizarre, for USAF and Navy.

NC-135A, NKC-135A Conversions (3) permanent testing for Atomic Energy Commission/AF Systems Command.

RC-135A* Model 739-700, four delivered to Military Air Transport Service 1965-66 (last of all USAF C/KC-135 new-builds) for mapping/surveying, then command posts with SAC and finally KC-135D.

VC-135A Convns (1 C/6 KC) staff transport.

C-135B* Model 717-158, 30 built as C-135A but with 18,000lb (8,165kg) TF33-5 turbofans, tailplane extended beyond elevators.

C-135B (TRIA) Three modified by Douglas as range instrumentation aircraft with 96in (2.44m) parabolic dish in extended nose.

KC-135B* Model 717-166, 17 with TF33-5 engines and extra fuel for use as SAC command posts, from 1964 EC-135C.

OC-135B WC-135B (3) converted to implement Open Skies treaty, titled "United States of America".

RC-135B* Model 739-445B, 10 built as electronic-reconnaissance derivative of KC-135B, became RC-135C.

TC-135B Trainer for OC-135B and Silk Purse.

VC-135B 5 staff-transport conv'ns of C-135B.

WC-135B Conversions (11) by Hayes for high-altitude weather reconnaissance, became C-135C and OC-135B.

C-135C Cargo aircraft retrofitted with TF33-102 engines (see KC-135A).

EC-135C KC-135B (17) converted as Looking Glass platforms for continuous SAC alert with new communication fits (VLF, Milstar, acoustic processor, teletypewriter etc).

RC-135C RC-135B (10) modified by Martin, boom replaced by camera station and fuel dump tube, large cheek sensors (see RC-135W), HF probes on wingtips. Later converted into RC-135V.

KC-135D Tankers (4) converted from RC-135A, later given TF33-102 engines.

RC-135D KC-135A (4) converted for electronic reconnaissance with large nose radome, wing-root antennas, wingtip pitot/static booms and other changes.

C-135E C-135A (3) retrofitted with TF33-102 and other changes.

EC-135E Electronic-warfare conversions with TF33-102 engines.

KC-135E KC-135As (149 active) retrofitted with TF33-102 and uprated wheel brakes.

NKC-135E NKC-135A (2) retrofit with TF33-102.

RC-135E C-135B (62-4137) with current from APU and environmental control in two underwing pods, glassfibre cover round forward fuselage.

C-135F* Model 717-164, KC-135A (12) for French Armée de l'Air, with drogue adapter for Mirage IVA/IVP and E-3F.

C-135FR C-135F (11, +3 added 1997) retrofitted with CFM F108 engines.

EC-135G KC-135A (4) converted as Minuteman ICBM launch-control centres, J57s retained.

EC-135H KC-135A (5) converted as airborne command posts for USAF Europe and TAC, TF33-102 engines.

EC-135J EC-135B (3) and EC-135C (1) converted as command posts for PACAF.

EC-135K KC-135A (3, one the original 55-3118,

Boeing KC-135R

1 Radome
2 Weather radar scanner
3 ILS glideslope antenna
4 Front pressure bulkhead
5 Underfloor equipment bay
6 Ventral access hatch
7 Rudder pedals
8 Instrument panel
9 Windscreen wipers
10 Instrument panel shroud
11 Windscreen panels
12 Overhead systems witch panel
13 Ditching handholds
14 Cockpit eyebrow windows
15 Copilot's seat
16 Pilot's seat
17 Pitot head
18 Nosewheel bay
19 Escape spoiler
20 Entry hatch
21 Twin nosewheels, forward retracting
22 Boarding ladder
23 Entry/escape hatch
24 Instructor's seat
25 Navigator's station
26 Flight refuelling receptacle
27 Star tracking windows, celestial navigation system
28 TACAN antenna
29 Cockpit doorway
30 Avionics equipment rack
31 Navigator's stool
32 Supernumerary crew seat
33 Electrical equipment rack
34 Flight deck air supply duct

35 Battery stowage
36 Wash basin
37 Crew toilet
38 Director lighting strip for receiving aircraft, port and starboard
39 Forward underfloor fuel cells (4), capacity 21,955-lit (4,830 Imp gal, 5,800 US gal)
40 Cargo door latches
41 Door aperture 2.9-m x 1.98-m (9-ft 6-in x 6-ft 6-in)
42 Cargo deck floor structure
43 Tie-down fittings
44 Cargo door hydraulic jacks and hinges
45 Upward opening cargo door
46 VHF/UHF antenna
47 Door mounted ADF antennas
48 Conditioned air risers to overhead distribution duct
49 Wing inspection light
50 Front spar attachment fuselage main frame
51 Centre section fuel tanks (6), cap, 27,656-lit (6,084-Imp gal, 7,306-US gal)
52 Overwing escape hatches, port and starboard
53 Wing centre-section carry-through structure
54 Floor beam structure
55 Fuselage frame and stringer structure
56 Cabin overhead air distribution duct

57 Inboard integral wing tank, capacity 8,612-lit (1,894-Imp gal, 2,275-US gal)
58 Tank filler
59 No 3, starboard inner engine nacelle
60 Nacelle pylon
61 Wing centre main integral tank, capacity 7,805-lit (1,717-Imp gal, 2,062-US gal)
62 Fuel venting channels
63 Leading edge flap hydraulic jacks
64 Kruger-type leading edge flap
65 No 4, starboard outer engine nacelle
66 Outboard nacelle pylon
67 Outboard reserve integral fuel tank, capacity 1,643-lit (361-Imp gal, 434-US gal)
68 Optional drogue-type refuelling pod, carried by French KC-135FR
69 Starboard navigation light
70 Outboard, low-speed aileron
71 Aileron internal balance panels

72 Spoiler interconnection linkage
73 Aileron hinge control linkage
74 Aileron tab
75 Outboard double-slotted Fowler-type flap segment, extended
76 Outboard spoiler panels, open
77 Spoiler hydraulic jacks
78 Flap guide rails
79 Flap screw jacks
80 Aileron geared tab
81 Inboard high-speed aileron
82 Gust damper
83 Aileron actuating linkage
84 Inboard spoiler panels, open
85 Inboard double-slotted Fowler-type flap segment, extended
86 Anti-collision beacon
87 Pressure floor above wheel bay
88 Rear spar attachment fuselage main frame
89 Port main undercarriage wheel bay

90 Wheel bay bulkhead
91 Rear underfloor fuel cells (5), capacity 24,143-lit (5,311-Imp gal, 6,378 US gal)
92 Single cabin window panel
93 Centre-facing troop seating, 80-seats
94 Detachable overhead cargo rail
95 Cargo sling/winch
96 Rear cabin cargo loading deck

97 Rear escape hatch, starboard only
98 Troop seating, stowed position
99 Rear fuselage skin stiffeners

100 Air supply duct from APU
101 Access hatch to Boom Operator's position, port and starboard

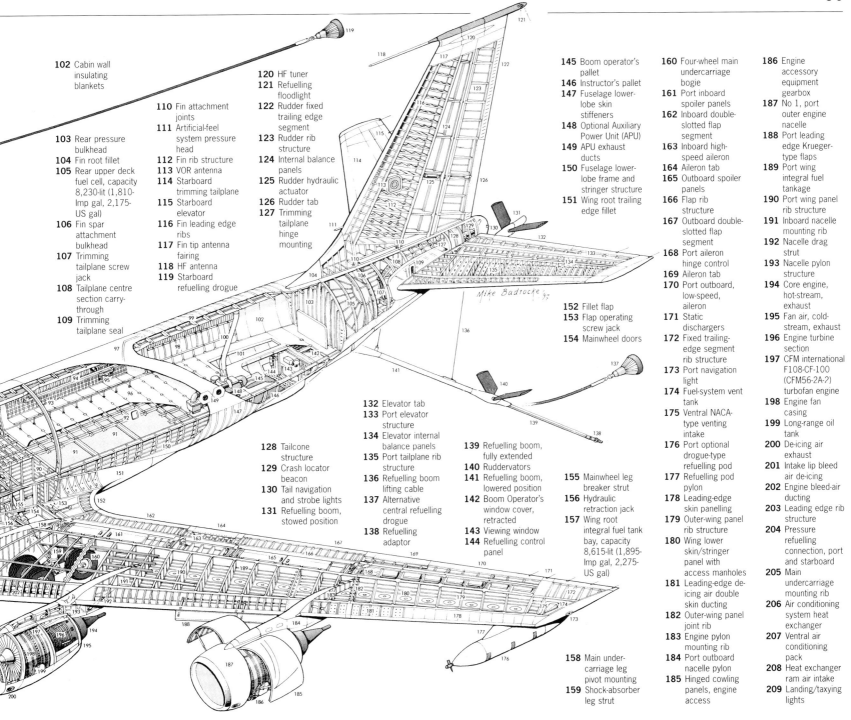

102 Cabin wall insulating blankets
103 Rear pressure bulkhead
104 Fin root fillet
105 Rear upper deck fuel cell, capacity 8,230-lit (1,810-Imp gal, 2,175-US gal)
106 Fin spar attachment bulkhead
107 Trimming tailplane screw jack
108 Tailplane centre section carry-through
109 Trimming tailplane seal

110 Fin attachment joints
111 Artificial-feel system pressure head
112 Fin rib structure
113 VOR antenna
114 Starboard trimming tailplane
115 Starboard elevator
116 Fin leading edge ribs
117 Fin tip antenna fairing
118 HF antenna
119 Starboard refuelling drogue

120 HF tuner
121 Refuelling floodlight
122 Rudder fixed trailing edge segment
123 Rudder rib structure
124 Internal balance panels
125 Rudder hydraulic actuator
126 Rudder tab
127 Trimming tailplane hinge mounting

128 Tailcone structure
129 Crash locator beacon
130 Tail navigation and strobe lights
131 Refuelling boom, stowed position

132 Elevator tab
133 Port elevator structure
134 Elevator internal balance panels
135 Port tailplane rib structure
136 Refuelling boom lifting cable
137 Alternative central refuelling drogue
138 Refuelling adaptor

139 Refuelling boom, fully extended
140 Ruddervators
141 Refuelling boom, lowered position
142 Boom Operator's window cover, retracted
143 Viewing window
144 Refuelling control panel

145 Boom operator's pallet
146 Instructor's pallet
147 Fuselage lower-lobe skin stiffeners
148 Optional Auxiliary Power Unit (APU)
149 APU exhaust ducts
150 Fuselage lower-lobe frame and stringer structure
151 Wing root trailing edge fillet

152 Fillet flap
153 Flap operating screw jack
154 Mainwheel doors

155 Mainwheel leg breaker strut
156 Hydraulic retraction jack
157 Wing root integral fuel tank bay, capacity 8,615-lit (1,895-Imp gal, 2,275-US gal)

158 Main under-carriage leg pivot mounting
159 Shock-absorber leg strut

160 Four-wheel main undercarriage bogie
161 Port inboard spoiler panels
162 Inboard double-slotted flap segment
163 Inboard high-speed aileron
164 Aileron tab
165 Outboard spoiler panels
166 Flap rib structure
167 Outboard double-slotted flap segment
168 Port aileron hinge control
169 Aileron tab
170 Port outboard, low-speed, aileron
171 Static dischargers
172 Fixed trailing-edge segment rib structure
173 Port navigation light
174 Fuel-system vent tank
175 Ventral NACA-type venting intake
176 Port optional drogue-type refuelling pod
177 Refuelling pod pylon
178 Leading-edge skin panelling
179 Outer-wing panel rib structure
180 Wing lower skin/stringer panel with access manholes
181 Leading-edge de-icing air double skin ducting
182 Outer-wing panel joint rib
183 Engine pylon mounting rib
184 Port outboard nacelle pylon
185 Hinged cowling panels, engine access

186 Engine accessory equipment gearbox
187 No 1, port outer engine nacelle
188 Port leading edge Krueger-type flaps
189 Port wing integral fuel tankage
190 Port wing panel rib structure
191 Inboard nacelle mounting rib
192 Nacelle drag strut
193 Nacelle pylon structure
194 Core engine, hot-stream, exhaust
195 Fan air, cold-stream, exhaust
196 Engine turbine section
197 CFM international F108-CF-100 (CFM56-2A-2) turbofan engine
198 Engine fan casing
199 Long-range oil tank
200 De-icing air exhaust
201 Intake lip bleed air de-icing
202 Engine bleed-air ducting
203 Leading edge rib structure
204 Pressure refuelling connection, port and starboard
205 Main undercarriage mounting rib
206 Air conditioning system heat exchanger
207 Ventral air conditioning pack
208 Heat exchanger ram air intake
209 Landing/taxiing lights

Mike Badrocke '93

717, KC-135 C-135 C-135

and another an ex-Astronaut zero-g trainer) converted as command posts for TAC, TF33-102 engines.

EC-135L KC-135A (8) converted as SAC post [nuclear] attack command systems.

RC-135M C-135B (6) converted for EW with numerous antennas, followed RC-135D/E, became RC-135W.

C-135N C-135A (4) rebuilt by Douglas with drooping swollen nose housing 7ft (2.13m) parabolic antenna as ARIA Apollo range instrumentation aircraft, redesignated Advanced instead of Apollo.

EC-135N C-135A (4) converted by Douglas as Airborne-Lightweight Optical Tracking System aircraft with tracker in external fuselage pod, 2 retrofitted with TF33-102.

EC-135P First 5 EC-135A converted as TAC/PACAF command posts, two with TF33-102.

KC-135Q KC-135A (56) converted with Tacan and JP-7 fuel system to support SR-71, some later given TF33-102, later still F108-100.

KC-135R KC-135A (380 by 1998) retrofitted with 22,000lb (9,979kg) CFM F108-100 turbofan with reverser. Transfer fuel increased by 50 per cent, noise cut 98 per cent, see data. Seven for Turkey, four for Singapore.

RC-135S C-135B (61-2662/3/4) converted as highly classified Cobra Ball aircraft for monitoring foreign missile tests, using many prominent receivers and optical sensors, TF33-5 engines with reversers (2664 lost at Shemya in 1981, others still active).

TC-135S EC-135B converted as RC-135S operator trainer.

KC-135T KC-135Q (54) retrofit with F108-100.

RC-135T JKC-135A temporarily rebuilt as electronic systems trainer and support aircraft, later retrofitted with TF33-102.

RC-135U Two RC-135C rebuilt as Combat Sent Elint research, TF33-9 engines, no reversers.

RC-135V RC-135C (10) rebuilt for Rivet Joint Elint missions, TF33-9 engines without reversers, but with APR-17 Siren IR jammer behind each pylon, operational in Okinawa, Desert Shield, Desert Storm, and Bosnia.

RC-135W RC-135M (6) converted as Rivet Joint Elint aircraft, TF33-5 engines with reversers, Have Siren behind pylons, E-Systems upgraded and lengthened cheek fairings over multiple interferometer receivers of Automatic Elint Emitter/Locator System. Visibly differ from RC-135V by absence of turbocompressor inlet above engine.Two more being converted 1998.

TC-135W One aircraft (62-4129) converted as Rivet Joint trainer

RC-135X EC-135N ARIA aircraft with black starboard wing to assist large Cobra Eye optical/IR tracker in forward fuselage for Strategic Defense Initiative.

Boeing RC-135W

1 Radome
2 Forward radar antenna
3 Front pressure bulkhead
4 Ventral antennas
5 Extended nose radome fairing
6 Nose compartment framing
7 Cockpit floor level
8 Pilot's floor level
9 Rudder pedals
10 Control yoke
11 Instrument panel
12 Windscreen wipers
13 Windscreen panels
14 Cockpit eyebrow windows
15 Overhead systems switch panels
16 Copilot's seat
17 Direct-vision opening side window panel
18 Pilot's seat
19 Safely equipment stowage
20 Chart/plotting table
21 Navigator's instrument console
22 Boom type in-flight refueling receptacle, open
23 Dual navigators' seats
24 Retractable escape spoiler, stowed position
25 Entry-hatch floor grille
26 Nose undercarriage wheel bay
27 Crew entry hatch open
28 Retractable boarding ladder
29 Twin nosewheels, forward retracting
30 Nose undercarriage pivot fixing
31 Underfloor avionics equipment racks
32 Electrical equipment racking
33 Supernumerary crew seat
34 Star tracking windows, celestial navigation system
35 Cockpit doorway
36 Circuit-breaker panels
37 Overhead air distribution ducting
38 No 1 UHF/VHF antenna
39 Starboard side avionics equipment racks
40 Toilet compartment
41 Water heater
42 Wash basin
43 Water storage tanks
44 Toilet
45 Side-looking airborne radar (SLAR) antenna panels
46 SLAR equipment fairing
47 Cargo doorway, electronic equipment loading
48 Main cabin flooring
49 Modular equipment package
50 Cargo door hydraulic jacks and hinges
51 Cargo door, open
52 ADF antennas
53 Electronics equipment racks
54 Air conditioning ducting
55 Antenna lead-in
56 Front spar attachment fuselage main frame
57 Centre section fuel tanks, capacity 27,656 lit (6,084 Imp gal)
58 Overwing emergency exit hatch, port only
59 Floor beam construction
60 AN/ASD-1 avionics equipment racks
61 Tacan antenna
62 No 1 satellite navigation system aerial
63 Inboard wing fuel tank capacity 8,612 lit (1,894 Imp gal)
64 Fuel filler cap
65 Detachable engine cowling
66 No 3 starboard inboard engine nacelle
67 Intake cowling
68 Nacelle pylon
69 Pylon strut access panels
70 Wing centre main fuel tank, capacity 7,805 lit (1,717 Imp gal)
71 Fuel venting channels
72 Leading edge flap hydraulic jacks
73 Krueger-type leading edge flap down position
74 No 4 starboard outboard engine nacelle
75 Outboard nacelle pylon
76 Outer wing panel joint rib
77 Wing outboard fuel tank, capacity 1,643 lit (361 Imp gal)
78 HF antenna tuner
79 Lightning arrester panel
80 HF antenna mast
81 Pitot static boom
82 Starboard navigation light
83 Static dischargers
84 Outboard, low speed aileron
85 Aileron internal balance panels
86 Spoiler interconnection linkage
87 Aileron hinge control mechanism
88 Aileron tab
89 Outboard double-slotted Fowler-type flap, down position
90 Outboard spoilers, open
91 Spoiler hydraulic jacks
92 Flap guide rails
93 Flap screw jacks
94 Aileron control and trim tab
95 Inboard, high-speed aileron
96 Gust damper
97 Aileron hinge control linkage
98 Inboard spoilers, open
99 Spoiler hydraulic jacks

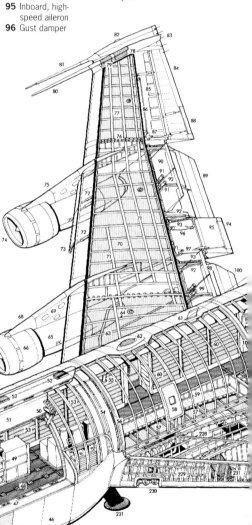

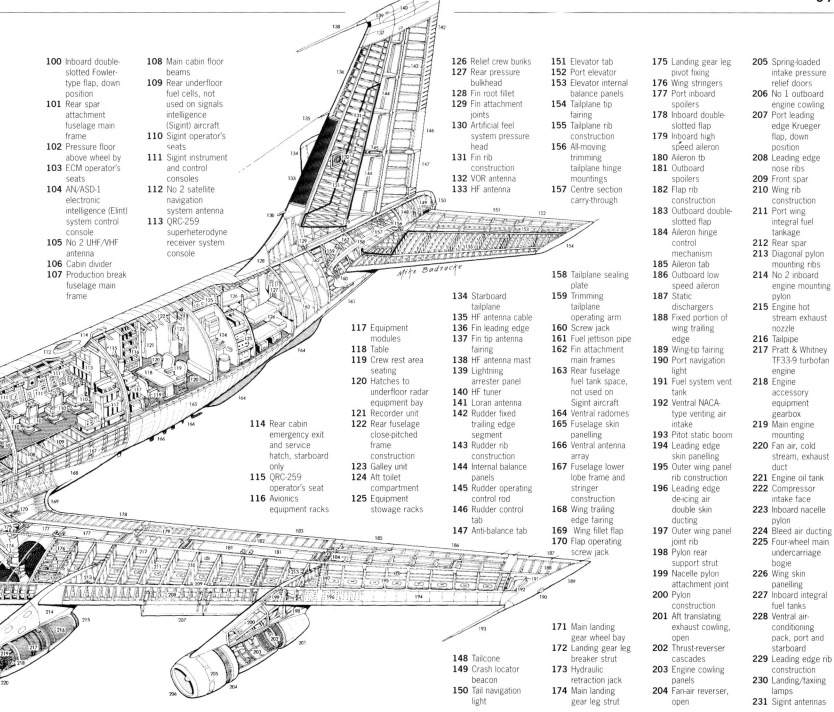

100 Inboard double-slotted Fowler-type flap, down position
101 Rear spar attachment fuselage main frame
102 Pressure floor above wheel by
103 ECM operator's seats
104 AN/ASD-1 electronic intelligence (Elint) system control console
105 No 2 UHF/VHF antenna
106 Cabin divider
107 Production break fuselage main frame

108 Main cabin floor beams
109 Rear underfloor fuel cells, not used on signals intelligence (Sigint) aircraft
110 Sigint operator's seats
111 Sigint instrument and control consoles
112 No 2 satellite navigation system antenna
113 QRC-259 superheterodyne receiver system console

114 Rear cabin emergency exit and service hatch, starboard only
115 QRC-259 operator's seat
116 Avionics equipment racks

117 Equipment modules
118 Table
119 Crew rest area seating
120 Hatches to underfloor radar equipment bay
121 Recorder unit
122 Rear fuselage close-pitched frame construction
123 Galley unit
124 Aft toilet compartment
125 Equipment stowage racks

126 Relief crew bunks
127 Rear pressure bulkhead
128 Fin root fillet
129 Fin attachment joints
130 Artificial feel system pressure head
131 Fin rib construction
132 VOR antenna
133 HF antenna

134 Starboard tailplane
135 HF antenna cable
136 Fin leading edge
137 Fin tip antenna fairing
138 HF antenna mast
139 Lightning arrester panel
140 HF tuner
141 Loran antenna
142 Rudder fixed trailing edge segment
143 Rudder rib construction
144 Internal balance panels
145 Rudder operating control rod
146 Rudder control tab
147 Anti-balance tab

148 Tailcone
149 Crash locator beacon
150 Tail navigation light

151 Elevator tab
152 Port elevator
153 Elevator internal balance panels
154 Tailplane tip fairing
155 Tailplane rib construction
156 All-moving trimming tailplane hinge mountings
157 Centre section carry-through
158 Tailplane sealing plate
159 Trimming tailplane operating arm
160 Screw jack
161 Fuel jettison pipe
162 Fin attachment main frames
163 Rear fuselage fuel tank space, not used on Sigint aircraft
164 Ventral radomes
165 Fuselage skin panelling
166 Ventral antenna array
167 Fuselage lower lobe frame and stringer construction
168 Wing trailing edge fairing
169 Wing fillet flap
170 Flap operating screw jack

171 Main landing gear wheel bay
172 Landing gear leg breaker strut
173 Hydraulic retraction jack
174 Main landing gear leg strut

175 Landing gear leg pivot fixing
176 Wing stringers
177 Port inboard spoilers
178 Inboard double-slotted flap
179 Inboard high speed aileron
180 Aileron tb
181 Outboard spoilers
182 Flap rib construction
183 Outboard double-slotted flap
184 Aileron hinge control mechanism
185 Aileron tab
186 Outboard low speed aileron
187 Static dischargers
188 Fixed portion of wing trailing edge
189 Wing-tip fairing
190 Port navigation light
191 Fuel system vent tank
192 Ventral NACA-type venting air intake
193 Pitot static boom
194 Leading edge skin panelling
195 Outer wing panel rib construction
196 Leading edge de-icing air double skin ducting
197 Outer wing panel joint rib
198 Pylon rear support strut
199 Nacelle pylon attachment joint
200 Pylon construction
201 Aft translating exhaust cowling, open
202 Thrust-reverser cascades
203 Engine cowling panels
204 Fan-air reverser, open

205 Spring-loaded intake pressure relief doors
206 No 1 outboard engine cowling
207 Port leading edge Krueger flap, down position
208 Leading edge nose ribs
209 Front spar
210 Wing rib construction
211 Port wing integral fuel tankage
212 Rear spar
213 Diagonal pylon mounting ribs
214 No 2 inboard engine mounting pylon
215 Engine hot stream exhaust nozzle
216 Tailpipe
217 Pratt & Whitney TF33-9 turbofan engine
218 Engine accessory equipment gearbox
219 Main engine mounting
220 Fan air, cold stream, exhaust duct
221 Engine oil tank
222 Compressor intake face
223 Inboard nacelle pylon
224 Bleed air ducting
225 Four-wheel main undercarriage bogie
226 Wing skin panelling
227 Inboard integral fuel tanks
228 Ventral air-conditioning pack, port and starboard
229 Leading edge rib construction
230 Landing/taxiing lamps
231 Sigint antennas

Mike Badrocke

717, KC-135 C-135

707

BECOMING NUMBER ONE

While the 367-80 prototype was company property, and could be demonstrated to airlines, the Air Force placed its initial order of October 1954 with the stipulation that, for the time being, Boeing would build the KC-135A only. This restriction did little to harm commercial sales, because with few exceptions the airlines were reluctant to commit themselves to expensive (and, as the Comet showed, high-risk) aircraft which the US industry had proclaimed to be "uneconomic".

On 13 July 1955 Boeing was given Air Force clearance to build the commercial 707. By this time a competitor had emerged. Without Air Force backing, Douglas had the courage to launch the DC-8, and as this aircraft existed only on paper it could match the needs of possible customers exactly. The DC-8 was given a fuselage diameter of 146in (3.71m), to accommodate 3+3 seating. This was impossible with the 132in body of the Dash-80, but Boeing hoped the 144in demanded by the Air Force would satisfy the market. This would permit costly KC-135 tooling to be used for the 707, enabling the commercial derivative to be sold at a lower price than the DC-8. To the company's deep chagrin this proved not to be the case: the first airline to place an order (PanAm, in September 1955) signed secretly for 25 DC-8s. Apart from having a wider cabin than the 707 they would be heavier and longer-ranged, because their engines would be the bigger Pratt & Whitney JT4A.

For several years Boeing had built nothing in the commercial transport category, and had almost lost touch with the airlines. Now, even after its courageous investment in the Dash-80, it seemed to be on the verge of losing the commercial jet market to Douglas. Boeing virtually had no option but to increase the width of the fuselage upper lobe a second time, to 148in (3.76m). On 13 October 1955 PanAm, while keeping its order for the DC-8 (which it then believed to be superior), signed for six 707-121s, to be delivered as fast as possible. The key customer

On 29 July 1959, Qantas' short-bodied 707-138s inaugurated its transpacific service.

demanding a wider cabin was American Airlines, which on 8 November 1955 signed for 30, at an announced $135 million (this order was later modified). Nevertheless, the JT4A-engined DC-8 promised transatlantic range, and Boeing decided it had to develop a larger and much heavier "707 Intercontinental", powered by the same engine. This would demand a financial risk approaching that required by the 367-80. As described later, on 24 December 1955 PanAm signed for 15 of these larger aircraft.

These orders unleashed a flurry of others. Almost overnight it could be seen that the DC-7 and L-1049 were obsolete (and they never were converted to turboprops). Instead the airlines queued to buy the DC-8 and 707. Despite Boeing's efforts, and offer of two sizes of aircraft, by the end of 1955 seven airlines had ordered 98 DC-8s while six had ordered 73 707s. However, nine months later the 707 overtook its rival. Despite a major fuselage stretch in the 1960s the DC-8 line ended at No 556, while the 707 continued to No 1,010, excluding all versions of Model 717/739. From then onwards, Boeing was No 1.

707-100
This was the first version, based on the Dash-80 and Model 717. The major difference was that the upper lobe of the fuselage was 10ft (3.05m) longer and had a diameter of 148in, making possible an internal cabin

width of 140in (3,556mm). An outward-opening plug-type door 34 x 72in (86.4 x 183cm) was provided on the left at each end of the upper deck The underfloor cargo/baggage holds had doors 48 x 50in (122 x 127cm) on the starboard side. A similar arrangement became standard on all subsequent Boeing jetliners. The flight deck was arranged for a flight crew of four, as in the 367-80. They boarded via the forward passenger door, the tanker's low-level door and escape chute being eliminated. The 707-100 was designed for 3+3 seating for up to 125 tourist passengers, but was eventually certificated to carry up to 179.

Initially the engine was the Pratt & Whitney JT3C-4, a significantly lighter derivative of the military J57. Its takeoff rating was 11,200lb (5,080kg) dry or 13,000lb (5,897kg) with water injection. Especially when using water, the noise and smoke on takeoff were intrusive, and though in the 1950s public awareness was embryonic, it was decided to fit a noise-suppressing nozzle. This matured as a heavy welded assembly which discharged the jet through 21 separate tubes, which rapidly became coated with soot. With this fitted, wet rating was

12,500lb (5,670kg).

Prompted by de Havilland's experience with the Comet, a distinctive feature was the use of numerous (two per seat row) passenger windows only 12.5 x 9in (31.75 x 22.86cm), with the frames reinforced by a doubler plate running the length of the cabin. This typified the fail-safe philosophy followed throughout the airframe, also seen in every detail of the primary structure. The ruling material was 2024, not as strong as the 7178 used in the B-52 and KC-135 but selected to resist cracking even after millions of stress reversals.

The wing was thus heavier than that of the tanker, and it differed in the addition of a Krueger flap, 12ft x 14in (3.66m x 356mm) immediately inboard of each outer pylon. This rotated hydraulically out of the underside of the wing when the flaps were extended beyond 9.5°, smoothing flow over the otherwise fixed leading edge. Between the spars the wing was sealed to form seven integral tanks with provision for both pressure and gravity filling. Boeing left a dry bay (a compartment without fuel) adjacent to each pylon. The main gears were stressed for use as airbrakes, and had Bendix multi-disc brakes with Hydro-Aire anti-skid units. The

cabin pressurization differed considerably from that in the KC-135A, where bleed air was used directly. Instead ram inlets above three (in some aircraft, all four) of the engines supplied fresh air to bleed-air turbocompressors, which was then fed to two air-cycle packs under the centre section. The first 707 was a PanAm 707-121, N707PA, which began its flight-test programme on 20 December 1957. FAA certification was granted on 18 September 1958. The author still has the flight bag, emblazoned "Jet Clipper passenger", handed out on the first Press

flight from London to New York and back. The 707-100 family were not designed for the North Atlantic, and scheduled services – which began to Paris on 27 October – invariably made a refuelling stop at Gander or Keflavik.

Boeing produced 138 of the 707-100 series. Three VIP aircraft were bought by the USAF as the VC-137A, redesignated VC-137B after being retrofitted with JT3D-3 turbofans. These used callsign Air Force One when the President was aboard. They were replaced in this duty by the VC-137Cs, described later. Qantas was the

DATA FOR 707-100:

Span	**130ft 10in (39.88m)**
Length	**144ft 6in (44.04m)**
Wing area	**2,433 sq ft (226m²).**
Weight empty	**118,000lb (53,525kg)**
Maximum takeoff weight	**247,000lb (112,039kg)** *initially*
	257,000lb (116,575kg) *later*
Cruising speed	**549-571mph (884-919km/h)** *at 28,000ft (8,534m);*
Initial climb	**2,290ft (698m)/min**
Range	**3,075 miles (4,949km)**
	maximum 52,000lb,23,587kg, payload, no reserves

DATA FOR 707-120B:

Dimensions unchanged except	
Wing area	**2,521 sq ft (234.2m²).**
Weight empty	**129,300lb (58,650kg)**
Maximum takeoff weight	**258,000lb (117,029kg).**
Cruising speed	**up to 618mph (995km/h)** *at 25,000ft (7,620m)*
Initial climb	**5,050ft (1,539m)/min**
Range	**4,235 miles (6,815km)**
	maximum 53,000lb, 24,041kg, payload, no reserves

only purchaser of the "707 Short Body", buying seven Dash-138s with the fuselage shortened by 10ft to reduce empty weight, and thus enable a heavier payload (limited by weight, not capacity) to be carried on long sectors.

A more important development was the 707-100B, with performance dramatically improved by fitting JT3D-1 turbofans, later replaced by the JT3D-3B, in each case with water injection as an option. This version also incorporated the wing aerodynamic improvements originally designed for the 720 and the long-span tailplane and taller fin later adopted on the Intercontinental versions. The first of these fan-engined versions, a converted 707-123 of American, flew on 22 June 1960. Braniff was the only customer for the 707-220, similar to the standard Dash-100 but powered, like the early 707-300 Intercontinental, by JT4A-3 turbojets in order to improve takeoff at hot/high airports.

720

From the earliest days of Boeing's jetliner studies the project staff had looked at short/ medium sectors: but while the high fuel consumption of turbojets made it difficult to achieve a long range, on shorter journeys the jet's higher speed could not save more than a few minutes, compared with a turboprop aircraft burning much less fuel. Nevertheless, once the 707 had customers it was easier to carry out a minor redesign to match the aircraft to shorter sectors.

The result, initially called the 707-020 and then (because it returned to the length of the tanker) the 717-020, finally was marketed as the 720. Though it looked like an early 707, it was aerodynamically and structurally different. The leading edge of the wing inboard of the inner engines was redesigned to increase chord at the root. The result-

ing slight increase in sweep, and reduction in thickness/ chord ratio, increased critical Mach number from 0.88 to 0.9, and slightly improved takeoff run and cruising speed. To permit operation from shorter runways, each leading edge was provided with two more Krueger flaps (making three on each wing) rotated open hydraulically to increase lift at low speeds. Other visible changes, compared with the 707-100, were that the fuselage upper lobe was made 100in (2.54m) shorter, providing for up to 149 tourist passengers (later increased to 165).HF radio was rarely specified.

The airframe was made

lighter by shortening the fuselage, and by carrying out a concomitant total detail redesign. The main saving was to reduce fuel capacity. Scantlings (metal thicknesses) were carefully reduced in the wing and certain other areas, and the landing gears were made lighter and fitted with smaller tyres inflated to slightly higher pressure. The engine chosen was the JT3C-7, rated at 12,000lb (5,443kg), the water system being eliminated. This engine weighed 3,495lb (1,585kg), compared with the 4,234lb (1,921kg) of the JT3C-6. Later the 720 was offered with the fractionally heavier JT3C-12. There was no prototype, the first (N7201U for United) flying on 23 November 1959. Certification was gained on 30 June 1960, and revenue service began on 5 July. By this time hard-over rudder problems had led to the introduction of a powered rudder, and yaw limitations (see 707-436) had required an increase in the height of the fin and the addition of a ventral fin; all these modifications were retrofitted to the 720. Renton built 154 Model 720s, most built or converted as the 720B, powered by the JT3D-1 (17,000lb) or JT3D-3B (18,000lb). New-build 720Bs had far greater fuel capacity.

DATA FOR 720:

Span	**130ft 10in (39.88m)**
Length	**136ft 2in (41.5m)**
Wing area	**2,521 sq ft (234.2m²).**
Weight empty	**110,800lb (50,259kg)**
Maximum takeoff weight	**203,000lb (92,081kg)** *at certification*
	229,000lb (103,874kg) *later*
Cruising speed	**up to 601mph (967km/h)** *at 25,000ft (7,620m)*
Range	**2,850 miles (4,587km)**
	with capacity (37,000lb, 16,783kg) payload

DATA FOR 720B:

Dimensions unchanged.	
Weight empty	**115,500lb (52,391kg)**
Maximum takeoff weight	**221,000lb (100,246kg)** *initially*
	234,000lb (106,142kg) *later*
Cruising speed	**up to 608mph (978km/h)**
Range	**4,110 miles (6,614km)**
	with capacity (40,500lb, 18,371kg) payload

ENLARGEMENT

While the original 707-100 was initially – and briefly – called the Jet Stratocruiser, the enlarged overwater model was called the Intercontinental. It was made possible by the availability of a commercial version of the Pratt & Whitney J75 military turbojet. Designated JT4A, this engine did not use water injection. It was initially produced as the JT4A-3, rated at 15,800lb (7,167kg) and with a dry weight of 5,020lb (2,277kg). In the 1960s it was given modest increases in rotational speed as the JT4A-9 and JT4A-11.

This more powerful engine made possible a major increase in fuel weight. To provide adequate volumetric capacity and lift, this demanded a larger wing with better high-lift systems. It was also found possible to lengthen the fuselage to carry greater payloads. The stretch in the parallel section of fuselage was a modest 101in (2.565m). This increased the length of the passenger

cabin from 104ft 10in to 111ft 6in (33.99m), enabling the certificated passenger load to be increased to 189, later raised to 215. The aft underfloor hold was unchanged, but the hold ahead of the wing was lengthened to increase its volume from 680 cu ft (19.25m³) to 870 cu ft (24.64m³).

The wing was considerably redesigned, with an extra 69.5in (1.77m) section added at the root on each side. The main recognition feature was that the trailing edge was given a slight kink at the inboard engine. Combined with slight chord extension at the leading edge, this increased the root chord from the 28ft 0in (8.53m) of the 707-100 to 33ft 10.7in (10.33m). The outer panels and high-lift devices were generally unchanged. The extra wing inter-spar volume saw fuel

Intercontinentals dominated civil sales of the 707 series; N714PA was No 1.

capacity increased from the previous maximum of 11,223gal to 19,863gal (90,299 litres). This demanded a stronger landing gear, tyre pressures were increased (on the main gears from 135 to 160 lb/sq in, 11.25 kg/cm²) and the brake supplier was changed to B.F.Goodrich. Not least, the span of the tailplane was increased from the original 39ft 8in to 45ft 8in (13.92m), a much greater increase than that of the 707-100B.

The first Intercontinental was N714PA, the 16th 707 to be built, and the first of the 15 707-321s ordered by PanAm on Christmas Eve 1955. It made its first flight on 11 January 1959. The 707-321 entered

service with PanAm in August. On 24 April 1956 the British flag-carrier, then called BOAC, caused a storm by ordering 15 Boeing 707-436, costing $98 million. The storm arose because a few weeks previously the airline had said it had "no interest" in the British VC.7, a transatlantic aircraft of 707 size, to be powered by four Rolls-Royce Conway engines (it was the civil version of the RAF's V.1000), which accordingly had to be abandoned. BOAC then said it had to order the 707 "as an exceptional measure" because there was no alternative. This order was later increased to 16, plus two for affiliate BOAC-Cunard. The basic 707-400 differed from the -300 only in the Conway engine, which was a low-ratio turbofan rated at 17,500lb (7,938kg) in Mk 508 form, uprated to 18,000lb (8,165kg) in the Mk 508A. Compared with the JT4A, these engines were an astonishing 505lb (229kg) lighter, despite having a Greatrex multi-lobe nozzle and a twin-clamshell thrust reverser. They also offered 24 per cent lower fuel consumption, and made no visible smoke. Despite this, the British engine was selected by only four other airlines, and in any case was soon overtaken by the Pratt & Whitney JT3D.

The first BOAC 707-436 flew on 20 May 1959. It received FAA certification on 12 February 1960, but was refused a certificate by the British Air Registration Board. Their test pilot, D.P.Davies, reported that there were two problems. First, on takeoff, it was possible to over-rotate and reach a dangerous high-drag position with the tail scraping the runway and airspeed stagnant. Second, in flight the directional stability in some situations was dangerously inadequate. In such a highly charged political situation Davies needed courage not to give way, but the result was that Boeing made all 707s better, by increasing the height of the fin, adding area above the rudder, and adding a shallow underfin. The ARB was finally satisfied, and issued a British Certificate on 27 April 1960.

The bigger 707 was ideally suited to the JT3D engine. The first version of this commercial turbofan was already fitted to the 707-020B and -120B versions. For the 707-300B Pratt developed the 18,000lb JT3D-3B, and for the first time with an American engine the 707 was fitted with reversers. These blanked off the fan exit ring with airframe-mounted

blocker doors, ignoring the core jet (the Conway reverser diverted the whole jet). The core nozzle was a plain circular hole, with no noise suppressor.

The fan-engined Dash-300B also introduced a wing with three modifications. The first was a redesigned leading edge, with even more powerful Krueger flaps extending from the tip. The second was to enlarge the outer wings. Leading-edge chord outboard of the outer engines was extended 5in (127mm), and the new leading edge was extended in a spanwise direction to end in a more efficient Kächemann curved profile. The third change was that the Fowler flaps were twice improved, the final form having a second kink 6ft (1.8m) from the root, the innermost section being at 90° to the fuselage. These changes made it more difficult to over-rotate on takeoff, and aircraft with

the improved wing were able to dispense with the underfin.

Again the launch customer was PanAm, which purchased 31 Dash-321Bs. The first, N760PA, flew on 31 January 1962, and FAA certification was received on 31 May. PanAm was also the launch customer for the 707-300C convertible passenger/cargo aircraft. This had a reinforced floor with provisions for handling containers, but any part of the cabin could be furnished for passengers. In the cargo mode the windows could be protected by clip-on panels. Cargo space comprised 7,415 cu ft (later 7,612 cu ft, 210m³) on the upper deck and 1,700 cu ft (later 1,770 cu ft, 50.1m³) in the underfloor holds. For the third time the supplier of wheel brakes was changed, this time to Goodyear. The usual engine of the later 707-300B/C variants was the JT3D-7, rated at 19,000lb (8,618kg). The first

Dash-300C, 707-321C N765PA, entered service with PanAm Boeing produced a single 707-700, a test aircraft originally built as a Dash-300 which in 1977 was retrofitted with four CFM56 engines and re-registered N707QT. Though this engine was important for the DC-8, Boeing dropped the idea because it was judged to damage prospects for the 757. In the same way, stretched 707 versions were not proceeded with. The Dash-700 was later fitted with JT3D engines and, designated 707-3W6C, was sold to Morocco. This was the last 707 to be delivered by Boeing to a civil customer.

In January 1998 an agreement was signed to re-engine 707s and military versions, including KC-135 tankers, with the JT8D-219. The signatories are Pratt & Whitney and Seven Q Seven, a Texas grouping of Omega Air of Ireland and partners Ed Swearingen and Douglas Jaffe. Rated at 22,000lb (9,979kg), the JT8D-219 is used only in MD-80 versions. It is remarkable that, while Boeing decided against the 707-700 with modern engines, this proposal to fit newly built examples of a much older engine should attract sponsors. A demonstrator is to fly in late 1998, for FAA certification in summer 1999.

DATA FOR 707-300:

Span	**142ft 5in (43.41m)**
Length	**152ft 11in (46.61m)**
Wing area	**2,892 sq ft (268.67m²).**
Weight empty	**135,000lb (61,236kg)** typical
Maximum takeoff weight	**302,000lb (136,987kg)** initially
	312,000lb (141,523kg) later
Cruising speed	**545mph (877km/h)**
Maximum cruising speed	**602mph (969km/h)** at 25,000ft (7,620m)
Range with maximum	**4,784 miles (7,699km)**
	with 55,000lb, 24,948kg) payload, no reserves

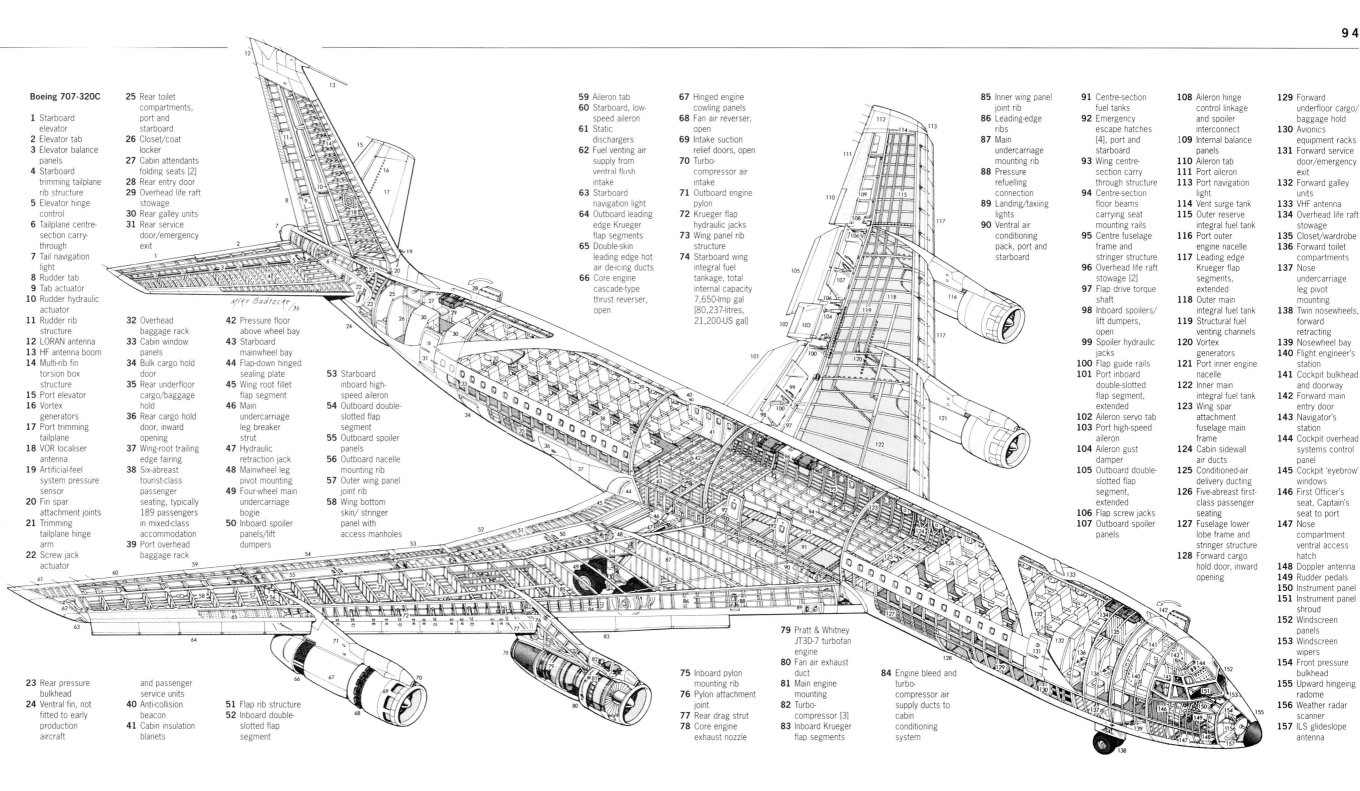

ATION

umber of
lified 707
e USAF
rces. From
derived
al military
poses other
and these
habetical
ation.
s made
e purchase
ondhand
ly by the
h-time

pares, but
7-331C)
tration
itles and
rve as
E-3A
ws.

ready been
raft for use by
ther special
dered off-the-
y were desig-
58-6970/2.
ed to -100B
ated VC-137B.
and later
53B, ordered as
l 72-7000).
urchased by

the USAF with designation C-137,
serial 68-11071/4, for the West
German Luftwaffe, with codes 10+01
to +04. The Canadian Armed Forces
snapped up five 707-347C cancelled
by Western Airlines and had them
converted as CC-137C multirole
tanker/transports, serial 13701/5,
with provision for Beech underwing
hose/drogue pods (these are now
being turned into E-8Cs, see below).
Argentina purchased a 707-3F3B as
Presidential aircraft TC-91, followed
by two ex-airline 707-372C with air
force serials TC-92 and -94, and later
operated six in the tanker/ trans-
port/ECM/Sigint roles. Five ex-airline
707-320Cs are used by the Royal
Australian AF. The Portuguese air
force operates two 707-3F5C, serial
8801/2. The Imperial, later Islamic,
Iranian air force purchased four
ex-Eastern 707-125 and 14 new
707-3J9C (called Peace Station by the
US), the 3J9Cs all having a Flying
Boom and two Beech hose/drogue
pods. Other national VIP aircraft
include a 707-3L5C of Libya, two
707-368C of Saudi Arabia, three used
707-320C of Pakistan and two
707-3P1C of Qatar, while among
operators of tanker/transports are
Brazil (four ex-airline -320C converted by Boeing and designated
KC-137), Saudi Arabia (eight new-
build KE-3A tankers with CFM56
engines), Morocco and Peru. On the

Boeing 707-320C

1 Starboard elevator
2 Elevator tab
3 Elevator balance panels
4 Starboard trimming tailplane rib structure
5 Elevator hinge control
6 Tailplane centre-section carry-through
7 Tail navigation light
8 Rudder tab
9 Tab actuator
10 Rudder hydraulic actuator
11 Rudder rib structure
12 LORAN antenna
13 HF antenna boom
14 Multi-rib fin torsion box structure
15 Port elevator
16 Vortex generators
17 Port trimming tailplane
18 VOR localiser antenna
19 Artificial-feel system pressure sensor
20 Fin spar attachment joints
21 Trimming tailplane hinge arm
22 Screw jack actuator
23 Rear pressure bulkhead
24 Ventral fin; not fitted to early production aircraft
25 Rear toilet compartments, port and starboard
26 Closet/coat locker
27 Cabin attendants folding seats [2]
28 Rear entry door
29 Overhead life raft stowage
30 Rear galley units
31 Rear service door/emergency exit
32 Overhead baggage rack
33 Cabin window panels
34 Bulk cargo hold door
35 Rear underfloor cargo/baggage hold
36 Rear cargo hold door, inward opening
37 Wing-root trailing edge fairing
38 Six-abreast tourist-class passenger seating, typically 189 passengers in mixed-class accommodation
39 Port overhead baggage rack
40 Anti-collision beacon
41 Cabin insulation blanets
42 Pressure floor above wheel bay
43 Starboard mainwheel bay
44 Flap-down hinged sealing plate
45 Wing root fillet flap segment
46 Main undercarriage leg breaker strut
47 Hydraulic retraction jack
48 Mainwheel leg pivot mounting
49 Four-wheel main undercarriage bogie
50 Inboard spoiler panels/lift dumpers
51 Flap rib structure
52 Inboard double-slotted flap segment
53 Starboard inboard high-speed aileron
54 Outboard double-slotted flap segment
55 Outboard spoiler panels
56 Outboard nacelle mounting rib
57 Outer wing panel joint rib
58 Wing bottom skin/ stringer panel with access manholes
59 Aileron tab
60 Starboard, low-speed aileron
61 Static dischargers
62 Fuel venting air supply from ventral flush intake
63 Starboard navigation light
64 Outboard leading edge Krueger flap segments
65 Double-skin leading edge hot air de-icing ducts
66 Core engine cascade-type thrust reverser, open
67 Hinged engine cowling panels
68 Fan air reverser, open
69 Intake suction relief doors, open
70 Turbo-compressor air intake
71 Outboard engine pylon
72 Krueger flap hydraulic jacks
73 Wing panel rib structure
74 Starboard wing integral fuel tankage, total internal capacity 7,650-Imp gal [80,237-litres, 21,200-US gal]
75 Inboard pylon mounting rib
76 Pylon attachment joint
77 Rear drag strut
78 Core engine exhaust nozzle
79 Pratt & Whitney JT3D-7 turbofan engine
80 Fan air exhaust duct
81 Main engine mounting
82 Turbo-compressor [3]
83 Inboard Krueger flap segments
84 Engine bleed and turbo-compressor air supply ducts to cabin conditioning system
85 Inner wing panel joint rib
86 Leading-edge ribs
87 Main undercarriage mounting rib
88 Pressure refuelling connection
89 Landing/taxiing lights
90 Ventral air conditioning pack, port and starboard
91 Centre-section fuel tanks
92 Emergency escape hatches [4], port and starboard
93 Wing centre-section carry through structure
94 Centre-section floor beams carrying seat mounting rails
95 Centre fuselage frame and stringer structure
96 Overhead life raft stowage [2]
97 Flap drive torque shaft
98 Inboard spoilers/ lift dumpers, open
99 Spoiler hydraulic jacks
100 Flap guide rails
101 Port inboard double-slotted flap segment, extended
102 Aileron servo tab
103 Port high-speed aileron
104 Aileron gust damper
105 Outboard double-slotted flap segment, extended
106 Flap screw jacks
107 Outboard spoiler panels
108 Aileron hinge control linkage and spoiler interconnect
109 Internal balance panels
110 Aileron tab
111 Port aileron
113 Port navigation light
114 Vent surge tank
115 Outer reserve integral fuel tank
116 Port outer engine nacelle
117 Leading edge Krueger flap segments, extended
118 Outer main integral fuel tank
119 Structural fuel venting channels
120 Vortex generators
121 Port inner engine nacelle
122 Inner main integral fuel tank
123 Wing spar attachment fuselage main frame
124 Cabin sidewall air ducts
125 Conditioned-air delivery ducting
126 Five-abreast first-class passenger seating
127 Fuselage lower lobe frame and stringer structure
128 Forward cargo hold door, inward opening
129 Forward underfloor cargo/ baggage hold
130 Avionics equipment racks
131 Forward service door/emergency exit
132 Forward galley units
133 VHF antenna
134 Overhead life raft stowage
135 Closet/wardrobe
136 Forward toilet compartments
137 Nose undercarriage leg pivot mounting
138 Twin nosewheels, forward retracting
139 Nosewheel bay
140 Flight engineer's station
141 Cockpit bulkhead and doorway
142 Forward main entry door
143 Navigator's station
144 Cockpit overhead systems control panel
145 Cockpit 'eyebrow' windows
146 First Officer's seat, Captain's seat to port
147 Nose compartment ventral access hatch
148 Doppler antenna
149 Rudder pedals
150 Instrument panel
151 Instrument panel shroud
152 Windscreen panels
153 Windscreen wipers
154 Front pressure bulkhead
155 Upward hingeing radome
156 Weather radar scanner
157 ILS glideslope antenna

Mike Badrocke/98

Boeing E-6 Mercury

1 Radome
2 AN/APS-133 weather radar
3 Glideslope antenna
4 Front pressure bulkhead
5 Underfloor equipment bay
6 Ventral access hatch
7 Rudder pedals
8 Control yoke
9 Instrument panel
10 Instrument panel shroud
11 Windscreen wipers
12 Windscreen panels
13 Overhead systems switch panel
14 Starboard side flight engineer's station
15 Cockpit eyebrow windows
16 Copilot's seat
17 Centre console
18 Pilot's seat
19 Side console and document stowage
20 Pitot head
21 Nosewheel bay
22 Twin nosewheels, forward retracting
23 Nose landing gear pivot mounting
24 Tactical navigator's station
25 Curtained cockpit bulkhead
26 Flight refuelling receptacle, open
27 Stowage lockers
28 Toilet compartment
29 Forward cabin door
30 Door latch
31 Lower VHF antenna

32 Forward underfloor hold avionics equipment racks
33 Food locker
34 Galley units
35 Spare crew rest area seating
36 UHF antenna
37 TACAN antenna
38 Forward SIGINT antenna
39 Dining table
40 Cargo door, open, used for systems equipment installation
41 Door mounted ADF antennae
42 Upper VHF antenna
43 Cargo door hydraulically powered hinged actuators
44 Individual swivelling seats
45 Starboard side lower hold access hatch
46 Underfloor air and cable ducting
47 Fire extinguisher
48 Bale-out hatch blast shield
49 Boarding ladder
50 Fuselage lower lobe frame and stringer structure
51 Bale-out/entry hatch
52 Portable oxygen bottle
53 Spare crew rest bunks (8)
54 Forward cabin air conditioning ducting
55 Curtained cabin divider
56 Front spar attachment fuselage main frame
57 Front spar attachment joint
58 Ventral heat exchanger air intake

59 Cabin air conditioning pack, port and starboard
60 Centre section fuel tanks, total fuel capacity 63,776 lit (14,034 Imp gal)
61 Overwing floor beam
62 Airborne Communications Officer's (ACO) seat
63 Operators' stations (5)
64 Communications consoles
65 Ancillary equipment stowage
66 Emergency escape hatches, port and starboard
67 Starboard wing inboard integral fuel tank
68 Overwing fuel filler
69 Dry bay
70 Starboard engine nacelles
71 Nacelle pylons
72 Starboard wing leading edge Krueger flaps
73 Vortex generators
74 Fuel venting channels
75 Starboard wing leading edge Krueger flaps
76 Krueger flap hydraulic jacks
77 Outboard fuel tank bay
78 HF antenna
79 Starboard navigation light
80 Wing tip pod housing ESM equipment and UHF SATCOM receiver

81 Static dischargers
82 Outboard, low-speed, aileron
83 Aileron internal balance panels
84 Hinge control linkage and spoiler interconnect
85 Aileron tab
86 Outboard double-slotted flap, down position
87 Outboard spoiler panels/airbrakes, open
88 Spoiler hydraulic jacks
89 Flap drive torque shaft and screw jacks
90 Flap guide rails
91 Aileron gust damper
92 Inboard, high-speed, aileron
93 Aileron servo tab
94 Inboard double-slotted, aileron segment, down position
95 Inboard spoilers/lift dumpers
96 HF aerial cable
97 Rear spar/fuselage attachment main frame
98 Communications section cabin divider
99 Pressure floor above wheel bay
100 Communications equipment racks

101 Rear cabin conditioned-air delivery ducting
102 Very Low Frequency (VLF) transmitting equipment rack
103 Long antenna cable reel housing
104 Trailing antenna operator's stations
105 Ant. cable drive
106 Starboard side APU bay
107 Rear SIGINT antennas
108 Satellite navigation system antenna
109 Starboard side bale-out door
110 Fin root fillet
111 Flight recorder and emergency locator transmitter
112 Artificial feel system pressure sensor
113 Fin spar attachment joint
114 Fin rib construction
115 VOR Localiser antenna
116 Starboard trimming tailplane
117 Vortex generators

118 Starboard elevator
119 HF antenna
120 Lightning arrestor panel
121 HF tuner housing
122 LORAN antenna
123 Rudder

124 Rudder rib construction
125 Hydraulic rudder actuator
126 Rudder tab
127 Trailing antenna drogue housing
128 VLF short (1,520m) trailing wire antenna (STWA)
129 Trailing antenna drogue
130 Tail navigation light
131 Elevator tab
132 Port elevator
133 Port trimming tailplane
134 Tailplane rib construction
135 Elevator hinge control
136 Tailplane pivot mounting
137 Tailplane sealing plate
138 Trimming tailplane hinge arm
139 Screw jack
140 Rear pressure bulkhead
141 Short trailing antenna winch and reel housing
142 Rear cabin door

143 Parachute stowage rack
144 Spares stowage
145 Long (8,530m) trailing wire antenna (LTWA)
146 Ventral dorgue housing
147 Rear underfloor equipment bay

148 Cooling air scoop
149 Vapour-cycle avionics cooling system
150 Liquid-oxygen bottle
151 Wing root trailing edge fillet
152 Inboard fillet flap segment
153 Main undercarriage wheel bay

154 Side stay/breaker strut
155 Hydraulic retraction jack
156 Mainwheel leg pivot mounting
157 Torque scissor links
158 Four-wheel main undercarriage bogie
159 Shock absorber leg strut
160 Port inboard spoiler panels/lift dumpers
161 Flap rib construction
162 Inboard double-slotted flap segment
163 Port inboard, high-speed, aileron
164 Outboard roll control spoiler panels/airbrakes
165 Outboard double-slotted flap segment
166 Aileron servo tab
167 Port aileron

168 Static dischargers
169 Port wing tip ECM pod
170 Aft ECM antenna
171 ECM and UHF SATCOM receiving equipment
172 Port navigation light
173 Ventral antenna mast
174 Port HF antenna
175 Forward ECM antenna
176 Wing tip fuel vent tank
177 Port leading edge Krueger flaps
178 Leading edge de-icing air ducts
179 Lower wing skin stringer panel
180 Access manholes
181 Outer wing panel joint rib
182 Outboard pylon mounting rib
183 Pylon attachment joint and lower support strut
184 Thrust reverser translating cowling, open

185 Thrust reverser cascades
186 Engine fan casing
187 Acoustically lined engine intake
188 Nacelle strake
189 Krueger flap pantographic hinge links
190 Flap hydraulic Jacks
191 Wing panel rib structure
192 Port wing integral fuel tankage
193 Inboard pylon mounting rib
194 Engine bleed air ducting
195 Nacelle pylon structure
196 Core engine hot stream exhaust
197 Fan air, cold stream exhaust
198 Engine turbine section
199 CFM International F108-CF-100 (CFM56-2A-2) turbofan engine
200 Long range oil tank
201 De-icing air exhaust
202 Intake lip bleed air de-icing
203 Inboard Krueger flap segments
204 Main undercarriage mounting rib
205 Pressure refuelling connection, port and starboard
206 Runway turn-off light
207 Landing/taxiing lights

Luxembourg re
ex-Sabena 707-
then equipped
the NATO fleet

C-18
In January 198
eight ex-Ameri
converted ther
serials 81-691/
transports and
passenger wind
other three we
EC-18B A/RIA
Advanced, Ran
Aircraft), repla
described earlie
fied as EC-18D
platforms, they
converted into

C-137C
This designatio
transports take
1965, a 707-38
drug smuggler
ex-Wardair.

E-3 Sentry
In 1962 NORA
Air Defense) re
veillance on 6
EC-121 Warnin
severe limitati
their age. On
issued a Specifi
Requirement v
major ORT (O
ogy) programr
for an aircraft
aircraft compe

DC-8-62 and 707-320C, and in June 1970 the latter was selected, with Boeing Aerospace, of Kent, Washington, as prime contractor. The system was called AWACS (Airborne Warning And Control System).

The key item was the radar, which among other things had to be able to detect small moving targets flying at very low level, and thus in the presence of intense ground clutter. Eventually two pulse-doppler radars competed, one by Hughes and the other by Westinghouse. To evaluate these in the sky two 707-320Bs were diverted from the Renton line and completed as EC-137D trials aircraft, one with each type of radar. The cabins were occupied by the radar racking and cooling systems, operator stations, data processors, communications and provisions for crew comfort. The obvious addition was the 30ft (9.14m)-diameter rotodome, which in operation rotates on twin 11ft (3.35m) pylons above the rear fuselage to sweep its radar beams and IFF signals to all points of the compass. The flight programme began on 9 February 1972, and on 5 October 1972 the Westinghouse installation was selected, with designation APY-1. In 1977-78 both trials aircraft were redelivered to the USAF after being refurbished as almost standard E-3As.

The plan to power production aircraft by four pairs of General Electric T34 engines was abandoned on the grounds of cost. Though this cut unrefuelled endurance from 14.5 hours to 11, the Sentry instead went into production with the Pratt & Whitney TF33-100/-100A. Each engine was rated at 21,000lb (9,526kg), and drove alternators with a combined output of 600kVA. Boeing later produced for the USAF 34 aircraft for inventory. The first 24 were E-3A Core aircraft, with first delivery to Tinker AFB in March 1977, becoming operational a year later. In Block 20 the two prototypes and 22 Core E-3As (Nos 4-9 and 11-26) were upgraded to E-3B standard, one result being the addition of limited performance over water. Nos 27-35 and the upgraded No 3 were delivered as US/NATO Standard E-3A, with full overwater capability. This was also the standard of 18 additional aircraft built for NATO, registered to Luxembourg, with multinational crews and home-based at Geilenkirchen. Under the Block 25 programme the E-3C added many further items, and all USAF aircraft have now been brought up to this standard. All the USAF and NATO aircraft are undergoing further progressive upgrades.

Boeing delivered to Saudi Arabia five E-3As with USAF serials, powered by the 24,000lb (10,886kg) CFM56-2A-2, and the same engine powers seven Sentry AEW.1 to E-3D standard of the RAF and four E-3F/SDA of the French Armée de l'Air. Normal crew is 17, 13 of them operators. All versions have a boom receptacle, and the Saudi, RAF and French aircraft also have a probe.

E-6A Hermes

In the 1970s the US Navy wished to procure a large high-flying jet to replace the EC-130Q in what it called the Tacamo (TAke Charge And Move Out) mission. This is the global communications relay mission, primarily to control missile-armed submarines, using AVLF (Airborne Very Low Frequency) radio. Among the necessary equipment are an LTWA (Long Trailing-Wire Antenna) with a length of 27,980ft (8,530m) and weight of 1,090lb (495kg) [ignoring aerodynamic drag of some 2,000lb, 907kg] and a Short TWA with a length of 4,990ft (1,520m) deployed from the tailcone to act as a dipole. After operating NC-135A and NKC-135A aircraft borrowed from the Air Force, the Navy ordered a prototype 707-320 with F108-100 (CFM56-2A-2) engines, followed by orders which eventually totalled 16 E-6A Mercury (Tacamo II) platforms. These were all newly built, and were the last aircraft of 707 type to be constructed. Painted white, they have many features common to the E-3. Whereas the E-3 is cleared to 332,500lb (150,822kg) the E-6 can take off at 342,000lb (155,128kg), and the tip pods (housing satcom and h.f. antennas) increase span to 148ft 2in (45.16m). The first E-6A was delivered to VQ-3 trials squadron at Barber's Point, Hawaii, on 2 August 1989.

E-8 J-Stars

The Joint Surveillance Target Attack Radar System does over a land battle what the AWACS does in the sky. The system was designed "to detect, locate, identify, classify, track and target hostile ground movement, in any condition, around the clock". It was launched in 1985 jointly by the US Army and USAF. The prime contract was won by Grumman's Melbourne (Florida) Systems Division, which (because the 707 production line had closed) integrated the airborne portions into two well-used airframes, an ex-American 707-323C and an ex-Qantas 707-338C. The main sensor is a large Norden multimode radar with its row of side-looking antennas in a 30ft (9.14m) "canoe" under the forward fuselage. The normal surveillance altitude is over 35,000ft (10,667m). These immature prototypes were pitchforked into the Gulf War, and did brilliantly. The original plan was to deploy 20 E-8B aircraft with F108 engines, but this has now been cut back to 14, to E-8C standard, retaining the JT3D-3B and -7 engines. Maximum takeoff weight is 336,000lb (152,407kg), and flyaway unit cost in 1996 was put at $266.2 million. They are Air Force aircraft, but transmit to Army ground stations. In March 1998, with deliveries continuing, Raytheon E-Systems began replacing the wing lower-surface stringers and skins to rectify "widespread fatigue". NATO, Japan, South Korea, Saudi Arabia and the RAF have discussed procuring the E-8, with CFM56-3B (F108) engines.

727

"THIS BUSINESS IS ONE-SIDED!"

In 1956 both Boeing and Douglas were breathing huge sighs of relief: they had a solid and growing list of customers for commercial jets. Accordingly, both began to consider whether there might be a market for a short-haul jet, such as France was already testing in the form of the Caravelle. By the end of the year Douglas was asking airlines about the DC-9, basically a much smaller DC-8 powered by four JT8 turbojets, while Boeing offered a small 707 (to be called the 727) with two JT3C engines. Airline interest was lukewarm, but in April 1957 the British airline BEA issued a requirement for a short-haul jet, and to Boeing's surprise said "preferably with three engines". Very quickly de Havilland, Avro and Bristol came up with proposals. Though Boeing made no attempt to meet the BEA specification, this triggered serious 727 work, which eventually was to lead to tunnel testing of 68 configurations selected from 150 design studies.

The author often visited Boeing at this time, and Jack Steiner told him "Three engines? Heck, that's the optimum worst!" But on his next visit he was intrigued to discover that three engines was exactly what the 727 would have, and they would probably be Allison/Rolls-Royce ARB.963 turbofans. The situation was, as ever in this industry, fraught. Boeing was nowhere near to breaking even on the 707, and though the 727 promised to be a more attractive short-hauler than the 720, there was no military market and no way it could be sold at a lower price than its larger predecessor. One could buy a 720 for $3.5 million, but the small 727 had to begin life at over $4.25 million.

Meanwhile, Pratt & Whitney, for the first time since 1925, had to emulate Boeing and grit its teeth and take a big risk. With no military requirement, its engineers were busy turning the JT8 turbojet into the JT8D turbofan. Rated at 14,000lb (6,350kg), this was considerably bigger and heavier than the ARB.963. The author, whose respect for his hosts at East Hartford was and is profound, deliberately needled them by commenting "You say your conservative temperatures permit the use of solid vanes and blades for greater durability. What you mean is, you have no experience of cooled blades,

The Model 727 takes its bow at Renton. Finished temporarily in company colours, N7001U was actually the first 'three holer' for United.

which is why the JT8D is so much bigger and heavier".

In the event Pratt's parent United Aircraft believed the prediction that the JT8D could win a market hesitantly guessed at 1,000 engines. It boldly voted $75 million, some of which went to affiliate SNECMA in Paris, who designed the nacelle complete with reverser. Chief Engineer Schmickrath told the author "The JT8D will be a nice engine. I just hope we find a customer". Little did he know it would outsell every other airline jet engine, and still be in production in 1998 with over 14,550 shipped.

In February 1960 United ordered 20 Caravelles. Within days Boeing had sent a mission headed by Schairer and Bruce Connelly to Sud-Aviation to discuss collaboration. They went on to de Havilland, where they studied the D.H.121 Trident in the greatest detail, telling their hosts "We'll invite you to Seattle to see plans for the 727". In the event Boeing decided to go it alone with the 727, and nobody was invited over from Hatfield. In passing, de Havilland designed the Trident specifically for the British airline BEA, which ordered it to be made smaller, with 9,850lb (4,468kg) engines. Amazingly, their sales staff were ordered not even to speak with any other airlines until they had tailored the Trident precisely to BEA's needs. This guaranteed disaster, and potential customers bought the 727 – except for the Chinese, who were not allowed to.

Soon Douglas said it would help Sud-Aviation to sell GE-engined Caravelles, and with the Trident and Convair's Coronado forging ahead Boeing knew it had to do something quickly. Though American still said it wanted something smaller (but certainly not the long-runway Trident), Boeing got encouraging responses from Eastern and United. In October 1960 Boeing issued the 727 start-work order to Manufacturing. On 30 November 1960 contracts were signed for 40 aircraft for Eastern and 20, plus 20 options, for United. It was a close-run thing, but at $420 million the combined launch orders were "the largest in commercial aviation ever made" (up to that time).

Apart from the unexpected choice of three engines grouped at the tail, there were several arguable features. Design accommodation was 70 First-class or up to 129 all-tourist. Many Boeing people said "Let's use KC-135 tooling or make the fuselage even narrower", but the final choice was to use the same 148in upper lobe as that of the 707/720, but shortened to give a cabin length of 72ft 8in (22.15m). At the front on the left was a plug-type door identical with those of the 707, but available with Weber electrically powered airstairs. At the back was an innovative hydraulic aft-facing stairway arranged axially under the centre engine, with a door in the aft pressure bulkhead.

The most prolonged arguments centred on the wing and flight controls. Especially in a smaller aircraft there is strong pressure to keep things simple. Complex systems increase cost, weight, and ongoing maintenance, and militate against reliability. In early 727 studies the wing was simpler than that of the 707, but the need to keep the wing small for comfortable high-speed flight through low-level turbulence was combined with stringent demands for short field-length (for example, New York La Guardia and Chicago Midway). The result was a wing more advanced than anything seen previously.

The leading edge was almost straight (there was a slight kink at one-third span), with sweep at $1/4$-chord reduced from the previous 35° to 32°. The entire leading edge was fitted with high-lift devices: three sections of Krueger flap over the inner one-third and four sections of hydraulically powered slat from there to the tip. The trailing edge followed the proven arrangement of the 707, but with two big differences: the flaps were triple-slotted and the ailerons powered.

Triple-slotted flaps, to achieve lift coefficients never previously even approached by a fast jet, were an innovation which required testing on the 367-80. As for the flight controls, whereas Boeing had previously done wonders with manual systems, they now decided hydraulic power was mature enough to be relied upon, and every control

Boeing Advanced 727-200

1 Radome
2 Radar dish
3 Radar scanner mounting
4 Pressure bulkhead
5 Windscreen panels
6 Instrument panel shroud
7 Back of instrument panel
8 Rudder pedals
9 Radar transmitter and receiver
10 Pitot tube
11 Cockpit floor control ducting
12 Control yoke
13 Pilot's seat
14 Cockpit eyebrow windows
15 Copilot's seat
16 Engineer's control panel
17 Flight engineer's seat
18 Cockpit door
19 Observer's seat
20 Nosewheel bay
21 Nosewheel doors
22 Twin nosewheels
23 Retractable airstairs (optional)
24 Handrail
25 Escape chute pack
26 Front entry door
27 Front toilet
28 Galley
29 Starboard galley service door
30 Cabin bulkhead
31 Closet
32 Window frame panel
33 Radio and electronics bay
34 First class passenger cabin, 18 seats in mixed layout
35 Cabin roof construction
36 Seat rails
37 Cabin floor beams
38 Cargo door
39 Anti-collision light
40 Air conditioning supply ducting
41 Forward cargo hold
42 Cargo hold floor
43 Baggage pallet container
44 Tourist-class passenger cabin, 119 seats in mixed layout
45 Communications antenna
46 Fuselage frame and stringer construction
47 Cabin window frame panels
48 Air conditioning system intake
49 Air conditioning plant
50 Overhead air ducting
51 Main fuselage frames
52 Escape hatches, port and starboard
53 Wing centre section No 2 fuel tank
54 Centre section stringer construction
55 Cabin floor construction
56 Starboard wing No 3 fuel tank
57 Inboard Krueger flaps
58 Krueger flap hydraulic jack
59 Leading edge fence
60 Outboard leading edge slat segments
61 Slat hydraulic jacks
62 Fuel vent surge tank
63 Navigation lights
64 Starboard wing tip
65 Fuel jettison pipe
66 Static dischargers
67 Outboard, low speed, aileron
68 Aileron balance tab
69 Outboard spoilers
70 Outboard slotted flap
71 Flap screwjack mechanism
72 Inboard, high speed, aileron
73 Trim tab
74 Inboard spoilers
75 Inboard slotted flap
76 Fuselage centre section construction
77 Pressurised floor over starboard main undercarriage bay
78 Auxiliary power unit (APU)
79 Port main undercarriage bay
80 Tourist class, six-abreast, passenger seating
81 Overhead hand baggage stowage bins
82 Cabin trim panels
83 Rear cargo door
84 Aft cargo compartment floor
85 Passenger overhead service panels
86 Starboard service door/rear emergency exit
87 Aft galleys
88 Closet
89 Toilets, port and starboard
90 Cabin rear entry door
91 Starboard engine cowling
92 Centre engine intake
93 Noise-attenuating intake lining
94 Intake S-duct
95 Duct de-icing
96 Fin root fairing construction
97 Fin construction
98 VOR antenna
99 Elevator control cables
100 Tailplane trim jack
101 Starboard tailplane
102 Elevator horn balance
103 Static dischargers
104 Starboard elevator
105 Elevator tab
106 Fin bullet fairing
107 VHF antenna
108 Elevator control jack
109 Port elevator
110 Tailplane construction
111 Port tailplane
112 Rudder upper section
113 Rudder control jacks
114 Rudder lower section
115 Lower section trim jack
116 Centre engine mounting pylon
117 Centre engine exhaust pipe
118 Thrust reverser
119 Centre engine
120 Rear fuselage construction
121 Side engine thrust reverser
122 Engine pylon fairing
123 Rear pressure bulkhead
124 Bleed air system pipes
125 Pratt & Whitney JT8D-9A turbofan engine
126 Detachable cowlings
127 Rear entry ventral airstairs
128 Engine air intake
129 Port rear service door/emergency exit
130 Lower lobe fuselage frame construction
131 Trailing edge fillet
132 Inboard flap
133 Flap track fairings
134 Flap track mechanism
135 Inboard spoilers
136 Main undercarriage leg pivot
137 Retraction mechanism
138 Rear spar
139 Wing rib construction
140 Front spar
141 Leading edge construction
142 Landing and taxiing lamp
143 De-icing air duct
144 Inboard Krueger flap segments
145 Landing lamp
146 Main undercarriage leg
147 Twin mainwheels
148 Wing stringer construction
149 Inboard, high speed, aileron
150 Aileron trim tab
151 Flaps down position

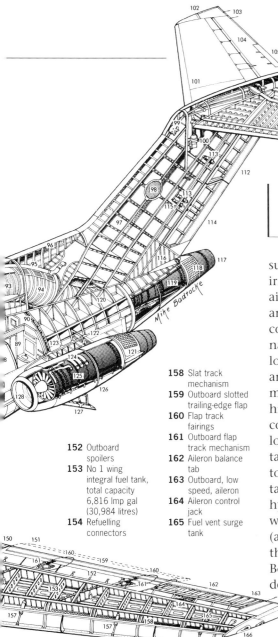

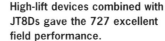

High-lift devices combined with JT8Ds gave the 727 excellent field performance.

152 Outboard spoilers
153 No 1 wing integral fuel tank, total capacity 6,816 Imp gal (30,984 litres)
154 Refuelling connectors

158 Slat track mechanism
159 Outboard slotted trailing-edge flap
160 Flap track fairings
161 Outboard flap track mechanism
162 Aileron balance tab
163 Outboard, low speed, aileron
164 Aileron control jack
165 Fuel vent surge tank

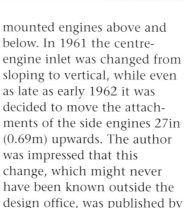

155 Leading edge fence
156 Leading edge slat segments
157 Slat hydraulic jacks

166 Port navigation lights
167 Static dischargers
168 Fuel jettison pipe

surface was driven by irreversible power units. The ailerons had dual actuators, and were provided with compound internal aerodynamic balance to ease pilot loads in the manual reversionary mode. To reduce hinge moments further, each inboard high-speed aileron had a control tab and each outboard low-speed aileron a balance tab. The T-type tail had elevators with q-feel, and spring tabs which were unlocked if hydraulic power was lost, while the lower double-hinged (anti-balance) rudder had a third hydraulic power channel. Both the upper and lower rudders were trimmed by displacing the neutral setting of the power units.

The centre engine was fed by a curved S-duct from an oval inlet above the fuselage. All engines incorporated internal twin-bucket reversers which discharged through cascade grills, the centre engine blasting laterally and the side-mounted engines above and below. In 1961 the centre-engine inlet was changed from sloping to vertical, while even as late as early 1962 it was decided to move the attachments of the side engines 27in (0.69m) upwards. The author was impressed that this change, which might never have been known outside the design office, was published by Boeing and explained in detail.

The fuel system was simple, with an integral tank in the centre section and one in each wing. System capacity was 5,829gal in 1962, 5,974 at first flight and eventually 6,796gal (30,895lit) in 727-100 production aircraft, with the option of extra bladder tanks housing up to 2,065gal (9,387lit). For the first time, Boeing considered that gravity filling could be omitted, and provided a single pressure coupling under the starboard wing.

The landing gears resembled shorter versions of those on the 707, but with twin main wheels. All three units retracted inwards or forwards hydraulically, as in the 707. The three 3,000lb/sq in (210kg/cm²) hydraulic systems, electrical systems energised by three 40kVA constant-speed alternators, bleed-air wing deicing and 8.6lb/sq in (0.6kg/cm²) cabin pressurization and environmental system were all based on 707 experience. To make the 727 self-sufficient an AiResearch auxiliary power unit was provided in the right mainwheel well to provide electric power and compressed air for cabin conditioning and engine starting. Sperry provided the SP-50 autopilot, and the weather radar was by RCA in early aircraft and Bendix later. Painted in company chocolate and yellow, the 727 prototype, N7001U, was ceremonially rolled out from Renton on 27 November 1962. While it was undergoing ground tests the 727 was ordered by a growing number of important world airlines, to the chagrin of many de Havilland people who had protested to their management that they ought to have designed the Trident for the world market. At last, on 9 February 1963, test pilots Lew Wallick and Dix Loesch opened the flight programme. Wallick said "She handles beautifully", omitting to mention that on the first take-off rotation bad airflow in the S-duct had stopped the centre engine. Within days, as the performance engineers plotted the data, it became clear that the figures were way off prediction. Often aircraft suffer higher drag than expected, but in the case of the 727 the results were almost unbelievably good. In cruise at most heights and engine settings the speed was 13-15 knots beyond prediction. In October 1963 Boeing cautiously admitted to "6.5 per cent more air-miles per pound", and at the time of certification, on Christmas Eve 1963, they announced "range figures generally 10 per cent beyond the guarantees". Sales Director George Sanborn said to the author "This business is one-sided: if we fall short, there's a financial penalty, but with the 727 we can't ask the customers to pay more !" Boeing delivered 408 727-100s, certificated for up to 131 passengers, one being the prototype which went to United. These were followed by 164 727-100C and QC (Quick Change) aircraft, with a 707-320C type cargo door and provisions for any mix of passengers or up to 44,730lb (20,290kg) of cargo on eight pallets. A few were sold to military, government or executive customers, and five ex-airline aircraft were passed to the US Air National Guard with the designation C-22A. The 727's good performance, coupled with Pratt's development of the JT8D to give increased thrusts up to 16,400lb (7,439kg), or 17,400lb (7,893kg) in emergency, allowed Boeing to stretch the fuselage by 20ft (6.1m) to seat up to 189 passengers. The new aircraft, which quickly became standard, was designated 727-200. It also had greater fuel capacity, and to handle the considerably increased weight a strengthened structure, and modified landing gear. The first 727-200 began flight testing on 27 July 1967. Boeing built 1,260 Dash-200s, ending with a batch of 15 727-252F freighters for FedEx. The last of these was delivered in September 1984, by which time the basic price of a 727 had climbed to over $22 million. Back in 1971 Boeing had schemed a stretched 727-300, with upgraded engines and other new features, but never got enough support to go ahead. While production continued on the 727-200, the Dash-300 project eventually gave rise to the 757. The 727's total of 1,832 was the all-time record production for any commercial aircraft, but is now far exceeded by the 737. Surviving aircraft face costly modifications at the 20-year point or 60,000 pressurization cycles, quite apart from the need to meet new environmental laws. Most are being fitted with noise-suppressors, which are heavy and degrade performance, but United Parcel Service's 727-100QC freighters have new 15,400lb (6,985kg) Rolls-Royce Tay engines.

DATA FOR 727-100:

Span	108ft 0in (32.92m)
Length	133ft 2in (40.59m)
Wing area	1,700 sq ft (157.9m²)
Weight empty	(for 142,000lb gross) 85,278lb (38,682kg)
	(QC for 169,000lb) 91,500lb (41,504kg)
Maximum takeoff weight	142,000lb (64,411kg) early aircraft
	169,000lb (76,658kg) final blocks
Cruising speed	570mph (917km/h)
Range	2,050 miles (3,299km)
	(maximum 40,500lb, 18,371kg, payload)

DATA FOR 727-200 ADVANCED:

Dimensions unchanged	
Except length	153ft 2in (46.69m)
Weight empty	101,773lb (46,164kg)
Maximum takeoff weight	209,500lb (95,027kg)
Cruising speed	538mph (866km/h)
Range	2,975 miles (4,788km)
	(maximum 41,000lb, 18,598kg, payload)

TWINJET, TWINJET, LITTLE STAR

The story of the 737 is almost beyond belief, and epitomizes the difficulty of taking strategic decisions in planemaking. With the 707 Boeing went ahead in fear and trepidation, despite having the assurance of massive orders for a closely related military aircraft. With the 727 the launch without military backing was even more of a gamble. With the 737 the prospect looked hopeless. Everyone except Eastern, United and Lufthansa had already bought short-haul twin-jets. Obviously, Boeing wanted to sign up all three, but in January 1965 Lufthansa's Gerhard Holtje said "We can't wait any longer". On 19 February 1965 a Boeing sales team went to Germany to sign Lufthansa alone, and launch the programme. On that very day Eastern bought the DC-9.

The team cabled Seattle and asked "What do we do? Lufthansa are afraid they will be left high and dry as the only 737 customer". Vice-

president Bruce Connelly said "Sign Lufthansa". The entire programme was launched on the basis of a single order for 21 (later increased to 24) from a foreign airline. Who would have thought, from this fraught beginning, that by 1998 the 737 would be developed in more major versions than any previous jet-liner, for more customers, and in far greater numbers than any previous commercial aircraft in history? Incidentally, though it was launched as the baby of the Boeing stable, the 737 would in an earlier era have been considered no mean aircraft. All current versions are actually longer than a B-29, and empty weights are greater.

Predictably, there was plenty of room for design argument, but, unlike the situation with the 727, decisions had to be taken very quickly. One of the most basic concerned the fuselage cross-section. General Bruner of the French Dassault company criticised the 737, saying that a circular tube as used in their Mercure was much lighter "but Boeing adopted a bad cross-section, the same as the 707 and 727, to save the cost of

The irresistible 737-200. Thai Airways' joined the jet set with HS-TBA.

tooling". He did not appreciate that the 737 adopted the same upper-lobe profile only after evaluation of 11 alternatives, one of which was a circle. In fact the lower lobe, under the floor, is shallower than in the 707 and 727, and the 737 body is quite close to a circular tube.

Of course, as the baby jet was designed for 80-100 passengers whilst retaining the same 3+3 seating as its prede-cessors, it was much shorter. At first it looked rather stumpy for a fast jet, but tunnel testing showed that fineness ratio (slenderness) was perfectly adequate. It was essential to devote a higher fraction of the fuselage length to seating, and this made it difficult to hang the engines on the rear fuse-

lage. Aft-mounted engines were also found to suffer from the big body ahead of the inlets. On the other hand, there was little room under the wing, unless long landing gears were used, but a further advantage of underwing engines was that (Steiner said) it saved 2,000lb (907kg) in weight.

The only area where there was no problem was that two Pratt & Whitney JT8D engines of 14,000lb (6,350kg) each fitted the bill perfectly. Boeing began to compile a list of advantages in commonality with previous Boeing jets, including engines, cockpit and many hardware items in the systems. After urgent studies, it was found possible to squeeze the engines directly under the wing, in tight nacelles in which the inlets were well ahead of the wing and the jet-pipes below the trailing edge. The cruise Mach would be

737

lower and this made it easier to avoid engine/wing interactions. Clamshell reversers similar to those of the 727 centre engine could just about be fitted without too much blast on the wing, or hot-gas ingestion by the inlet. Each inlet was provided with bleed-air anti-icing, together with a ring of six square suck-in auxiliary inlet doors which opened on takeoff. Three inter-spar tanks held 3,952gal (17,968lit).

The wing closely resembled a scaled version of that designed for the 727, even to the extent of using triple-slotted flaps. Differences were that $1/4$-chord sweep was reduced to 25°, with a slightly greater kink on the leading edge (at the engine), and the number of sections of leading-edge Krueger and slat was in each case reduced by one. Likewise, there were three instead of four sections of flight spoiler ahead of the outer flaps, and a single ground spoiler aligned like the inboard flaps at 90° to the fuselage. For the first time on a Boeing, the slats had bleed-air anti-icing.

Despite the extra moment arm possible with a T-tail the tailplane was pivoted to the fuselage, with dihedral, with elevators similar to those of the 727. The rudder, however, was one-piece, with a balance area at the top but no tab. The cockpit was a near-duplicate of that of the 727, but (except for some early customers who wanted flight engineers) for two-pilot operation only.

The first off the line, company-owned N73700, flew on 9 April 1967. On its nose were the insignia of 16 airlines which by that time had signed for the twin-jet, and the company began slightly to relax. With the 727 selling like the proverbial hot cakes it was possible to think how the 737 might be improved. Early in the design process it had been decided to stretch the fuselage, and on 8 August 1967 the fifth off the line – N9001U, the first of 75 737-222s for United – began flight testing. The stretched 737-200 immediately became the standard, and after Lufthansa's batch only seven Dash-100s were built.

The 737-100 was certificated on 15 December 1967, and the Dash-200 six days later. Lufthansa began scheduled services on 10 February 1968, and United began using its growing fleet of Dash-222s on 28 April. Lufthansa fitted a maximum of 107 seats, but United's stretched aircraft had maximum seating for 119, a capacity later increased to 130.

Weight increases over time were made possible by modest increases in engine thrust. In July 1967 Pratt achieved certification on the JT8D-9 and -9A at 14,500lb (6,577kg), followed in April 1971 by the JT8D-15 and in February 1974 by the JT8D-17 at 16,000lb (7,258kg). These uprated engines were partnered by significant improvements in the installation. From aircraft No 135 the unsatisfactory reversers were replaced by target buckets which swung round from their normal stowage in a 45in (1.14m) extension at the back of the nacelle, which put the jet nozzles well behind the wing. Improvements were made to the flaps and leading-edge slats, and several minor changes reduced drag.

These modifications resulted in No 135 and subsequent aircraft being dubbed the Advanced 737-200. Improvements continued, and eventually structure weight was reduced by over 1,000lb (454kg) by making the ailerons, elevators and rudder mainly from graphite composite, with honeycomb filling. A unique feature, prompted by frequent engine damage from contaminated runways, was a gravel kit. This comprised a large deflector plate behind the nosewheels, which lay externally under the nose in flight, and a tube projecting ahead from the bottom of each engine inlet from which bleed air could be blasted to destroy vortices which could suck up stones and foreign matter.

Boeing went on to produce the 737C convertible, able in all-cargo configuration to carry 34,966lb (15,860kg) of cargo. The USAF selected the 737-200 as its navigation trainer, buying 19 designated T-43A. The TNI-AU (Indonesian air force) bought three Surveillers with Motorola Slammr (Side-looking airborne multi-mission radar) with unique antennas above the rear fuselage, extending on each side of the fin.

DATA FOR ADVANCED 737-200:

Span	**93ft 0in (28.35m)**
Length	**100ft 2in (30.53m)** *original 737-100 93ft 9in, 28.58m*
Wing area	**1,098 sq ft (102m²)**. *100, 980 sq ft, 91.0m²*
Weight empty	**61,630lb (27,955kg)** *100, 56,893lb, 25,807kg*
Maximum takeoff weight	**115,500-128,000lb (52,391-58,061kg)**
Cruising speed	**Mach 0.73**, *at 33,000ft (10,060m) 483mph (777km/h)*
Maximum cruising speed	**532mph (856km/h)** *at 100,000lb (45,360kg) at 33,000ft, (10,060m)*
Range	**2,913 miles (4,688km)** *with 100 passengers*

Boeing-Vertol CH-46A Sea Knight visiting Wichita in the mid-1960s, when B-52Ds were being modified for saturation bombing.

The RAF operates a large fleet of CH-47D Chinooks in support of the British Army, from the Falklands to Bosnia. (Photo: John Ailes)

Ryanair found the 737-200 ideal for low fare flights within Europe. Promoting Jaguar Cars, EI- CJE rotates at London Gatwick. The carrier is acquiring 45 -800s.

Production of the 737-200 ended in 1988 after some 1,144 aircraft had been delivered. The cargo door identifies this example as a 737-200C.

In mid-1998 around 170 JT3D-powered 707-300 series aircraft were still earning a good living as freighters, including JY-AJO of Royal Jordanian Cargo.

One of more than 100 727-200s delivered to mighty Delta Air Lines, N522DA is seen departing Toronto on 1 June 1984.

Sporting a special Aboriginal colour scheme, VH-OTB *Wunula Dreaming* is one of 18 747-400s delivered to Qantas with RB.211-524G turbofans.

The smart new look of the world's largest private airline was perfectly suited to the 777. In mid-1998 Everett was assembling seven 777s a month.

Pictured on 22 October 1997 in approach configuration, this Canada 3000 757-200 can expect to perform 100,000 cycles before retirement.

American Airlines is one of several carriers which use 767-300ERs routinely for 180min extended range twinjet operations (ETOPS).

Before this artist's impression becomes a reality, Boeing will have to build and flight test two prototypes of its Joint Strike Fighter (JSF) concept, and customers as diverse as the USAF, Navy, Marines, and the Royal Navy's Fleet Air Arm will have to agree on their service-specific variants. If JSF reaches production, a Boeing fighter will arrive on a carrier deck for the first time in 70 years.

707-320

727-200

737-200

737-300

747-200

767-200

777

CFM VICTORIOUS

In 1979 Boeing began to firm up studies for a second stretch of the 737, to be called the 737-300. A key factor was a change of engine. It was evident that, despite the JT8D's huge background of experience, it was obsolescent, and had been overtaken by later turbofans with higher bypass ratio. Such engines offered better fuel economy and dramatically reduced noise, essential to meet impending FAR-36 Stage 3 legislation.

Pratt already had the refanned JT8D-200 series, launched in 1977 and selected for the MD-80 derivatives of the DC-9. One of the most significant of Boeing's decisions was to look beyond this derivative engine, at much more efficient and quieter engines with a bypass ratio of 5 or over. Pratt was uncertain that many more 737s would be sold, and in any case was heavily committed on other fronts. Losing the 737 was one of the biggest mistakes it ever made, and it is only now in the late 1990s that it is trying to produce a JT8D

successor, the PW6000. This could have been launched specifically for later 737s, with very different results for the Connecticut company.

Instead, Boeing saw two possible engines: the Rolls-Royce RJ500 and the CFM56. Again, one company got it right and the other didn't. The RJ500 ran at Bristol, but was abandoned in favour of a later engine, the V2500 for which a five-nation team was formed in March 1983. The V2500 is a superb engine, but by then it was too late for Boeing, which, having no alternative, picked CFM in 1981. By 1998 new versions of 737 had provided a market for an extra 5,572 CFM56 engines, with thousands more to come. Soon the CFM56 will overtake the JT8D's record sales total. CFM is a partnership between General Electric of the USA and SNECMA of France.

The key factor distinguishing modern engines is a proportionately larger fan. The JT8D, with an overall diameter of 49.2in (1.25m), was already a tight fit under the 737 wing. CFM designed a new engine, the CFM56-3, rated at 20,000lb (9,072kg). This had the fan

Much more than a stretched and re-engined 737, the -300 was bound to be competitive.

diameter reduced from 68.3 to 60in (1,524mm), and by moving the accessories away from the underside of the fan case it was found possible to fit the new engine in a short pod with an almost flat bottom giving just adequate ground clearance. This pod was then hung on a short pylon with its top aligned with the top of the wing. Thus, whereas the JT8D was under the wing, the CFM56 is in front of it. Boeing apprehensively expected the new engine to "nod" seriously; instead they cause hardly any twisting of the wing, and anti-flutter booms on the wingtips were not needed. Again unexpectedly, the fact the much larger inlet is further forward actually reduces foreign-object ingestion. A translating-cowl

and cascade reverser is fitted in the fan duct.

The new engine first ran in April 1982, and was FAA-certificated on 12 January 1984. By this time production of the 737-300 was well under way, and the first (for USAir, but temporarily in Boeing colours and registered N73700) was flown on 24 February 1984. Airframe modifications were to stretch the fuselage by inserting a 44in (1.12m) plug ahead of the wing and a 60in (1.52m) plug aft. This increased all-tourist seating to 149, and increased underfloor baggage/ freight volume from 875 cu ft (24.78m^3) to 1,068 cu ft (30.24m^3). Span was increased at each wingtip, and other changes included broader and more "droopy" slats giving a 4.4 per cent chord increase outboard of the engines, modified flaps, and addition of a fourth roll spoiler on each wing. Tailplane span

737-300 TO -900

was increased from 36ft 0in (10.97m) to 41ft 8in (12.7m), and a definite dorsal fin was added. To lift the engine inlets, the nose gear was mounted 6in (152mm) lower. Standard fuel capacity of 4,422gal (20,104 litres) could be increased in the High Gross Weight (HGW) version to 5,242gal (23,830 litres) by fitting a tank in the aft cargo compartment.

The 737-300 sold not only to short/medium-haul customers but also to operators needing trans-US capability.

DATA FOR 737-300:

Span	**94ft 9in (28.88m)**
Length	**109ft 7in (33.4m)**
Wing area	**1,135 sq ft (105.4m²)**
Weight empty	**72,490lb (32,881kg)**
Maximum takeoff weight	**124,500lb (56,470kg)**
	139,500lb (63,276kg) HGW version
Cruising speed	**Mach 0.745**
	equal at 34,000ft (10,363m) to 494mph (795km/h)
Range	**1,680 miles (2,703km)** still air, 140 passengers
	2,570 miles (4,136km) HGW

DATA FOR 737-400

Dimensions as 737-300, except:	
Length	**119ft 7in (36.45m)**
Weight empty	**76,200lb (34,564kg)**
	76,780lb (34,827kg) HGW
Maximum takeoff weight	**138,500lb (62,820kg)**
	150,000lb (68,040kg) HGW
Cruising speed	**Mach 0.745**
	at 31,700ft (9,662m) equal to 501mph (807km/h)
Design range	**2,405 miles (3,870km)** HGW with 136 passengers

DATA FOR 737-500:

Dimensions as 737-300, except:	
Length	**101ft 9in (31.01m)**
Weight empty	**70,510lb (31,983kg)**
Maximum takeoff weight	**115,500lb (52,390kg)**
	133,500lb (60,555kg) HGW
Cruising speed	**Mach 0.745**
	at 34,250ft (10,440m) equal to 496mph (798km/h)
Design range	**2,784 miles (4,481km)** with 138 passengers

Boeing 737-300

1 Radome
2 Weather radar scanner
3 Scanner tracking mechanism
4 Lightning-conductor strips
5 ILS glideslope antenna
6 Front pressure bulkhead
7 Rudder pedals
8 Control column
9 Instrument panel
10 Instrument panel shroud
11 Windscreen wipers
12 Windscreen panels
13 Overhead systems switch panel
14 Co-pilot's seat
15 Cockpit eyebrow windows
16 Pilot's seat
17 Nosewheel steering control
18 Flight bag stowage
19 Nose undercarriage wheel bay
20 Nosewheel doors
21 Twin nosewheels
22 Torque scissor links
23 Nosewheel steering jacks
24 Nose undercarriage pivot fixing
25 Pitot heads (2)
26 Crew wardrobe
27 Observer's folding seat
28 Cockpit doorway
29 Forward galley unit
30 Starboard side service door
31 Toilet compartment
32 Forward entry door open
33 Door latch
34 Escape chute stowage

35 Retractable airstairs
36 Folding handrail
37 Entry lobby
38 Cabin attendant's folding seat
39 First-class cabin, four-abreast seating (eight-passengers)
40 Overhead stowage bins
41 Curtained cabin divider
42 Passenger emergency oxygen bottles
43 Underfloor avionics equipment bay
44 Cabin window panels
45 Seat rail support structure
46 Lower VHF ant.
47 Forward under-floor freight/baggage hold, capacity 425-cu ft (12.03 m³)
48 Forward freight hold door
49 Overhead air conditioning distribution ducting
50 Tourist class cabin, six-abreast seating (114 to 140 passengers)
51 Air system ducting
52 Wing inspection light
53 Conditioned-air riser

54 Wing root leading edge fillet
55 Ventral air conditioning intake
56 Landing and taxying lamps
57 Wing panel/fuselage bolted root joint
58 Ventral air conditioning pack, port and starboard
59 Centre section fuel tanks
60 Floor beam construction
61 Front spar/fuselage main frame
62 Anti-collision light
63 Starboard nacelle pylon
64 Starboard engine nacelle
65 Engine air intake
66 Hinged cowling panels
67 Pressure refuelling connection
68 Starboard wing integral fuel tank Total system capacity 4,422 Imp gal (20,104 litres)
69 Fuel venting channels

70 Overwing fuel filler cap
71 Vortex generators
72 Leading edge slat segments, open
73 Slat drive shaft
74 Screw jacks
75 Guide rails
76 Vent surge tank
77 Wing tip fairing
78 Starboard navigation light (green) and strobe light (white)
79 Tail navigation light (white)
80 Starboard aileron
81 Aileron hinge control
82 Aileron tab
83 Outboard triple-slotted Fowler-type flap, down position
84 Flap guide rails
85 Screw jacks
86 Flap track fairings

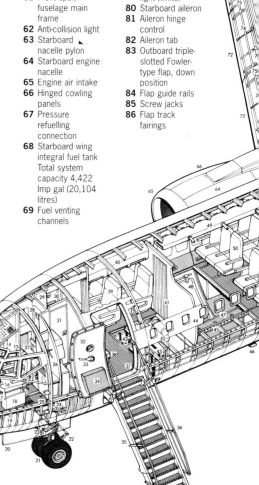

87 Outboard (flight) spoilers, open
88 Spoiler hydraulic jacks
89 Nacelle tail fairing
90 Inboard flap screw jack
91 Inboard (ground) spoiler, open
92 Fuselage skin panelling
93 Upper VHF ant.
94 Centre fuselage frame and stringer construction
95 Emergency exit window hatches, port and starboard
96 Pressure floor above starboard wheel bay

97 Cabin soundproofing lining
98 Rear spar/fuselage main frame
99 Overhead stowage bins
100 Passenger service units
101 Cabin roof lighting panels
102 Rear freight hold door
103 Cockpit voice recorder
104 Cabin wall trim panelling
105 Cabin roof frames

106 Rear cabin tourist class seating
107 Starboard side rear galley unit
108 Fin root fillet construction
109 Fin spar attachment joints
110 Optional flush HF antenna
111 Starboard tailplane
112 Starboard elevator mass balance
113 Fin rib construction

114 VOR antenna
115 Fin tip antenna fairing
116 Rudder mass balance
117 Static dischargers
118 Rudder
119 Honeycomb rudder panel construction

120 Rudder hydraulic actuators
121 Tailcone
122 Rear position light (white)
123 Elevator tab
124 Port elevator honeycomb construction

125 Elevator mass balance
126 Static dischargers
127 Port tailplane construction
128 APU exhaust duct
129 Elevator hinge control
130 Trimming tailplane pivot fixing
131 Garrett GTCP85-129(C) Auxiliary Power Unit (APU)
132 Fin/tailplane support main frame
133 Tailplane trim screw jack

134 APU intake duct
135 Rear pressure dome
136 Rear toilet compartments, port and starboard
137 Rear entry and service doors, port and starboard
138 Cabin attendant's folding seat
139 Wardrobe/closet
140 Rear cabin window panels
141 Rear underfloor freight/baggage hold, capacity 643cu ft (18.21m³)
142 Rear fuselage frame and stinger construction
143 DME antenna
144 Wing root trailing-edge fillet
145 ADF sense ant.

146 Central flap drive hydraulic motor
147 Port main undercarriage wheel bay
148 Main undercarriage mounting beam
149 Hydraulic retraction jack
150 Spoiler hydraulic jack
151 Inboard (ground) spoiler

152 Inboard triple-slotted Fowler-type flap
153 Flap guide rails and screw jacks
154 Flap down position
155 Flap thrust gate segments
156 Nacelle tail fairing
157 Outboard triple-slotted Fowler-type flap
158 Outboard flap screw jacks and guide rails
159 Outboard four-segment (flight) spoilers
160 Flap track fairings
161 Flap down position
162 Aileron tab
163 Port aileron
164 Fixed portion of trailing-edge
165 Static dischargers
166 Tail navigation light (white)
167 Port navigation light (red) and strobe light (white)
168 Leading-edge slat segments, open

169 Slat screw jacks
170 Guide rails
171 Telescopic de-icing air ducts
172 Front spar
173 Port wing integral fuel tank
174 Wing rib construction
175 Rear spar
176 Wing stringers
177 Wing skin panelling
178 Engine pylon mounting ribs
179 Twin mainwheels
180 Main undercarriage leg strut
181 Undercarriage leg pivot
182 Inboard wing rib construction
183 Engine bleed air ducting
184 Krueger flap jacks
185 Inboard two-segment Krueger flaps, open
186 Nacelle strake
187 Nacelle pylon construction
188 Intake lip de-icing air duct
189 Port engine air intake
190 CFM International CFM56-3 turbofan engine
191 Engine fan casing
192 Laterally mounted accessory equipment gearbox
193 Thrust reverser cascades
194 Engine turbine section
195 Fan air (cold stream) exhaust duct
196 Core engine (hot stream) exhaust duct
197 Tailcone fairing
198 Cowling open position to expose reverser cascades

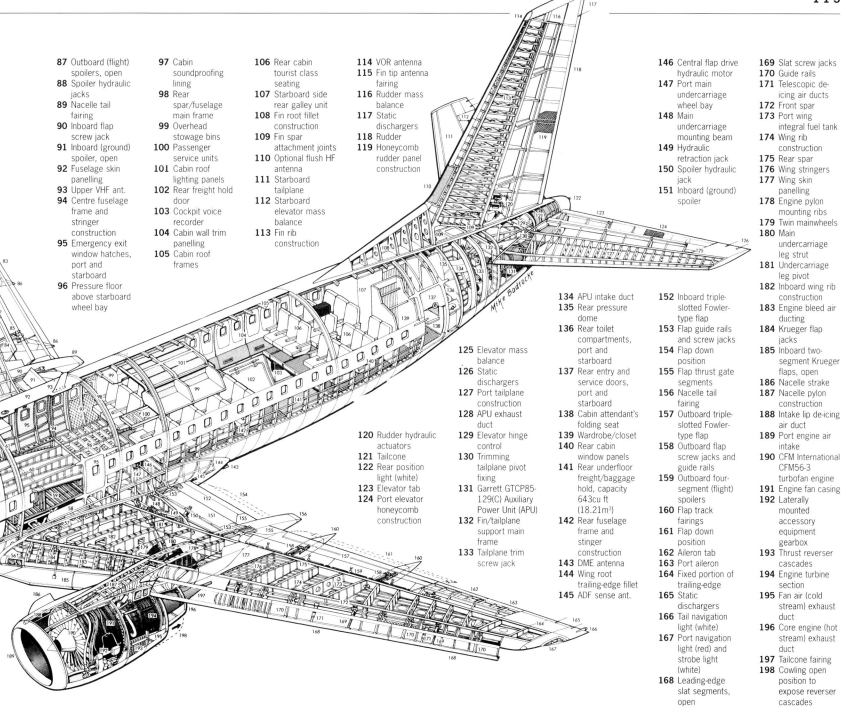

Mike Badrocke

737-300 TO -900

Boeing 737-800

1 Radome with lightning conductor strips
2 Weather radar scanner
3 ILS glideslope
4 Radar scanner tracking mechanism
5 Front pressure bulkhead
6 Rudder pedals
7 Control yoke
8 Instrument panel, EFIS displays
9 Instrument panel shroud
10 Windscreen wipers
11 Windscreen panels
12 Cockpit eyebrow windows
13 Overhead systems control panel
14 Co-Pilot's seat
15 Captain's seat
16 Flight bag/document stowage
17 Nose undercarriage wheel bay
18 Nosewheel doors
19 Twin nosewheels, forward retracting
20 Torque scissor links
21 Hydraulic steering jacks
22 Nosewheel leg pivot mounting
23 Dual pitot heads
24 Cockpit bulkhead
25 Observer's folding seat
26 Forward toilet compartment
27 Cockpit door
28 Starboard service door
29 Forward galley units
30 Closet compartment
31 Cabin attendant's folding seat

32 Entry lobby
33 Forward entry door
34 Door mounted escape chute/slide
35 Airstairs
36 Folding handrail
37 Underfloor avionics equipment bay
38 Fuselage lower lobe frame and stringer structure
39 Passenger oxygen bottle
40 Floor beam structure
41 Forward underfloor freight hold door
42 Cabin wall trim panelling
43 Overhead conditioned-air distribution ducting
44 Cabin floor with continuous seat rails
45 lower UHF antenna
46 Six abreast passenger seating, 184 passengers in all economy layout or 160 passengers in mixed class arrangement
47 Cabin window panels
48 Conditioned-air distribution system

49 Wing inspection light
50 Wing spar bulkhead
51 Conditioned air risers to overhead ducting
52 Forward and min cabin air distribution ducting, rear cabin air duct on starboard side
53 Starboard engine nacelle
54 Hinged cowling panels
55 Nacelle pylon
56 Pressure refuelling connection
57 Starboard wing integral fuel tank, total fuel capacity 26.035 lit (5,729 Imp gal)
58 Fuel venting channels
59 Overwing filler cap
60 Starboard leading edge slat segments, extended
61 Leading edge de-icing air duct
62 Slat guide rails
63 Slat screw jacks, torque shaft driven via central hydraulic motor

64 Starboard navigation and strobe lights
65 Aft strobe light
66 Starboard aileron
67 Aileron hinge control
68 Aileron tab
69 Outboard double-slotted flap segment, down position
70 Flap guide rails and carriages
71 Outboard (flight) spoilers
72 Spoiler hydraulic jacks
73 Single slotted portion of flap (thrust gate segment)
74 Inboard flap segment
75 Inboard (ground) spoiler
76 Upper UHF antenna
77 Anti-collision beacon light
78 Overwing emergency exits, two per side

79 Fuselage centre section frame and stringer structure
80 Wing front spar attachment main frame

81 Floor beams
82 Wing centre section carry-through
83 Centre section integral fuel tank
84 Air conditioning pack, port and starboard, in ventral fairing beneath wing box
85 Wing root joint strap

86 Port main undercarriage wheel bay
87 Central flap drive hydraulic motor
88 Pressure floor above wheel bay
89 Cabin wall insulation blankets
90 Rear spar attachment main frame
91 Overhead passenger service units
92 ADF antenna
93 Cabin roof trim/lighting panels
94 Overhead baggage lockers
95 Rear underfloor freight hold door

96 Cockpit voice recorder
97 Flight data recorder
98 Fin root fillet structure
99 Fin spar attachment joints
100 Rudder tandem hydraulic actuators
101 Fin rib structure
102 Starboard trimming tailplane
103 Starboard elevator
104 Two-spar fin torsion box

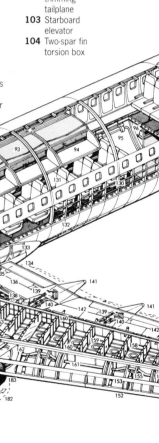

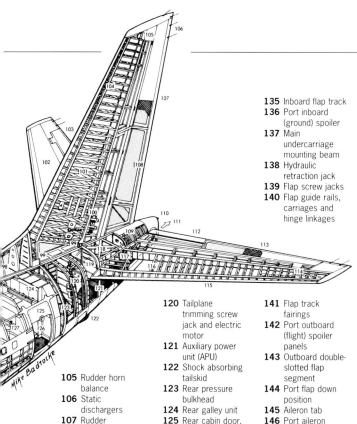

135 Inboard flap track
136 Port inboard (ground) spoiler
137 Main undercarriage mounting beam
138 Hydraulic retraction jack
139 Flap screw jacks
140 Flap guide rails, carriages and hinge linkages

105 Rudder horn balance
106 Static dischargers
107 Rudder
108 Composite rudder skin
109 Elevator hinge control
110 Tail navigation light
111 APU exhaust
112 Elevator tab
113 Port elevator
114 Elevator horn balance
115 Port trimming tailplane
116 Two-spar tailplane torsion box structure

117 Tailplane pivot mounting
118 Tailplane centre-section structure
119 Fin mounting bulkhead

120 Tailplane trimming screw jack and electric motor
121 Auxiliary power unit (APU)
122 Shock absorbing tailskid
123 Rear pressure bulkhead
124 Rear galley unit
125 Rear cabin door, port and starboard
126 Cabin attendant's folding seat
127 Rear toilet compartments, port and starboard
128 Rear cabin passenger seating
129 Cabin window panels
130 Aft fuselage frame and stringer structure
131 Mid cabin seating

132 Fuselage lower lobe skin
133 Wing root trailing edge fillet
134 Port inboard double-slotted flap segment

141 Flap track fairings
142 Port outboard (flight) spoiler panels
143 Outboard double-slotted flap segment
144 Port flap down position
145 Aileron tab
146 Port aileron
147 Fixed portion of trailing edge
148 Static dischargers
149 Rear strobe light
150 Wing tip fairing
151 Port navigation and strobe lights
152 Port leading edge slat segments, extended
153 Telescopic de-icing air ducts
154 Slat guide rails
155 Slat screw jacks
156 Wing rib structure
157 Port wing integral fuel tank
158 Wing bottom skin/stringer panel
159 Access manholes
160 Two-spar wing torsion box structure
161 Leading edge de-icing air duct

162 Port twin mainwheels
163 Main undercarriage leg strut
164 Folding side stay
165 Inboard machined wing ribs
166 Leading edge ribs
167 Engine bleed air duct to conditioning system
168 Landing and taxiing lights
169 Leading edge wing root fillet
170 Ventral ram air intake to conditioning system heat exchangers
171 Inboard Krueger flap, extended
172 Nacelle strake
173 Nacelle pylon structure
174 Intake de-icing air duct
175 Engine intake, flattened at lower edge
176 CFM56-7 turbofan engine with FADEC control
177 Engine fan casing
178 Side mounted accessory equipment gearbox, oil tank on starboard side
179 Thrust reverser cascades
180 Engine turbine section
181 Fan air (cold stream) exhaust duct
182 Translating cowling, reverser cascade opening
183 Core engine (hot stream) exhaust duct
184 Pylon attachment joints

A 1997 order for seven was priced at $41 million per aircraft. By early 1998 this version had passed the 1,114 sales total of the 737-200.

737-400

This even more capacious version was made possible by the CFM56-3B2 of 22,000lb (9,979kg), certificated in 1984, and the CFM56-3C1 of 23,500lb (10,660kg) certificated in 1986. This aircraft introduced a further stretched fuselage, with a 72in (1.83m) plug ahead of the wing and a 48in (1.22m) plug aft, increasing all-tourist seating to 168. The longer rear fuselage made a tail bumper desirable, and the landing gears were strengthened. Tankage was the same as in the Dash-300, but the HGW version with the 5,242gal option requires careful disposition of the payload to avoid the centre of gravity being dangerously far aft. The first Dash-400 flew on 19 February 1988, and was certificated on 2 September. The HGW version was certificated on 21 March 1989. In mid-1998 sales of the 737-400 totalled 484.

737-500

Announced as the 737-1000, this version mates the shorter fuselage of the 737-200 with the new features and tankage of the Dash-300. The basic (not HGW) aircraft can have the CFM56-3C1 engines derated to 18,500lb (8,392kg). Normal seating is 108-138. The first flight was on 20

June 1989, and in mid-1998 sales totalled 387.

737 Next-Generation

In the 1990s Boeing recognised that it had to respond to the competitive threat posed by the single-aisle Airbus products (A319, A320 and A321), whose later technology and wider cabins were winning many 737 customers. Boeing made only cosmetic changes to the 737 cabin, but decided upon major modifications to the wing and tail, and also introduced an improved CFM56 engine, low-noise APU, long-stroke nose leg, larger centre tank and modern "glass" cockpit, but not FBW.

The wing is of totally different profile, with mean chord increased by 18in (0.46m) and with each outer wing extended no less than 107in (2.72m). The vertical tail is increased in height by 5ft (1.52m) by adding 60 sq ft (5.57m²) at the root, and the horizontal tail is increased in span for the second time, to 47ft 1in (14.35m). The new wing enables standard tankage to be increased to 5,727gal (26,036 litres), and this makes the NG737 a US transcontinental aircraft. The engine is the CFM56-7B, which combines an upgraded core with a modern snubberless wide-chord fan, advanced electronic control and active clearance control. Fan diameter is 61in (1.55m), and the inlet is more nearly circular than before. Specific fuel consumption is typically 8 per cent better than that of the 3C1 engine, and maintenance costs are expected to be 15 per cent lower. The Dash-7B engine is rated at different thrust levels for each of the NG models:

737-600

Smallest of the NG aircraft, this is designed for 108-132 passengers. The fuselage is basically that of the 737-500, and the engine is rated at 22,000lb (9,979kg). First flight January 1998, first delivery (to SAS) due later in 1998. At mid-1998 sales totalled 117.

737-700

This was the first NG version to be launched (in 1993, by a 63-aircraft order by Southwest, which has always used the 737 exclusively and will shortly have a fleet numbering over 325). The fuselage is basically that of the 737-300, seating 128-149, and the engine is rated at 24,000lb (10,886kg). The first flight was on 9 February 1997. A high-frequency tailplane flutter required the addition of light-alloy reinforcing flanges on the composite trailing edge, and the Dash-700 then entered service with Southwest two months late in December 1997. The reinforced tailplane will go on all New Generation 737s. The US Navy is using the HGW QC (quick-change passenger/cargo) version to replace the C-9B Skytrain II; payload is 38,500lb (17,464kg), and the first two aircraft were together priced at $111 million. In mid-1998 sales totalled 383.

737-800

Originally known as the 737-400X Stretch, this was launched in September 1994 as the longest 737. Two-class seating is for 162, the tourist capacity being 189. The engine is rated at 26,200lb (11,884kg). First flight July 1997, service entry (with Hapag Lloyd) February 1998. By 31 May 1998 total sales of the -800 stood at 372 aircraft.

737-900

In 1997 it was found possible to stretch the 737 even further. This is the longest and heaviest of all 737 versions, made possible by certificating (in December 1996) the CFM56-7B at 27,300lb (12,383kg). Tankage is unchanged, but the stretched cabin will be certificated in 2000 for up to 200 passengers, or 177 two-class. Service entry (with launch customer Alaska) is due in 2001.

737 BBJ

The Boeing Business Jet was launched in July 1996, when Boeing formed a joint marketing company with General Electric, which bought two. The BBJ combines the fuselage of the 737-700, strengthened behind the wing, with the wing, engines and landing gear of the 737-800. Powered by CFM56-7 engines rated at 26,400lb (11,975kg), the main modification is to provide tankage for a remarkable 9,308gal (42,313 litres) of fuel. This brings MTO weight to almost twice that of the 737-100. Boeing expects to sell 40.

DATA FOR 737-600:

Span	**112ft 7in (34.31m)**
Length	**102ft 6in (31.24m)**
Wing area	**1,345.5 sq ft (125.0m²)**
Weight empty	**81,470lb (36,954kg)**
Maximum takeoff weight	**124,000lb (56,245kg)**
Cruising speed	**Mach 0.785**
	at 39,100ft (11,915m) equal to 518mph (834km/h)
Design range	**3,717 miles (5,981km)** with 132 passengers

DATA FOR 737-700:

Dimensions as 737-600 except:	
Length	**110ft 4in (33.63m)**
Weight empty	**83,790lb (38,006kg)**
Maximum takeoff weight	**133,000lb (60,330kg)**
Cruising speed	as 737-600
Design range	**3,710 miles (5,970km)** with 128 passengers (standard tankage)

DATA FOR 737-800:

Dimensions as 737-600, except:	
Length	**129ft 6in (39.47m)**
Weight empty	**91,610lb (41,554kg)**
Maximum takeoff weight	**155,500lb (70,535kg)**
Cruising speed	as 737-600
Design range	**3,371 miles (5,426km)** with 162 passengers

DATA FOR 737-900:

Dimensions as 737-600:	
Except length	**138ft 2in (42.1m)**
Weight empty	93,610lb (42,460kg)
Cruising speed	as 737-600
Design range	**3,140 miles (5,050km)** with 189 passengers

DATA FOR 737 BBJ:

Dimensions as 737-700.	
Weight empty	**94,000lb (42,638kg)**
Maximum takeoff weight	**171,000lb (77,565kg)**
Cruising speed	**Mach 0.8,**
	at 33,200ft (10,120m) equal to 534mph (859km/h)
Range	**7,134 miles (11,482km)** with 8 passengers

REDESIGN THE AIRPORTS ...

It is ironic that this aircraft, one of the largest heavier-than-air machines in the world, should be known only by such a short designation. Of course, to most people it is better known as the Jumbo Jet. At Boeing Commercial Airplane Company it is also identified by numerous Model numbers, but these have not been made public.

After 32 years without a rival it has sold just over 1,300. This is 1,275 more than Boeing could count on when this huge programme was launched. It was yet another case of Boeing girding its loins and launching a programme that risked more than the net worth of the company. Several Boeing people have told the author "We ought never to have attempted it on our own". I believe the bumblebee's wing loading is so high that it cannot take off, but it is too stupid to know this, so it goes ahead and flies. The birth of the 747 was like this. Now Boeing cry all the way to the bank.

Of course, if Boeing hadn't built the 747, such a vehicle would have been created by someone else. It all resulted from the invention in 1961-63 of giant turbofan engines of high bypass ratio, for the US Air Force CX-HLS competition. Boeing fought hard to win this, and submitted its 4,272-page proposal on 14 September 1964. The Boeing C-5A was the unanimous choice of the Air Force, but Senator Henry Jackson of Washington was out-clouted by two Georgians, Senator Richard Russell, Chairman of the Senate Armed Services Committee, and Representative Carl Vinson, Chairman of the House Armed Services Committee. The huge contract was awarded to Lockheed.

When the blow fell, in August 1965, Boeing had already established a group of design engineers to work on what would become the 747, a commercial jet in the same size class as the C-5A, using similar engines. The prospect was awesome. At a time when the 707 was still the biggest, heaviest and most powerful commercial jet transport, the aim was to create something dramatically larger, twice as heavy and more than twice as powerful. More-

An early customer, KLM bought the 747-200B in standard and Combi form.

over, such an aircraft would demand a complete rethink of airport gates and lounges, servicing facilities, passenger handling and even car parking. Almost the only thing unaffected would be the runway, provided it was strong enough.

Boeing had begun by talking to possible customers. By far the most important was PanAm, the only one likely to place a launch order. Others would be scared even to follow, but Juan T.Trippe was still at the helm of PanAm and intensely interested in the next great plateau in air transport. In April 1965 Douglas had stretched the DC-8 into the Super Sixty series. This could have been countered by a

stretched 707, but such a machine cut no ice with PanAm. The upgraded DC-8s were not the next generation, but a prolongation of the last. In any case, a few old-timers recalled how Boeing's 247 had been stopped in its tracks by the DC-2. This time Boeing had to use the giant new fan engines to get better fuel economy, and incidentally much less noise. The question was, did the airlines want 200, 300 or 400 passengers, in other words two, three or four engines?

Trippe instinctively picked the biggest, and so did the other airlines canvassed. This confirmed an aircraft of C-5A size, but Boeing could see that not many parts of its C-5A proposal could be used. Even the wing would have to be designed afresh, because for a 747 high cruising speed mattered more than short field length. Faster than any previous piloted Boeing, the new giant's wing had to be swept at 37.5° at the $1/4$-chord line, with a ruling thickness of 7.8 to 8 per cent, rising to 13.4 at the enormous root. Though planned for Mach 0.88, and theoretically capable of cruising at 0.92, most airlines actually operate the 747 at about 0.84. Boeing continued the 707 arrangement of movable surfaces, but with upgrades. The flaps were triple-slotted, and enormous. On the leading edge were Kruegers, in 13 sections (oddly, these stopped 10ft, 3m from the root). Uniquely, as these swung down under hydraulic screwjacks, they were designed to bend into a curved profile.

The biggest arguments concerned the enormous fuselage. Boeing even studied side-by-side double tubes and giant flattened ovals. The cross-section had to be got absolutely right, yet in the author's opinion Boeing got it wrong. With a cabin differential pressure of 8.9 lb/sq in (0.63kg/cm^2) the basic cross section has to be a perfect circle, but at 747 size it is impossible to draw in a single floor without having too much underfloor cargo space and a vast empty area over the passengers' heads. A double-deck layout with intermeshing circles solves the problem. In 1965 the airlines were introducing a range of standard cargo/baggage containers, the largest being the LD3 which weighs about 2,500lb (1,134kg) loaded. Boeing soon arrived at an excellent cross-section (just like today's A3XX), with space under the lower deck for two LD3s back-to-back.

Trippe was delighted with his "double-deck clipper", but the picture suddenly became clouded. Another Boeing team was working on the Model 2707 SST (this was never built, and so does not feature in this book). There seemed little doubt that before long most of the world's long-haul passengers would fly at Mach 2.7. This would mean that the 747s would be relegated to being freighters. The logical outcome was that the cross-section ought to be dictated by containers. Cargo is packed either in pallets or into a container 8ft x 8ft (2.44m square) and 10, 20 or 40ft long. These dimensions are the international standard for land, sea and air. The 747 could hardly have been more wrong, because it failed by a few inches to take two containers side-by-side.

After much agonizing a new shape was drawn, based on a circle of 21ft 4in (6.5m) diameter. The floor was added at such a height that side-by-side LD3s just fitted with a gap. The result was a floor 20ft 1.$^1/_2$in (6.13m) wide, just right for two rows of ISO containers. This was fine for cargo, but switching from the double-decker considerably reduced passenger capacity, did little to reduce aerodynamic drag, and resulted in lots of empty space; with the ceiling trim removed, passengers could have a headroom of 13ft (4m). As the global fleets of SSTs never happened, not many 747s are freighters, and for 25 years Boeing has been worrying over how to return the 747 to being a double-decker – but they haven't had to worry too much, because nothing else was on offer !

Having at last selected the cross-section, the obvious next task was to stick what Boeing call the cab section on the front. However, if you expect most aircraft to be freighters, it helps if containers can be loaded through the nose (Boeing never seriously thought of a C-5A back end). Thus, the nose has to be some kind of door, so the cab has to go either on the door itself or be further back. Boeing even built a model with the cab under the door, ahead of the underfloor area. Like today's Belouga, it looked funny and was christened "The Anteater". A more sensible location was on top at the front of the main deck, creating a distinct bump – which someone said enables 747 captains to sit on their wallets (billfolds). This bump has gradually enabled Boeing to move in a timid way back towards a double-deck layout, but the upper deck has to be narrow.

The cab itself was arranged for two pilots and a flight engineer. Increasingly the latter was himself a type-rated pilot, and eventually 747s were delivered with two-pilot cockpits. For the space behind the cab Boeing produced artwork showing bars, lounges and playrooms, but Trippe said "Seats". He got 32, accessed by a spiral staircase. He asked

December 1966, eight months after PanAm's first order for 25 747s; Northrop would become the major (fuselage) subcontractor.

about windows round the nose for First-class, but Boeing said this would cost 700lb (318kg) and make it difficult to instal radar.

Late in the design process it was decided that, as modern engines are so reliable that asymmetric problems were going to be rare, to reduce wing weight the four engines were moved much further apart. Pratt, like Boeing the loser in the C-5A programme, was from the start PanAm's choice. Their JTF14 matured by 1966 as the JT9D, rated at 43,500lb (19,732kg) and designed with community noise levels in mind. The JT9D ran in December 1966 and flew on a B-52 in 1968. Boeing solved thorny problems in designing the enormous nacelle, with a reverser in the fan duct and a core spoiler. Fuel was housed in a 14,154gal (64,345lit) centre-section integral tank, two 10,240gal (46,555lit) inboard tanks, two 3,680gal (16,730lit) outer tanks and wingtip surge tanks. Soon customers had the option of two outer-wing tanks, which added 666gal (3,028lit) each. These brought the maximum to 43,326gal (196,971lit).

The landing gear was straightforward. By this time Boeing had long experience with bogie main gears, and for the 747 it merely doubled their number. Behind the main wing box was pivoted an MLG (main landing gear) retracting inwards, as on the 707. Further back and inboard was a second MLG pivoted to the end of a fuselage beam and retracting forwards. These body-mounted gears were arranged to steer up to ±7° at low speeds whenever the forward-retracting twin-wheel nose gear was steered through an angle greater than 20°. The fuselage itself was fitted with radar in the nose, and the APU (driving two 90kVA alternators) in the extreme tail. Along each side were five doors, plus one in the upper deck, but for passengers it is usual to use only the two left-hand doors ahead of the wing. Flight crew use the front door and climb up to the cockpit.

On 13 April 1966 Boeing announced that PanAm would sign for 25 of the giants, costing with spares $525 million. This was then by far the biggest airline contract ever signed. Trippe bet Bill Allen that Boeing would not dare to go ahead within four months,

but in July Lufthansa and Japan Air Lines each signed for three, and Boeing launched on July 25th. Not least of their tasks was to refurbish and extend Paine Field, at Everett, 35 miles north of Seattle, and erect a completely new assembly plant which (with later extensions) has never been toppled from its perch as the largest building in the world.

Here, on 9 February 1969 Jack Waddell and test crew climbed aboard N7470, outside the still-unfinished factory. Among other problems, gross weight had climbed from 650,000lb to 680,000lb and then to 710,000lb (322,056kg), while the JT9D was not even giving the promised initial 42,000lb (19,051kg). The first flight was encouraging, apart from a flap malfunction which made Waddell fly cautiously and keep the gear extended. N7470 landed at Boeing Field, where certification flying was based. The 747-100 was certificated for up to 490 passsengers on 30 December 1969.

PanAm had intended to begin services in 1969, with the 747-121 arranged for about 360 passengers, but Pratt had trouble with the JT9D, which was an immature engine and a big challenge in every sense. Five weeks late, N735PA taxied out from New York JFK bound for London on 21 January 1970. One engine played up, and it was not until eight hours later that the first scheduled service actually departed on N733PA.

One problem was starting in a crosswind, which caused airflow distortion and overheated turbines. A more intractable fault was ovalizing of the casings, especially around the turbines, which caused gas leakage, blade rubbing and serious loss in power. The eventual cure was to design a massive Y-frame to pick up the engine at three widely spaced locations, but it took time. PanAm's Harold Graham had predicted "In August 1970 we'll dispatch eight 747s between 6.30 and 8 each evening". What actually happened was that they dispatched up to two, while at Everett 17 PanAm 747s were parked with concrete blocks hung on the engine pylons. Later 33 of the giants were waiting for engines.

This was a hard time. Pratt was also in deep trouble with F-111 engines, while an airline recession resulted in deliveries of new jets coming almost to a standstill. Between 1969 and 1971 Boeing's workforce at Seattle shrank from 103,450 to 35,400, and someone stuck up a famous notice saying LAST ONE OUT PLEASE TURN OFF THE LIGHTS.

747-200

From that low point, it could only get better. Basically a massive and tough engine, the JT9D got well, and with water injection gave 45,000, 48,000 and by 1982 thrusts up to 54,750lb (24,835kg) with the 7R4G version. General Electric's CF6-50 and the Rolls-Royce RB.211 gave customers a choice. For more than ten years these engines powered the standard aircraft, the 747-200B, certificated on 23 December 1970, and the 200C Combi, both strengthened for weights up to 833,000lb (377,840kg).

Reflecting the way Boeing saw the future, all early aircraft were built as PIs (Passenger, with Insurance provision for conversion as freighter). In March 1971 the SST was cancelled, and at the 31st aircraft

Boeing 747-200

1 Radome
2 Radar dish
3 Pressure bulkhead
4 Radar scanner mounting
5 First class cabin
6 Windscreen
7 Instrument panel shroud
8 Rudder pedals
9 Control column
10 Flight deck floor construction
11 First-class bar unit
12 Window panel
13 Nose u/c bay
14 Nosewheel door
15 Steering mechanism
16 Twin nosewheels
17 Radio and electronics racks
18 Captain's seat
19 Copilot's seat
20 Flight engineer's panel
21 Observer's seats
22 Upper deck door, port and starboard
23 Circular staircase between decks
24 Cockpit air conditioning duct
25 First-class galley
26 First-class toilets
27 Plug-type forward cabin door, No 1
28 First-class seats
29 Cabin dividing bulkhead
30 Anti-collision light
31 Cabin roof construction
32 Upper deck toilet
33 Upper deck seating, up to 32 passengers
34 Window panel
35 Air conditioning supply ducts
36 Forward fuselage construction
37 Baggage pallet containers
38 Forward under-
floor freight compartment
39 Communications antenna
40 Upper deck galley
41 Meal trolley elevator
42 Lower deck forward galley
43 No 2 passenger door, port and starboard
44 Air conditioning system intake
45 Wing-root fairing
46 Air conditioning plant
47 Wing spar bulkhead
48 Fresh water tanks
49 Forward economy-class cabin, typically 141 seats
50 Wing centre section fuel tank, capacity 17,000 US gal (64,345l)
51 Centre section stringer construction
52 Cabin floor construction
53 Fuselage frame and stringer construction
54 Main fuselage frame
55 Air distribution duct
56 Air conditioning cross-feed ducts
57 Risers to distribution ducts
58 Machined main frame
59 Satellite navigation antenna
60 Starboard wing inboard fuel tank, capacity 12,300 US gal (46,555 litresl)
61 Fuel pumps
62 Engine bleed-air supply
63 Krueger flap operating jacks
64 Inboard Krueger flap
65 Starboard inner engine
66 Starboard inner engine pylon
67 Leading edge Krueger flap segments
68 Krueger flap drive mechanism
69 Krueger flap motors
70 Refuelling panel
71 Starboard wing outboard fuel tank, capacity 4,420 US gal (16,730 litres)
72 Starboard outer engine
73 Starboard outer engine pylon
74 Outboard Krueger flap segments
75 Krueger flap drive mechanism
76 Extended range fuel tank, capacity 800 US gal (3028 litres) each wing
77 Surge tank
78 Starboard wing tip
79 Navigation light
80 VHF antenna boom
81 Fuel vent
82 Static dischargers
83 Outboard, low-speed, aileron

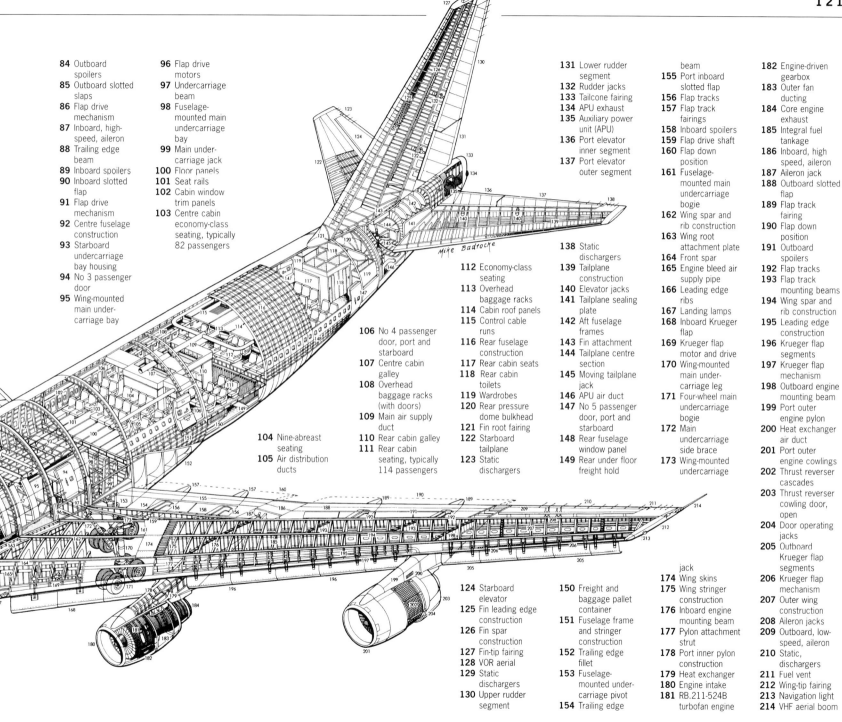

84 Outboard spoilers
85 Outboard slotted slaps
86 Flap drive mechanism
87 Inboard, high-speed, aileron
88 Trailing edge beam
89 Inboard spoilers
90 Inboard slotted flap
91 Flap drive mechanism
92 Centre fuselage construction
93 Starboard undercarriage bay housing
94 No 3 passenger door
95 Wing-mounted main undercarriage bay

96 Flap drive motors
97 Undercarriage beam
98 Fuselage-mounted main undercarriage bay
99 Main undercarriage jack
100 Floor panels
101 Seat rails
102 Cabin window trim panels
103 Centre cabin economy-class seating, typically 82 passengers
104 Nine-abreast seating
105 Air distribution ducts

106 No 4 passenger door, port and starboard
107 Centre cabin galley
108 Overhead baggage racks (with doors)
109 Main air supply duct
110 Rear cabin galley
111 Rear cabin seating, typically 114 passengers
112 Economy-class seating
113 Overhead baggage racks
114 Cabin roof panels
115 Control cable runs
116 Rear fuselage construction
117 Rear cabin seats
118 Rear cabin toilets
119 Wardrobes
120 Rear pressure dome bulkhead
121 Fin root fairing
122 Starboard tailplane
123 Static dischargers

124 Starboard elevator
125 Fin leading edge construction
126 Fin spar construction
127 Fin-tip fairing
128 VOR aerial
129 Static dischargers
130 Upper rudder segment

131 Lower rudder segment
132 Rudder jacks
133 Tailcone fairing
134 APU exhaust
135 Auxiliary power unit (APU)
136 Port elevator inner segment
137 Port elevator outer segment
138 Static dischargers
139 Tailplane construction
140 Elevator jacks
141 Tailplane sealing plate
142 Aft fuselage frames
143 Fin attachment
144 Tailplane centre section
145 Moving tailplane jack
146 APU air duct
147 No 5 passenger door, port and starboard
148 Rear fuselage window panel
149 Rear under floor freight hold
150 Freight and baggage pallet container
151 Fuselage frame and stringer construction
152 Trailing edge fillet
153 Fuselage-mounted undercarriage pivot
154 Trailing edge

155 Port inboard slotted flap
156 Flap tracks
157 Flap track fairings
158 Inboard spoilers
159 Flap drive shaft
160 Flap down position
161 Fuselage-mounted main undercarriage bogie
162 Wing spar and rib construction
163 Wing root attachment plate
164 Front spar
165 Engine bleed air supply pipe
166 Leading edge ribs
167 Landing lamps
168 Inboard Krueger flap
169 Krueger flap motor and drive
170 Wing-mounted main undercarriage leg
171 Four-wheel main undercarriage bogie
172 Main undercarriage side brace
173 Wing-mounted undercarriage
174 Wing skins
175 Wing stringer construction
176 Inboard engine mounting beam
177 Pylon attachment strut
178 Port inner pylon construction
179 Heat exchanger
180 Engine intake
181 RB.211-524B turbofan engine

beam
155 Port inboard slotted flap
156 Flap tracks
157 Flap track fairings
158 Inboard spoilers
159 Flap drive shaft
160 Flap down position
161 Fuselage-mounted main undercarriage bogie
162 Wing spar and rib construction
163 Wing root attachment plate
164 Front spar
165 Engine bleed air supply pipe
166 Leading edge ribs
167 Landing lamps
168 Inboard Krueger flap
169 Krueger flap motor and drive
170 Wing-mounted main undercarriage leg
171 Four-wheel main undercarriage bogie
172 Main undercarriage side brace
173 Wing-mounted undercarriage

182 Engine-driven gearbox
183 Outer fan ducting
184 Core engine exhaust
185 Integral fuel tankage
186 Inboard, high speed, aileron
187 Aileron jack
188 Outboard slotted flap
189 Flap track fairing
190 Flap down position
191 Outboard spoilers
192 Flap tracks
193 Flap track mounting beams
194 Wing spar and rib construction
195 Leading edge construction
196 Krueger flap segments
197 Krueger flap mechanism
198 Outboard engine mounting beam
199 Port outer engine pylon
200 Heat exchanger air duct
201 Port outer engine cowlings
202 Thrust reverser cascades
203 Thrust reverser cowling door, open
204 Door operating jacks
205 Outboard Krueger flap segments
206 Krueger flap mechanism
207 Outer wing construction
208 Aileron jacks
209 Outboard, low-speed, aileron
210 Static, dischargers
211 Fuel vent
212 Wing-tip fairing
213 Navigation light
214 VHF aerial boom

jack
174 Wing skins
175 Wing stringer construction
176 Inboard engine mounting beam
177 Pylon attachment strut
178 Port inner pylon construction
179 Heat exchanger
180 Engine intake
181 RB.211-524B turbofan engine

the PI provisions were omitted. However, as the basic design of the 747 was tailored to cargo it was natural that airlines should have called for the 747-200F. Whereas the 747-100 cargo conversions have a wide door behind the wing, the dedicated -200F has an upward-hinged nose and no passenger windows. Lufthansa bought the first, No 180 off the line, and from 10 March 1972 D-ABYE shuttled every day of the year between NY and Frankfurt with 100 tons of containers. To bolster the US Civil Reserve Air Fleet 19 ex-PanAm 747-121s have been modified as passenger/cargo aircraft with designation C-19A.

747SR

One of the first distinct variants was the 747SR, for Short Range. This went in the opposite direction, eschewing cargo in favour of more passengers. Particularly appealing to Japan Air Lines, this was restressed for reduced gross weights combined with attention to fatigue caused by more rapid cycling with shorter flight-times. Reduction of amenities resulted in certificated capacity rising to 550. Services began

DATA FOR 747-200:

Span	**195ft 8in (59.64m)**
Length	**231ft 10in (70.66m)**
Wing area	**5,500 sq ft (510.95m²)**
Weight empty	**375,170-383,600lb (170,177kg-174,001kg)**
Maximum takeoff weight	**833,000lb (377,840kg)**
Cruising speed	**557mph (897km/h)** at 35,000ft (10,667m)
Range	**7,085 miles (11,402km)** with 440 passengers

DATA FOR 747-400:

Span	**213ft 0in (64.92m)** full tanks
Length	unchanged
Wing area	**5,825 sq ft (541.16m²)**
Weight empty	**398,500-401,800lb (180,760-182,256kg)**
Maximum takeoff weight	**800,000-875,000lb (362,875-396,895kg)**
Cruising speed	**584mph (940km/h)** typical)
Design range	**8,350 miles (13,438km)** 875k, 420 passengers

between Tokyo and Okinawa in October 1973.

Special variants

Several early aircraft were supplied with VIP furnishings to governments and other customers. Two 747-2G4Bs were equipped as special vehicles for the US President, with a crew of 25, the USAF designation being C-25A. Even more special are the US AABNCPs (Advanced Airborne National Command Posts). Designated initially in 1973 as E-4As, the fleet was upgraded to comprise four E-4B aircraft powered by

CF6-50E engines and packed with the greatest array of communications ever fitted into any aircraft. They are distinguished by a "doghouse" fairing over the superhigh-frequency antenna. In 1974 NASA purchased a 747-123 from American and had it modified as the 747SCA Shuttle Carrier Aircraft) to carry and release the Shuttle Orbiter on its initial flight tests. In 1975 the Imperial (now Islamic) Iranian air force purchased 12 used 747-100s and had them converted into military aircraft, three having Fly-

ing Booms for air refuelling.

747SP

The first new-build variant to look different was the 747SP. Special Performance was an odd way of saying "tailored to long thin routes". In the author's opinion it is unwise to start with a huge aircraft and then cut it down to seat fewer (288-332) passengers. The SP looked odd, with a body 48ft 4in (14.73m) shorter, with a visible kink, which demanded a larger tail with double-hinged rudders. Other changes, expensive to introduce, included simple pivoted flaps and a structure restressed for gross weights below 700,000lb (317,520kg). The 747SP first flew on 4 July 1975. Only 44 were built.

747-300

In June 1980 Boeing at last moved a little way back to two decks with the SUD (Stretched Upper Deck) option. By extending the upper level 23ft 4in (7.1m) towards the tail, this area was made to seat not 32 but up to 91. Seven of the extra seats resulted from Boeing's discovery, after 14 years, that the spiral staircase could profitably be replaced by a straight flight (a few aircraft had a stair with a right-angle bend in the centre). The inward-sloping walls make it difficult to see the ground from the upper level, but the SUD not only made the 747 look better but reduced drag, raising cruise Mach at a given engine setting from 0.84 to 0.85. New aircraft were designated 747-300, while a few earlier models were modified with the suffix SU.

747-400

In May 1985 Boeing announced the 747-400. Outwardly a 747-300 with winglets, this was actually a major redesign, cleared to higher weights (see data). Customers have a choice of the Pratt & Whitney PW4056 at 56,750lb (25,742kg) thrust, or the General Electric CF6-80C2B1F at the same power, or the Rolls-Royce RB.211-524H at 58,000lb (26,309kg), with various higher-power versions on option. Fuel capacity is increased to 47,700gal (216,846lit) [slightly less with GE engines], including 2,748gal (12,492lit, considerably more than the total capac-

ity of a Lancaster) in the tailplane, which must be full before taking off at high weights.

The 747-400 introduced an airframe structurally redesigned throughout, making extensive use of aluminium-lithium alloys, which save a claimed 6,000lb (2,722kg) in the wing box alone. The winglets are added on extra tip sections which increase span by 12ft (3.66m). Other updates include digital avionics and a modern "glass cockpit" arranged for a two-pilot crew. The landing gears were improved in detail, and

It's 19 May 1975, and Boeing folk are celebrating the rollout of the 747SP, alongside the prototype 747.

among other things fitted with carbon brakes.

Many of these upgrades could have been introduced a decade earlier, but Boeing was forever conservative. The Dash-400 first flew on 29 April 1988, and two years later Boeing announced that this was the only model on offer. In April 1993 it announced the PIP (Performance Improvement Package), which increases MTO

weight from 870k to 875k (see data) and introduces a longer dorsal fin made of carbon fibre. In 1999 Boeing expects to deliver the concept demonstrator for the USAF AL-1A anti-missile defence aircraft, armed with a colossal TRW laser aimed by Lockheed Martin electro-optics and fire control. A squadron of seven is to be operational by 2008.

Today the Dash-400 has outsold all other versions, with a total of 573 including 747-400D 568-seat domestic versions, -400F freighters with a payload of 249,125lb (113 tonnes) and the -400M Combi

Boeing 747-400

1 Radome
2 Weather radar scanner
3 Front pressure bulkhead
4 Scanner tracking mechanism
5 Wardrobe
6 First-class cabin, 30 or 34 seats at 62-in [1.57-m] pitch
7 Nose undercarriage wheel bay
8 Nosewheel doors
9 Twin nosewheels
10 Hydraulic steering jacks
11 Nose undercarriage pivot mounting
12 Underfloor avionics equipment racks
13 Cabin window panels
14 First-class bar unit
15 Flight deck floor level
16 Rudder pedals
17 Control yoke
18 Instrument panel, five-CRT EFIS displays
19 Instrument panel shroud
20 Windscreen panels
21 Overhead systems switch panel
22 First Officer's seat
23 Captain's seat [two-crew cockpit]
24 Observer's folding seats [2]
25 Starboard side toilet compartments [2]
26 Cockpit bulkhead
27 Crew rest bunks [2]
28 Upper deck window panel
29 Conditioned-air distribution ducting
30 Forward main deck galley unit

31 Plug-type forward cabin door, No 1 port and starboard
32 Business-class passenger seating, 24 seats typical at 36-in [91-cm] pitch
33 Fuselage lower lobe skin panelling
34 Baggage/cargo pallet containers
35 Forward under-floor cargo hold, capacity 2,768 cu ft [78.4 cu m]
36 Forward fuselage frame and stringer construction
37 Upper deck doorway, port and starboard
38 Cabin roof frames
39 Anti-collision beacon light
40 No.1 UHF communications antenna
41 Upper deck passenger cabin, 52 business-class or 69 economy-class seats
42 Lower deck sidewall toilet compartment
43 No 2 passenger door, port and starboard
44 Air conditioning system heat exchanger intake ducting
45 Ventral ram air intakes
46 Faired wing root leading edge fillet
47 Ventral air conditioning packs, port and starboard
48 Wing spar bulkhead
49 Economy-class seating
50 Staircase to upper deck level
51 Fresh-water tanks
52 Wing centre-section fuel tankage, capacity

16,990 US gal [64,315 litres]
53 Centre-section stringer construction
54 Floor beam structure
55 Front spar/fuselage main frame
56 Upper deck lobby area
57 Curtained bulkhead
58 Galley units
59 Starboard wing inboard main fuel tank, capacity 12,546 US gal [47,492 litres]
60 Fuel pumps
61 Engine bleed air supply ducting
62 Kruger flap operating mechanism
63 Inboard Kruger flap segments
64 Starboard inner Pratt & Whitney PW4256 engine nacelle
65 Inboard nacelle pylon
66 Leading-edge Krueger flap segments
67 Pressure refuelling connections, port and starboard
68 Krueger flap drive shaft
69 Krueger flap rotary actuators
70 Starboard wing outer main fuel tank, capacity 4,482 US gal [16,966 litres]

71 Starboard outer engine nacelle
72 Outer nacelle pylon
73 Starboard wing reserve tank provision, capacity 534 US gal 2,021 litres]
74 Outboard Krueger flap
75 Krueger flap drive mechanism
76 Outer wing panel dry bay
77 Vent surge tank
78 Wing-tip extension
79 Starboard navigation [green] and strobe [white] lights
80 Starboard winglet
81 Fixed portion of trailing edge
82 Fuel vent
83 Static dischargers
84 Outboard, low-speed, aileron
85 Outboard four-segment spoilers
86 Outboard triple-slotted Fowler-type flap, extended
87 Flap screw jacks and segment linkages
88 Flap drive shaft
89 Inboard, high speed, aileron
90 Inboard triple-slotted flap, extended

91 Inboard two-segment spoilers/lift dumpers
92 Inboard triple-slotted flap, extended
93 Auxiliary trailing edge wing spar
94 Cabin air distribution ducting
95 Extended upper deck rear bulkhead

96 Upper deck floor beams
97 Air system cross-feed ducting
98 Conditioned-air risers
99 Machined wing spar attaching main frames
100 Central flap drive motors
101 Wing-mounted outboard main undercarriage wheel bay
102 Undercarriage mounting beam
103 Central keel section
104 Pressure floor above wheel bay
105 Centre fuselage frame and stringer construction
106 Dual navigation antennas

107 Cabin wall trim panelling
108 Seat mounting rails
109 Main cabin floor panelling
110 Fuselage-mounted inboard, main undercarriage wheel bay
111 Hydraulic retraction jack
112 Cabin window panel
113 Overhead conditioned-air distribution ducting
114 Economy-class seating, 302 to 410 seats at 34-in [86-cm] pitch
115 Overhead stowage bins

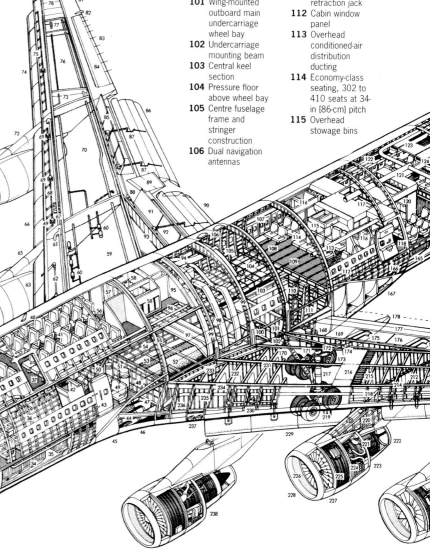

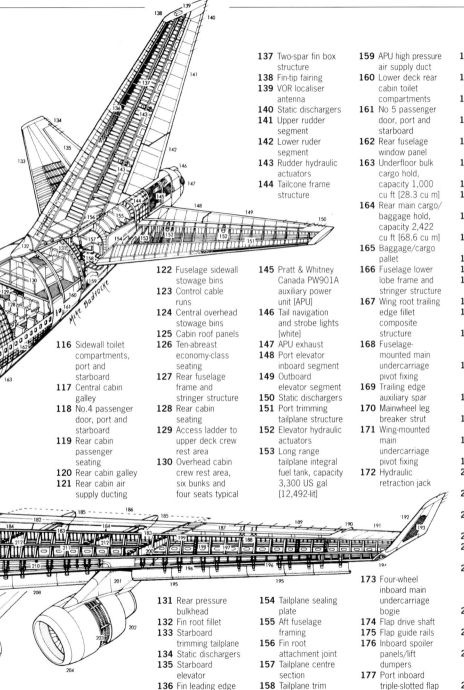

137 Two-spar fin box structure
138 Fin-tip fairing
139 VOR localiser antenna
140 Static dischargers
141 Upper rudder segment
142 Lower ruder segment
143 Rudder hydraulic actuators
144 Tailcone frame structure

122 Fuselage sidewall stowage bins
123 Control cable runs
124 Central overhead stowage bins
125 Cabin roof panels
126 Ten-abreast economy-class seating
127 Rear fuselage frame and stringer structure
128 Rear cabin seating
129 Access ladder to upper deck crew rest area
130 Overhead cabin crew rest area, six bunks and four seats typical

116 Sidewall toilet compartments, port and starboard
117 Central cabin galley
118 No.4 passenger door, port and starboard
119 Rear cabin passenger seating
120 Rear cabin galley
121 Rear cabin air supply ducting

145 Pratt & Whitney Canada PW901A auxiliary power unit [APU]
146 Tail navigation and strobe lights [white]
147 APU exhaust
148 Port elevator inboard segment
149 Outboard elevator segment
150 Static dischargers
151 Port trimming tailplane structure
152 Elevator hydraulic actuators
153 Long range tailplane integral fuel tank, capacity 3,300 US gal [12,492-lit]

131 Rear pressure bulkhead
132 Fin root fillet
133 Starboard trimming tailplane
134 Static dischargers
135 Starboard elevator
136 Fin leading edge structure

154 Tailplane sealing plate
155 Aft fuselage framing
156 Fin root attachment joint
157 Tailplane centre section
158 Tailplane trim screw jack

159 APU high pressure air supply duct
160 Lower deck rear cabin toilet compartments
161 No 5 passenger door, port and starboard
162 Rear fuselage window panel
163 Underfloor bulk cargo hold, capacity 1,000 cu ft [28.3 cu m]
164 Rear main cargo/baggage hold, capacity 2,422 cu ft [68.6 cu m]
165 Baggage/cargo pallet
166 Fuselage lower lobe frame and stringer structure
167 Wing root trailing edge fillet composite structure
168 Fuselage-mounted main undercarriage pivot fixing
169 Trailing edge auxiliary spar
170 Mainwheel leg breaker strut
171 Wing-mounted main undercarriage pivot fixing
172 Hydraulic retraction jack

173 Four-wheel inboard main undercarriage bogie
174 Flap drive shaft
175 Flap guide rails
176 Inboard spoiler panels/lift dumpers
177 Port inboard triple-slotted flap
178 Flap track fairings

179 Flap extended position
180 Aileron hydraulic actuator
181 Inboard, high-speed, aileron
182 Outboard triple-slotted flap
183 Outboard flap tracks
184 Outboard spoiler panels
185 Flap track fairings
186 Flap extended position
187 Outboard, low-speed, aileron
188 Aileron hydraulic actuators
189 Static dischargers
190 Fuel vent
191 Fixed portion of trailing edge
192 Port winglet
193 Winglet composite structure
194 Port navigation [red] and strobe [white] lights
195 Outboard leading edge Krueger flap segments
196 Krueger flap drive mechanism
197 Outer wing panel rib structure
198 Wing bottom skin access manholes
199 Rear spar
200 Outboard engine mounting rib
201 Port outer nacelle pylon
202 Thrust reverser cowling door
203 Reverser cascades
204 Outboard engine nacelle
205 Rolls-Royce RB211-524G/H alternative engine installation
206 Full length nacelle cowling
207 Internal exhaust stream mixer duct
208 Central leading edge Krueger flap segments
209 Krueger flap drive mechanism

210 Leading-edge rib structure
211 Main wing panel three-spar torsion box structure
212 Wing ribs
213 Rear spar
214 Front spar
215 Wing stringers
216 Wing skin panelling
217 Wing-mounted main under-carriage leg strut
218 Pylon attachment strut
219 Four-wheel outer main under-carriage bogie
220 Nacelle pylon structure
221 Engine bleed air pre-cooler
222 Core engine, hot stream, exhaust duct
223 Fan air, cold stream, exhaust duct
224 Ventral engine accessory equipment pack
225 Pratt & Whitney PW4256 turbofan engine
226 Engine intake with acoustic lining
227 Detachable cowling panels
228 Bleed air de-icing intake lip
229 Inboard Krueger flap segments
230 Krueger flap motor and drive shaft
231 Machined spar booms
232 Inboard wing ribs
233 bolted wing root attachment joint strap
234 Front spar
235 Engine bleed air ducting
236 Leading edge nose ribs
237 Twin landing lamps
238 GE CF6-80C2 alternative engine installation

versions. In early 1998 the total for all variants was 1,297.

Whereas PanAm paid $21 million for each of the first Jumbos, the current price is more than ten times as much, hence the comment about crying all the way to the bank. Nobody could argue about price, because there was no alternative.

Throughout the 1990s Boeing worked on where to go from the 747. One idea was the all-new NLA (New Large Airplane), which would get it right and be a double-decker. In 1992 Boeing published a sketch showing one NLA study, seating 612-750 and with MTO weight of 1,201,500lb (545 tonnes). The other avenue was the stretched and re-winged 747-500X and -600X, but these received a lukewarm response.

On 20 January 1997 Boeing announced that it was terminating these two derivative projects, and would instead work on the NLA and improved 767/777 versions (though it is still quietly working on 747 derivatives). The result is that the immediate successors to the 747 are the A340-500/-600 and the twin-engined 777-300.

MODEL 953 YC-14

MISSED OPPORTUNITY

In 1971 it seemed essential to replace the Lockheed C-130, which had been designed 20 years previously. In early 1972 Requests For Proposals were sent to Boeing and McDonnell Douglas for an AMST, Advanced Medium STOL (Short Take-Off and Landing) Transport.

Boeing based the Model 953 on a supercritical wing profile developed at NASA, coupled with USB, Upper-Surface Blowing. The two 51,000lb (23,133kg)-thrust General Electric CF6-50D turbofans were mounted in drum-like cowlings completely ahead of the wing, so that their entire (fan plus core) efflux was blasted out through a broad but shallow slit above the wing, fitted with an upward-hinged reverser. Spread laterally by diagonal deflectors, the Coanda effect kept this high-energy flow attached to the wing, so that when the extremely powerful flaps were depressed to 90° the relatively small wing gave tremendous lift. Further outboard were powerful double-slotted flaps, while the entire leading edge

was occupied by variable-camber Kruegers blown from the main engines.

A special flight-control system was needed to provide control power at airspeeds down to 52 knots (96km/h). Each wing was fitted with small wingtip ailerons and five sections of spoiler (747 inboard and 727 outboard). The tail was relatively huge. The rudder was made in three double-hinged sections, while the pivoted tailplane carried inner and outer sections of double-hinged elevator. Marconi-Elliott supplied the advanced autopilot, and for the first time in a large aircraft the flight-control system was fly-by-wire.

For operation from soft airstrips there were four pairs of mainwheels, retracting into large fairings which also housed the pressurization and air-conditioning systems. The main cargo compartment was 47ft (14.33m) long by about 11.7ft (3.55m) square, appreciably less-constricted than the C-130. Payloads could include 81,000lb (36,742kg) of cargo, loaded through the rear ramp, or up to 150 troops. Paratroops could leave via the ramp or side doors. The view from the

Boeing YC-14

1 Radome
2 Radar scanner
3 Nose bulkhead
4 Windscreen panels
5 Windscreen wipers
6 Windscreen panel shroud
7 Nose frames
8 Pilot's downward-view window
9 Nose under-carriage bay
10 Nose under-carriage leg (Boeing 707 unit)
11 Twin nosewheels
12 Nosewheel door
13 Crew entry door
14 Door operating cylinder
15 Flight-deck stairs
16 Handrail
17 Radio and electronics racks
18 Pilot's seat
19 Cabin roof window
20 Observer's seat
21 Ditching hatch
22 Air-conditioning supply pipe
23 Cabin bulkhead frame
24 Fuselage frame and stringer construction
25 Observation windows
26 Port engine intake
27 Main cargo floor
28 Cargo hold floor construction
29 Roller-track loading rails
30 Engine access panels
31 General Electric YF103-GE-100 (CF6-50D) turbofan
32 Engine mounting beam
33 Engine pylon frame
34 Bleed air pipes
35 Fan flow duct
36 Core engine

37 Firewall
38 Engine turbine section
39 Engine mounting struts
40 Reverser door jack
41 Wing centre-section construction
42 Engine pylon fairing
43 Starboard engine nacelle
44 Engine access doors
45 Thrust reverser panel
46 Thrust reverser lip door
47 Door jack
48 Leading edge Krueger flap sections (modified Boeing 747 units)
49 Krueger flap drive shafts
50 Boundary layer control air pipe
51 Starboard wingtip
52 Navigation light
53 Starboard aileron
54 Supercritical wing aerofoil profile
55 Flap actuating mechanism fairing
56 Starboard wing fuel tank
57 Outboard spoilers (Boeing 727 units)
58 Outboard flaps
59 Inboard spoilers (Boeing 747 units)
60 Inboard flaps
61 Vortex generators, closed
62 Trailing edge fairing
63 Fuselage semi-monocoque construction
64 Main fuselage frames
65 Door opening box beam

66 Aft main frame
67 Door guide rail and roller
68 Upward opening cargo hold door
69 Fin attachment frames

70 Constant section fin construction
71 Fin leading edge
72 Tailplane controls
73 Tail lighting
74 Fin/tailplane leading edge fairing
75 Tailplane jacks

76 Moving tailplane centre section
77 Centre section sealing plate
78 Starboard tailplane

79 Starboard elevator sections
80 Tailplane bullet fairing
81 Port elevator controls
82 Elevator controls

83 Honeycomb panels
84 Tailplane construction
85 Split rudder sections, three interchangeable units

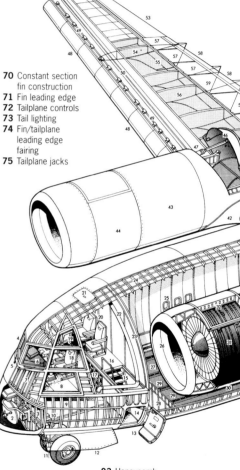

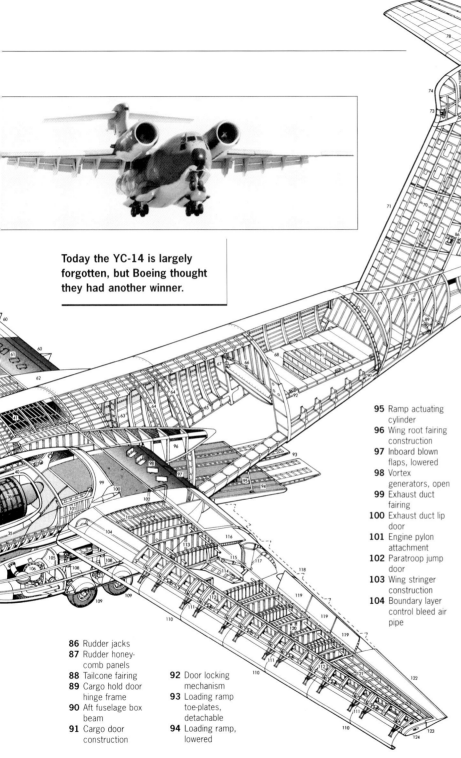

Today the YC-14 is largely forgotten, but Boeing thought they had another winner.

three-man cockpit was better than in commercial jets.

In November 1972 Boeing received a contract for two Model 953s, designated YC-14. Built in the company Developmental Center on Boeing Field (King County airport), the first was USAF 72-1873. Finished in natural metal, it was flown by Ray McPherson and Major Dave Bittenbinder on 9 August 1976. The second, 72-1874, was camouflaged. To the author — whose 30 minutes on a YC-14 demo flight are an awesome memory — it was amazing that these outstanding aircraft, and the rival YC-15s, should have been dropped like hot bricks. The old narrow-body C-130, with longer field length and cruising at 290kt instead of 400, will be the only tactical transport available into the Millennium.

86 Rudder jacks
87 Rudder honey-comb panels
88 Tailcone fairing
89 Cargo hold door hinge frame
90 Aft fuselage box beam
91 Cargo door construction
92 Door locking mechanism
93 Loading ramp toe-plates, detachable
94 Loading ramp, lowered
95 Ramp actuating cylinder
96 Wing root fairing construction
97 Inboard blown flaps, lowered
98 Vortex generators, open
99 Exhaust duct fairing
100 Exhaust duct lip door
101 Engine pylon attachment
102 Paratroop jump door
103 Wing stringer construction
104 Boundary layer control bleed air pipe
105 Main landing gear sponson
106 Air conditioning plant
107 Air conditioning intake
108 Main landing gear units, two interchangeable legs
109 Twin-wheel bogies (Boeing 737 wheels)
110 Leading edge Krueger flap segments (Boeing 747 units)
111 Krueger flap mechanism
112 Leading edge construction
113 Wing ribs
114 Flap hinge mechanism fairing
115 Flap jack
116 Inboard spoiler
117 Double slotted flap sections, lowered
118 Flap hinge fairing and trailing edge location
119 Outboard spoilers, open (Boeing 727 units)
120 Integral wing fuel tank
121 Outer wing dry bay construction
122 Port aileron
123 Port wing-tip fairing
124 Port navigation light

DATA FOR 953 YC-14:

Span	**129ft 0in (39.32m)**
Length	**131ft 8in (40.13m)**
Wing area	**1,762 sq ft (163.69m²)**
Weight empty	**117,500lb (53,297kg)**
Maximum takeoff weight	**251,000lb (113,854kg)**
Cruising speed	**449-472mph (723-760km/h)**
Takeoff or landing run	**1,100ft (335m)**
Range	**980 miles (1,577km)**
	27,000lb payload, 1,800ft, 570m, runway
	1,150 miles (1,851km)
	81,000lb payload, long runway)

M. Badrocke

953 YC-14

STRAIGHT AND NARROW

757

In the early 1970s Boeing began far-ranging studies into new commercial jet designs for the 1980s and beyond. In 1973 these gained impetus from the dramatic increase in fuel prices. Another factor was the emergence of Airbus as a competitor. The A300B first flew in May 1972, but for several years it was ignored by the market, and accordingly by Boeing also. Gradually the airlines awoke, and Boeing recognised that it faced a potentially serious rival.

The first study to be allotted real manpower was the wide-body 7X7 (see 767). Five months later another team began trying to determine what might profitably continue the traditional body cross-section first seen in the 707, and subsequently the 727 and 737. The Model number 751 was used for numerous studies, one of which – in partnership with Aeritalia – was a high-wing STOL with four underwing engines resembling an enlarged BAe 146. Further studies had the Model number 761. As these progressed in

1976 they became grouped under the generic title of 7N7. They homed in on seating for 120-180 over sectors up to 2,300 miles (3,700km) – basically a successor to the 727. The 7N7 replaced the 727-300, which had never attracted enough customers to be launched. By late 1976 the decision had been taken to use two underwing engines. As in the 737, removing engines from the rear fuselage enabled the cabin to be made significantly longer, and use of just two engines matched the 7N7 to proposed high-bypass

engines of excellent fuel economy. At the 1976 Farnborough airshow the studies ranged from the 125-seat 761-119 with CFM56 engines of 22,000lb (9,979kg) thrust to the 180-seat 761-143 with General Electric CF6-32 engines of 30,000lb (13,608kg) thrust. By 1977 the 7N7 had put on weight, and the engine choice had narrowed to the Pratt & Whitney JT10D-4 of 27,000lb (12,247kg) and the CF6-32 and Rolls-Royce 535 rated at 32,000lb (14,515kg).

The British engine manufacturer had never shown any interest in Airbus, but fought hard to get on the 7N7. In this it was eagerly supported by British Airways, which was one of the principal operators who worked with Boeing to define the form the 7N7 should take. Seeing this, in August 1976 British Aerospace sent a team to Seattle to see if Boeing would let them participate, with responsibility for the wing, landing gear and engine pods. This appeared to the author ironic, because the 7N7 had now become virtually identical in shape, dimensions, weights and performance to the Hawker Siddeley HS.134 of

Unlike the majority of 757 customers, TWA selected PW2043 engines. Its -200s have replaced a large fleet of 727-100Cs.

January 1967, which had never got off the drawing board.

By September 1978 Boeing was ready to sign BA and Eastern as launch customers. By this time the design was almost firm, the key factor being a new wing with an advanced Boeing aerofoil and sweep at the $1/4$-chord line of only 25°, the same as the 737. As far as possible, commonality with the 727 was preserved; indeed, Boeing initially tried to make the 7N7 a 727 with new engines hung under a new wing. However, in January 1979 the reduced overall length and structure weight of a conventional tail led to the T-tail being abandoned. Later that year the nose was redesigned to resemble that of the 767, giving a longer full-width tube and wider cockpit, redesigned for two-pilot operation. The extended main cabin was long enough for 239 passengers seated 3+3. The underfloor holds had doors on the left, and offered 700 cu ft (19.8m³) ahead of the wing, 1,000 cu ft (30.87m³) behind.

By 1979 the objective was no longer commonality with the 727 but with the 767. This extended to the vertical tail,

Collins FCS-700 digital flight-control system, Honeywell navigation and flight-management and air-data computer systems, electrical and hydraulic systems, cabin environmental system and the AlliedSignal GTCP-331 APU in the tailcone. Menasco was chosen to supply both the inwards-retracting bogie main landing gears and the forward-retracting twin-wheel nose gear. All landing-gear doors were made of graphite/Kevlar. In relation to its capacity of 9,389gal (42,684 litres) the fuel system was simple, comprising just three integral tanks plus wingtip surge tanks beyond small dry bays. Features distinguishing this aircraft from the 767 include the narrow body, downward-pointing nose, less wing sweep and the graphite/Kevlar fairings over the tracks along which the flaps travel (double-slotted inboard and single-slotted outboard).

Final tweaking of the design in 1979 was accompanied by signatures from BA and Eastern, and Boeing announced the go-ahead on 23 March. Both airlines picked the Rolls-Royce 535C engine, which by that time had been developed

to 37,400lb (16,965kg) thrust. Each was hung on a shallow Rohr pylon in a pod incorporating a cascade-type reverser in the fan duct.

Before go-ahead Boeing had assembled a global network of suppliers. Apart from systems components, these included Boeing Renton for the main section of fuselage and the five slat sections on each wing, Boeing Military Airplanes for the cab section, Boeing Vertol (later Boeing Helicopters) for the fixed leading edges, LTV (later Vought) for the rear fuselage and tail, IAI for the dorsal fin, Shorts for the inboard flaps, CASA for the outboard flaps, Northrop Grumman for the five flight and one ground spoiler sections on each wing, Hawker de Havilland of Australia for the inter-spar wing ribs, Heath Tecna for the flap-track fairings and the wing/fuselage fairing, Schweizer for the wingtips and Fleet Industries for the APU doors.

The first off the line, N757A, was designated as a 757-225, and retained by Boeing for future development and demonstration. On 13 January 1982 it emerged from the Renton plant in the distinctive

company livery of red/white/blue stripes first seen five months earlier on the first 767. Using five aircraft FAA certification was achieved on 21 December 1982. Revenue service began with Eastern on 1 January 1983.

Boeing had continued to offer the CF6-32 engine, and in April 1980 this was picked by Aloha and Transbrasil. However, GE decided not to develop this downsized CF6 version. The next customer, Delta, announced a massive order for 60 in November 1980, leaving the engine option open. Eventually Delta placed the launch order for a specially developed derivative of the JT10D to be designated PW2000. Their first 757-232 flight was on 14 March 1984, powered by the PW2037, rated at 38,200lb (17,328kg).

The Pratt & Whitney engine later won further large orders from US airlines, but the superior reliability of the British engine won it more than 80 per cent of the customers. In 1987 Pratt certificated the PW2040 at 40,900lb (18,552kg), and in September that year the same engine was certificated on the 757PF

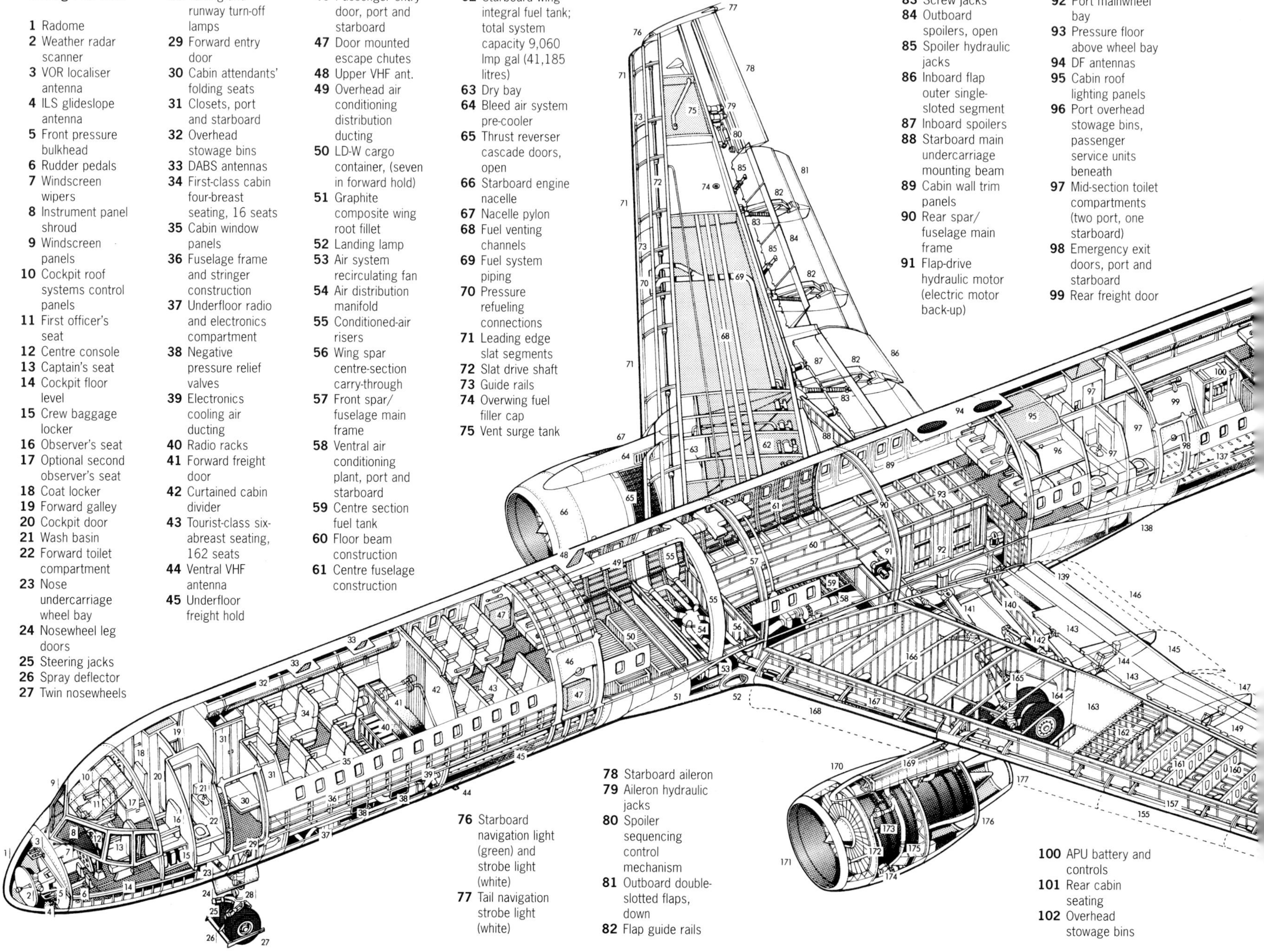

Boeing 757-200

1 Radome
2 Weather radar scanner
3 VOR localiser antenna
4 ILS glideslope antenna
5 Front pressure bulkhead
6 Rudder pedals
7 Windscreen wipers
8 Instrument panel shroud
9 Windscreen panels
10 Cockpit roof systems control panels
11 First officer's seat
12 Centre console
13 Captain's seat
14 Cockpit floor level
15 Crew baggage locker
16 Observer's seat
17 Optional second observer's seat
18 Coat locker
19 Forward galley
20 Cockpit door
21 Wash basin
22 Forward toilet compartment
23 Nose undercarriage wheel bay
24 Nosewheel leg doors
25 Steering jacks
26 Spray deflector
27 Twin nosewheels

28 Taxiing and runway turn-off lamps
29 Forward entry door
30 Cabin attendants' folding seats
31 Closets, port and starboard
32 Overhead stowage bins
33 DABS antennas
34 First-class cabin four-breast seating, 16 seats
35 Cabin window panels
36 Fuselage frame and stringer construction
37 Underfloor radio and electronics compartment
38 Negative pressure relief valves
39 Electronics cooling air ducting
40 Radio racks
41 Forward freight door
42 Curtained cabin divider
43 Tourist-class six-abreast seating, 162 seats
44 Ventral VHF antenna
45 Underfloor freight hold

46 Passenger entry door, port and starboard
47 Door mounted escape chutes
48 Upper VHF ant.
49 Overhead air conditioning distribution ducting
50 LD-W cargo container, (seven in forward hold)
51 Graphite composite wing root fillet
52 Landing lamp
53 Air system recirculating fan
54 Air distribution manifold
55 Conditioned-air risers
56 Wing spar centre-section carry-through
57 Front spar/ fuselage main frame
58 Ventral air conditioning plant, port and starboard
59 Centre section fuel tank
60 Floor beam construction
61 Centre fuselage construction

62 Starboard wing integral fuel tank; total system capacity 9,060 Imp gal (41,185 litres)
63 Dry bay
64 Bleed air system pre-cooler
65 Thrust reverser cascade doors, open
66 Starboard engine nacelle
67 Nacelle pylon
68 Fuel venting channels
69 Fuel system piping
70 Pressure refueling connections
71 Leading edge slat segments
72 Slat drive shaft
73 Guide rails
74 Overwing fuel filler cap
75 Vent surge tank

76 Starboard navigation light (green) and strobe light (white)
77 Tail navigation strobe light (white)

78 Starboard aileron
79 Aileron hydraulic jacks
80 Spoiler sequencing control mechanism
81 Outboard double-slotted flaps, down
82 Flap guide rails

83 Screw jacks
84 Outboard spoilers, open
85 Spoiler hydraulic jacks
86 Inboard flap outer single-sloted segment
87 Inboard spoilers
88 Starboard main undercarriage mounting beam
89 Cabin wall trim panels
90 Rear spar/ fuselage main frame
91 Flap-drive hydraulic motor (electric motor back-up)

92 Port mainwheel bay
93 Pressure floor above wheel bay
94 DF antennas
95 Cabin roof lighting panels
96 Port overhead stowage bins, passenger service units beneath
97 Mid-section toilet compartments (two port, one starboard)
98 Emergency exit doors, port and starboard
99 Rear freight door

100 APU battery and controls
101 Rear cabin seating
102 Overhead stowage bins

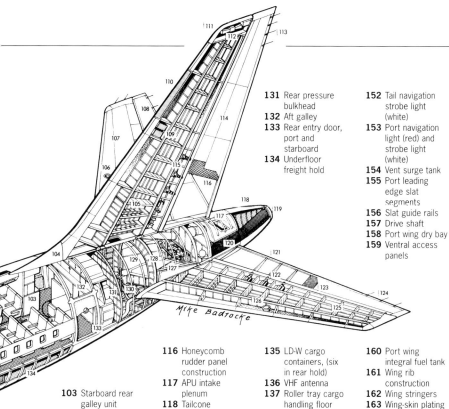

131 Rear pressure bulkhead
132 Aft galley
133 Rear entry door, port and starboard
134 Underfloor freight hold

152 Tail navigation strobe light (white)
153 Port navigation light (red) and strobe light (white)
154 Vent surge tank
155 Port leading edge slat segments
156 Slat guide rails
157 Drive shaft
158 Port wing dry bay
159 Ventral access panels

103 Starboard rear galley unit
104 Fin root fillet
105 Fin construction
106 Fin 'logo' spotlight
107 Starboard tailplane
108 starboard elevator
109 HF antenna couplers
110 Leading edge HF antenna
111 Fin tip antenna fairing
112 VOR antennas
113 Static dischargers
114 Rudder
115 Rudder power units

116 Honeycomb rudder panel construction
117 APU intake plenum
118 Tailcone
119 APU exhaust
120 AlliedSignal GTCP331-200 auxiliary power plant (APU)
121 Port elevator
122 Elevator power units
123 Honeycomb panel construction
124 Static dischargers
125 Tailplane construction
126 Fin 'logo' light
127 Tailplane sealing plate
128 Fin support frame
129 Tailplane centre-section
130 Tailplane trim control jack

135 LD-W cargo containers, (six in rear hold)
136 VHF antenna
137 Roller tray cargo handling floor
138 Graphite composite wing root fillet
139 Port inboard double slotted flap
140 Main undercarriage mounting beam
141 Undercarriage leg side strut
142 Hydraulic retraction jack
143 Inboard spoilers
144 Flap hinge linkage
145 Inboard flap single slotted outer segment
146 Flaps down position
147 Flap track fairings
148 Outboard double slotted flap
149 Outboard spoilers
150 Aileron hydraulic jacks
151 Port aileron honeycomb construction

160 Port wing integral fuel tank
161 Wing rib construction
162 Wing stringers
163 Wing-skin plating
164 Four-wheel main undercarriage bogie
165 Main undercarriage leg strut
166 Inboard wing ribs
167 Bleed air ducting
168 Inboard leading edge slat
169 Engine mounting pylon
170 Detachable engine cowlings
171 Port engine intake
172 Intake de-icing air duct
173 Rolls-Royce RB.211-535C or E4B turbofan (PW2037 or PW2043 turbofans optional fit)
174 Engine accessory gearbox
175 Oil cooler
176 Fan air exhaust duct
177 Hot stream exhaust nozzle

(Package Freighter) at 41,700lb (18,915kg), and has remained the only engine of that version, 80 of which are used by UPS. Hurt by its rejection by most customers, Pratt fought back and has introduced a succession of modifications which improve the PW2040's reliability. Today customers can select the RR E4 of 40,100lb (18,189kg) or E4B of 43,100lb (19,550kg) or the PW2043 of 43,850lb (19,890kg).

The US government's VIP transports, replacing the VC-137, are four 757s designated C-32A. The original prototype is testing avionics for the Lockheed Martin/ Boeing F-22A Raptor, with a portion of F-22A wing with conformal antennas

behind the cockpit. Boeing offer Combi and Freighter versions, as well as the stretched 757-300. While the original 757 could be identified by its long and thin look, the Dash-300 is grotesque. The body is stretched 13ft 4in (4.06m) ahead of the wing and 10ft (3.05m) behind. Maximum seating is 289, and the underfloor holds provide 1,070 cu ft (30.3m³) ahead of the wing and 1,312 cu ft (37.2m³) behind. Features include a new flight-management system, improved environmental system, new furnishings and a tailskid. The first flight was due in August 1998, for delivery to launch customer Condor Flugdienst in January 1999.

DATA FOR 757-200:	
Span	**124ft 10in (38.05m)**
Length	**155ft 3in (47.32m)**
Wing area	**1,994 sq ft (185.25m²)**
Weight empty	**127,810lb (57,975kg)** RR 535E4
Maximum takeoff weight	**240,000lb (108,860kg)**
Cruising speed	**Mach 0.8**
	equivalent at 38,200ft (11,643m) to 528mph (850km/h)
Range	**3,926 miles (6,318km)** with 186 passengers

DATA FOR 757-300:	
Dimensions unchanged except:	
Length	**178ft 7in (54.43m)**
Weight empty	**142,400lb (64,950kg)**
Maximum takeoff weight	**270,000lb (122,470kg)**
Cruising speed	**Mach 0.8**
Range	**3,763 miles (6,056km)** with 240 passengers

767

WIDE-BODIED WONDER

When this big twin was announced in July 1978 it appeared to be a straight copy of the Airbus 300B. In fact, the 767 had been preceded by a typically exhaustive Boeing study lasting eight years, and encompassing some 900 permutations of more than ten basic configurations. By 1975 nearly all the proposals were either big twins or trijets, many with a T-tail and in some cases even with USB (upper-surface blowing) as tested on the YC-14. In that year the re-use of the traditional 707/727/737 cross-section was abandoned, and opinion hardened on a circular section of either 188in (4.78m) or 206.5in (5.25m) diameter.

At the 1975 Paris airshow the author was told that Boeing's New Airplane Program involved two projects, the 727-derivative aircraft called 7N7 and the all-new 7X7. By this time the latter was confidently expected to be a twin, with the intermediate body diameter of 198in (5.03m). To the author this was astonishing because,

after discussing the 7X7 with nearly 40 airlines, led by United, Boeing appeared deliberately to be aiming at a body 2ft (0.61m) narrower than the rival A300B and A310, and therefore unable to carry standard LD3 containers side-by-side in the underfloor holds. Ever since, Boeing has claimed the narrower body to be an advantage, seating passengers 2+3+2 "with no passenger more than one seat away from an aisle". Airbus reply "Our 222in body can seat 2+3+2 with wider seats and huge aisles, and we can also seat 3+3+3 in comfort".

767-200

Despite this, the narrower body was what the airlines wanted, and on 14 July 1978 United announced the purchase of 30 aircraft designated 767-200, at a price of $1.2 billion. The engines were to be the Pratt & Whitney JT9D-7R4 rated at 44,300lb (20,094kg). With a full load of 197 passengers the new Boeing was to operate from a 7,300ft (2,225m) runway and fly a sector of 2,200 miles (3,540km). Though it had a smaller body than the A300B, it had a much larger wing. United wanted this in order to climb from Denver straight over the Rockies, and other

Boeing 767-200

1 Radome
2 Radar scanner dish
3 VOR localiser aerial
4 Front pressure bulkhead
5 ILS glideslope aerials
6 Windscreen wipers
7 Windscreen panels
8 Instrument panel shroud
9 Rudder pedals
10 Nose undercarriage wheel bay
11 Cockpit air conditioning duct
12 Captain's seat
13 Opening cockpit side window
14 Centre console
15 copilot's seat
16 Cockpit roof systems control panels
17 Flight engineer's station
18 Observer's seat
19 Pitot tubes
20 Angle of attack probe
21 Nose undercarriage steering jacks
22 Twin nosewheels
23 Nosewheel doors
24 Waste system vacuum tank
25 Forward toilet compartment
26 Crew wardrobe
27 Forward galley
28 Starboard overhead sliding door
29 Entry lobby
30 Cabin divider
31 Port entry door
32 Door control handle
33 Escape chute stowage
34 Underfloor electronics racks
35 Electronics

36 Skin heat exchanger
37 Fuselage frame and stringer construction
38 Cabin window panel
39 Six-abreast first class seating compartment (18 seats)
40 Overhead stowage bins
41 Curtained cabin divider
42 Sidewall trim panels
43 Negative pressure relief valves
44 Forward freight door
45 Forward underfloor freight hold
46 LD-2 cargo containers, 12 in forward hold
47 Centre electronics rack
48 Anti-collision light
49 Cabin roof frames
50 VHF antenna
51 Seven-abreast tourist class seating (193 seats)
52 Conditioned-air riser
53 Air conditioning distribution manifolds
54 Wing spar centre

cooling air system
55 Floor beam construction
56 Overhead air conditioning ducting
57 Front spar/ fuselage main frame
58 Starboard emergency exit window
59 Starboard wing integral fuel tank; total system capacity 12,955 Imp gal (58,895 litres)
60 Thrust reverser cascade door, open
61 Starboard engine nacelle
62 Nacelle pylon
63 Fixed portion of leading edge
64 Leading edge slat segments, open
65 Slat drive shaft
66 Rotary actuators
67 Fuel system piping
68 Fuel venting channels
69 Vent surge tank
70 Starboard navigation light (green)
71 Anti-collision light (red)

section carry through
72 Tail navigation strobe light (white)
73 Static dischargers
74 Starboard outer aileron
75 Aileron hydraulic jacks
76 Single slotted outer flap, down
77 Flap hinge fairings
78 Flap hinge control links
79 Outboard spoilers, open
80 Spoiler hydraulic jacks
81 Rotary actuator
82 Flap drive shaft
83 Aileron hydraulic power units
84 Inboard aileron
85 Inboard double slotted flap, down
86 Flap hinge control linkage
87 Fuselage centre section construction

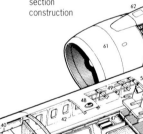

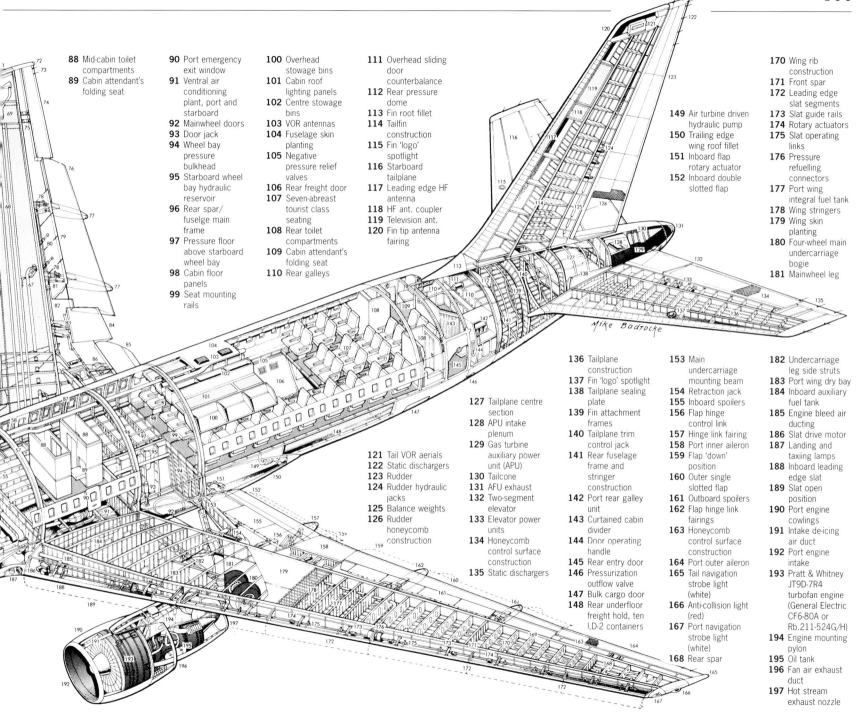

88 Mid-cabin toilet compartments
89 Cabin attendant's folding seat
90 Port emergency exit window
91 Ventral air conditioning plant, port and starboard
92 Mainwheel doors
93 Door jack
94 Wheel bay pressure bulkhead
95 Starboard wheel bay hydraulic reservoir
96 Rear spar/fuselge main frame
97 Pressure floor above starboard wheel bay
98 Cabin floor panels
99 Seat mounting rails

100 Overhead stowage bins
101 Cabin roof lighting panels
102 Centre stowage bins
103 VOR antennas
104 Fuselage skin planting
105 Negative pressure relief valves
106 Rear freight door
107 Seven-abreast tourist class seating
108 Rear toilet compartments
109 Cabin attendant's folding seat
110 Rear galleys

111 Overhead sliding door counterbalance
112 Rear pressure dome
113 Fin root fillet
114 Tailfin construction
115 Fin 'logo' spotlight
116 Starboard tailplane
117 Leading edge HF antenna
118 HF ant. coupler
119 Television ant.
120 Fin tip antenna fairing

149 Air turbine driven hydraulic pump
150 Trailing edge wing roof fillet
151 Inboard flap rotary actuator
152 Inboard double slotted flap

170 Wing rib construction
171 Front spar
172 Leading edge slat segments
173 Slat guide rails
174 Rotary actuators
175 Slat operating links
176 Pressure refuelling connectors
177 Port wing integral fuel tank
178 Wing stringers
179 Wing skin planting
180 Four-wheel main undercarriage bogie
181 Mainwheel leg

121 Tail VOR aerials
122 Static dischargers
123 Rudder
124 Rudder hydraulic jacks
125 Balance weights
126 Rudder honeycomb construction

127 Tailplane centre section
128 APU intake plenum
129 Gas turbine auxiliary power unit (APU)
130 Tailcone
131 AFU exhaust
132 Two-segment elevator
133 Elevator power units
134 Honeycomb control surface construction
135 Static dischargers

136 Tailplane construction
137 Fin 'logo' spotlight
138 Tailplane sealing plate
139 Fin attachment frames
140 Tailplane trim control jack
141 Rear fuselage frame and stringer construction
142 Port rear galley unit
143 Curtained cabin divider
144 Door operating handle
145 Rear entry door
146 Pressurization outflow valve
147 Bulk cargo door
148 Rear underfloor freight hold, ten LD-2 containers

153 Main undercarriage mounting beam
154 Retraction jack
155 Inboard spoilers
156 Flap hinge control link
157 Hinge link fairing
158 Port inner aileron
159 Flap 'down' position
160 Outer single slotted flap
161 Outboard spoilers
162 Flap hinge link fairings
163 Honeycomb control surface construction
164 Port outer aileron
165 Tail navigation strobe light (white)
166 Anti-collision light (red)
167 Port navigation strobe light (white)
168 Rear spar

182 Undercarriage leg side struts
183 Port wing dry bay
184 Inboard auxiliary fuel tank
185 Engine bleed air ducting
186 Slat drive motor
187 Landing and taxiing lamps
188 Inboard leading edge slat
189 Slat open position
190 Port engine cowlings
191 Intake de-icing air duct
192 Port engine intake
193 Pratt & Whitney JT9D-7R4 turbofan engine (General Electric CF6-80A or Rb.211-524G/H)
194 Engine mounting pylon
195 Oil tank
196 Fan air exhaust duct
197 Hot stream exhaust nozzle

767

Boeing 767-300ER

1 Radome
2 Weather radar scanner
3 VOR localiser antenna
4 Front pressure bulkhead
5 ILS glideslope antennas
6 Windscreen wipers
7 Windscreen panels
8 Instrument panel shroud
9 Electronic flight instrumentation system CRT displays
10 Control yoke
11 Rudder pedals
12 Nose undercarriage wheel bay
13 Cockpit air conditioning duct
14 Captain's seat
15 Direct vision opening side window panel
16 Centre console
17 copilot's seat
18 Overhead systems control panel
19 Crew wardrobe
20 Observer's seat
21 Cockpit bulkhead doorway
22 Second observer's seat
23 Twin pitot heads
24 Angle of attack transmitter
25 Nose under-carriage hydraulic steering jacks
26 Twin nosewheels
27 Nosewheel leg doors
28 Waste system vacuum tank
29 Forward toilet compartment
30 Forward galley unit
31 Starboard side service door

32 Galley compart-ment curtain
33 Door latch
34 Forward entry door
35 Door-mounted escape chute
36 Underfloor avionics equipment racks
37 Avionics cooling air systems
38 Skin heat exchanger
39 Fuselage frame and stringer construction
40 Cabin window panels
41 Six-abreast first-class seating compartment (26 seats)
42 Overhead baggage bins
43 Curtained cabin divider
44 Cabin wall trim panelling
45 Anti-collison beacon
46 Centre electronics equipment
47 Negative pressure relief valves
48 Forward freight door
49 Total freight hold volume, 3,770 cu ft (106.7 m³)
50 LD-2 baggage container; 16 in forward hold
51 Cooling air ground connection
52 Cabin pressure relief valves
53 Mid cabin door, optional
54 Conditioned air delivery ducting
55 Seven-abreast tourist-class seating, [224 seats] alternative layouts for up to 325 passengers
56 Srs 300 stretched forward fuselage segment, 121 in [3.07m]

57 Starboard engine nacelle
58 VHF antenna
59 Sidewall toilet compartments, port and starboard
60 Conditioned-air distribution manifold
61 Wing spar centre-section carry-through
62 Front spar attachment fuselage main frame
63 Ventral air conditioning pack, port and starboard
64 Centre section fuel tankage; total capacity, 20,101 Imp gal [24,140 US gal/91 400 litres]
65 Floor beam construction
66 Overhead rear cabin air distribution ducting
67 Starboard wing integral fuel tank
68 Starboard engine thrust reverser cascades, open
69 Inboard slat segment
70 Nacelle pylon
71 Fixed portion of leading edge
72 Dry bay
73 Wing stringers
74 Wing skin panelling
75 Fuel system piping
76 Fuel venting channels
77 Leading-edge slat torque shaft
78 Rotary actuators
79 Outboard leading-edge slat segments, open
80 Starboard navigation light, green

81 Starboard navigation light, green
82 Rear position light, white
83 Static dischargers
84 Outboard, low-speed, aileron
85 Aileron power unit
86 Single-slotted outboard flap segment, down position
87 Flap hinge fairings
88 Flap hinge control linkages and rotary actuators
89 Outboard spoiler panels, open
90 Spoiler hydraulic jacks
91 Flap drive torque shaft
92 Inboard, high-speed, aileron
93 Aileron tandem power units
94 Inboard double-slotted flap segment, down position
95 Flap hinge linkages
96 Inboard spoilers/lift dumpers
97 Starboard main undercarriage hydraulic jack
98 Cabin wall

above wheel bay
100 Rear spar attachment fuselage main frame
101 Starboard wheel bay
102 Central flap drive motor
103 Port main undercarriage wheel bay
104 Mainwheel bay
105 Undercarriage bay rear pressure bulkhead
106 Centre cabin passenger seating
107 Passenger service units
108 Cabin wall stowage bins
109 Cabin roof trim/lighting panels
110 Centre stowage bins
111 ADF antennas
112 Rear fuselage stretch section, 132-in [3.35-m]
113 Rear freight hold door
114 LD-2 baggage containers, 14 in rear hold
115 Rear cabin seat

compartments, port and starboard
118 Starboard service door
119 Rear galley units
120 Fin root fillet
121 Fin spar box construction
122 Fin ribs
123 'Logo' light
124 Starboard tailplane
125 HFG antennar
126 TV antenna
127 Fin tip antenna fairing
128 Tail VOR antenna
129 Static dischargers
130 Rudder
131 Triplex rudder power units
132 Graphite composite rudder construction
133 Rudder mass balance weights
134 APU intake duct
135 Firewall

139 APU exhaust
140 Two-segment elevators

144 Tailplane rib construction
145 Fin 'logo' light
146 Tailplane sealing plate
147 Tailplane hinge point
148 Spar box centre-section carry-through
149 Tailplane trim control screw jack

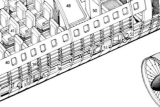

rows
116 Centre toilet compartment
117 Sidewall toilet

insulating blankets
99 Pressure floor

136 APU intake plenum
137 AlliedSignal GRCP 332 auxiliary power unit [APU]
138 Tailcone

141 Elevator triplex power units
142 Graphite composite elevator construction
143 Static dischargers

150 Fin attachment main frames
151 Rear fuselage frame and stringer construction

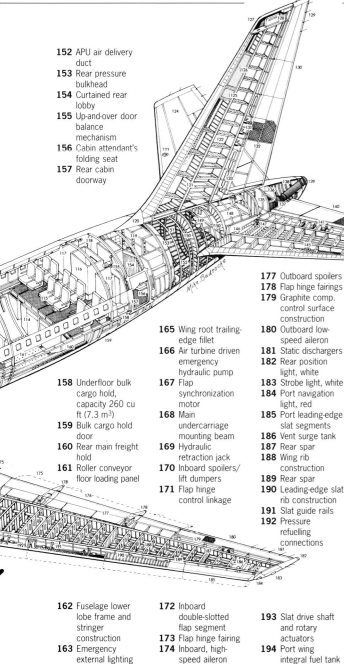

152 APU air delivery duct
153 Rear pressure bulkhead
154 Curtained rear lobby
155 Up-and-over door balance mechanism
156 Cabin attendant's folding seat
157 Rear cabin doorway

158 Underfloor bulk cargo hold, capacity 260 cu ft (7.3 m³)
159 Bulk cargo hold door
160 Rear main freight hold
161 Roller conveyor floor loading panel

162 Fuselage lower lobe frame and stringer construction
163 Emergency external lighting
164 Mid cabin emergency exit door

165 Wing root trailing-edge fillet
166 Air turbine driven emergency hydraulic pump
167 Flap synchronization motor
168 Main undercarriage mounting beam
169 Hydraulic retraction jack
170 Inboard spoilers/lift dumpers
171 Flap hinge control linkage

172 Inboard double-slotted flap segment
173 Flap hinge fairing
174 Inboard, high-speed aileron
175 Flap down position
176 Outer single-slotted flap

177 Outboard spoilers
178 Flap hinge fairings
179 Graphite comp. control surface construction
180 Outboard low-speed aileron
181 Static dischargers
182 Rear position light, white
183 Strobe light, white
184 Port navigation light, red
185 Port leading-edge slat segments
186 Vent surge tank
187 Rear spar
188 Wing rib construction
189 Rear spar
190 Leading-edge slat rib construction
191 Slat guide rails
192 Pressure refuelling connections

193 Slat drive shaft and rotary actuators
194 Port wing integral fuel tank
195 Four-wheel main undercarriage bogie

196 Main under-carriage leg strut
197 Undercarriage leg breaker strut
198 Port wing dry bay
199 Pylon attachment links
200 Port nacelle pylon
201 Rolls-Royce RB211-524G turbofan engine
202 Engine turbine section
203 By-pass air duct
204 Multi-lobe exhaust mixer
205 Combined exhaust nozzle
206 Pratt & Whitney PW4060 alternative powerplant
207 RB211 full-length engine nacelle
208 Thrust reverser cascades
209 Engine accessory equipment gearbox
210 Acoustically lined air intake
211 Nacelle strake
212 Inboard leading-edge slat segment
213 Inboard wing panel integral fuel tank
214 Wing root attachment rib
215 Leading-edge slat drive motor
216 Slat down position
217 Landing and taxiing lamps
218 Wing inspection light
219 Kevlar composite leading-edge root fillet
220 General Electric CF6-80C2B6 alternative power-plant

customers went along. The 767 was to be assembled at Everett, in an extension to the vast 747 plant.

The author was told that a key reason for the choice of 198in as body diameter was to minimise drag; privately, he was told "We couldn't select the same figure as Airbus, and decided on less rather than more". One result was the invention of a non-standard type of baggage/cargo container called LD2, with capacity only 62 per cent that of the LD3 of other wide-bodies. Boeing brought in Canadair, Grumman Aerospace (now Lockheed Martin), Mitsubishi and Kawasaki to help make the fuselage.

Compared with the 747 the wing of the 767, apart from being smaller, was designed for the lower cruise Mach number of 0.8. Thus, at the $1/4$-chord line the sweep angle was reduced from 37.5° to 31.5°, and the thickness/chord ratios of the super-critical profile were higher: 15.1 per cent at the root, never tapering below 10.3 at the tip. A remarkable decision was to use flaps simpler than in the 767's predecessors, double-slotted over the short inboard section and single-slotted outboard. Kruegers were abandoned in favour of full-span slats, hydraulically driven by spanwise rotary shafts in one large inboard section and five from the pylon to the tip. Other movables comprised four outboard and two inboard spoilers on each wing, inboard all-speed ailerons, and outboard ailerons locked in cruising flight. The tail comprised a trimming

tailplane with elevators, all made by Vought, and a fin and one-piece rudder from Alenia. All flight controls were fully powered. Boeing was so concerned about reliability that each surface had triple actuators, each in a different hydraulic system, but with mechanical (cable) signalling.

Boeing said use of Kevlar and Nomex composites saved 1,000lb (454kg) in structure weight. Cleveland Pneumatic were assigned the bogie main landing gears, with Bendix wheels, steel brakes and Fuji-made doors, and Menasco the forwards-retracting nose gear. Apart from dry bays around the pylons, the entire volume between the wing spars was sealed to form a simple three-tank system. By 1983 the standard system had been modified to 13,905gal (63,216lit). Surprisingly, the cockpit went into production with an engineer station; early aircraft were modified for two-crew operation.On 4 August 1981 the Boeing-owned 767 prototype N767BA was rolled out. Flight testing began on 26 September 1981. By then the price to new customers had reached $50 million, and thrust required had begun to climb. At rollout the JT9D-7R4 had been uprated to 48,000lb (21,773kg); General Electric had offered the CF6-80A at the same thrust, but that was just the start.

767-200ER

The 767 was certificated with the JT9D engine in July 1982. The first customer delivery, to United, was on

767

19 August 1982. The first CF6-80A-engined aircraft was delivered to Delta on 25 October. By then the JT9D-7R4E4 and CF6-80A2 were flat-rated at 50,000lb (22,680kg). There was a second centre-section tank, raising total capacity to 17,029gal (77,412lit). On 1 June 1984 the first 767-200ER was delivered 7,500 miles (12,070km) to Ethiopian Airlines at Addis Ababa, the longest flight by a commercial twin-jet.

767-300

In February 1983 Boeing announced this stretched version, with a 10ft 1in (3.07m) plug ahead of the wing and 11ft (3.35m) added behind. This increased mixed-class seating from 224 to 269. Structure and main landing gear were strengthened. In 1987 British Airways ordered 11 (increased to 25) with the RB.211-524H.

767-300ER

Initially this extended-range version had the same extra centre-section tank as the -200ER, but the availability of more powerful engines enabled MTO weight to be increased. Options eventually included the RB.211-524H, and the significantly upgraded G/H-T version, also the PW4060 and CF6-80C2B6, both rated at 60,000lb (27,216kg). These engines allowed the second centre-section tank to be enlarged, to a capacity of 20,100gal (91,379lit).

767 Military

As part of the Strategic Defense Initiative, the original prototype was rebuilt as the AOA (Airborne Optical Adjunct) aircraft. First flown in this form on 21 August 1987, it featured an enormous dorsal cupola housing sensors for detecting ICBMs, requir-ing the addition of two ventral tail fins. This aircraft became the AST (Airborne Surveillance Testbed). In December 1992 Japan ordered four 767-AWACS. Based on the 767-200ER, the fuselage houses the Northrop Grumman APY-2 radar, with antennas in a rotodome similar to that of the E-3. Engines are the CF6-80C2. The first aircraft was delivered in March 1998. Unit price has been published as $403 million. Boeing expects to sell a further 20, plus 75 of other 767 military derivatives. One 767 has been modified by E-Systems as a medevac aircraft for the US Civil Reserve Air Fleet.

767 Freighter

In January 1993 UPS ordered 30 plus 30 options of the General Market Freighter version. This has no cabin windows, a reinforced wing, landing gear and cargo floor, with provision for loading 24 containers.

767-400ER

This introduces a remarkable further fuselage stretch, with an 11ft 0³⁄₄in (3.36m) plug ahead of the wing and a 10ft 0³⁄₄in (3.07m) plug aft. With this doubly-stretched version Boeing has come some way to equalling the 440-seat capacity of the A330 by offering a very long cabin seating 305 in two-class. Other modifications include a reinforced wing with a 14ft 6in (4.42m) increase in span, plus highly swept 7ft 5in (2.26m) winglets, an increase in underfloor cargo volume, longer and stronger main landing gears, 120kVA alternators, and a more powerful APU. On 20 March 1997 Delta launched the 400ER with an order for 21, first delivery due in May 2000.

DATA FOR 767-200:

Span	**156ft 1in (47.57m)**
Length	**159ft 2in (48.51m)**
Wing area	**3,050 sq ft (283.3m²)**
Operating weight empty	**175,300-176,200lb (79,515-79,923kg)**
Maximum takeoff weight	**282,000-300,000lb (127,913-136,078kg)**
Cruising speed	**Mach 0.8** *equal at initial cruise altitude of 40,400ft (12,315m) to 528mph (850km/h)*
Design range	**2,787-3,783 miles (4,485-6,088km)**

DATA FOR 767-300:

Dimensions unchanged, except:	
Length	**180ft 3in (54.94m)**
Operating weight empty	**191,700-192,100lb (86,955-87,135kg)**
Maximum takeoff weight	**345,000-351,000lb (156,490-159,210kg)**
Cruising speed	**Mach 0.8** *but at initial 36,500ft*
Design range	**4,603-4,902 miles (7,408-7,889km)**

DATA FOR 767-300ER:

Dimensions as 767-300.	
Operating weight empty	**198,800-199,600lb (90,175-90,535kg)**
Maximum takeoff weight	**387,000-400,000lb (175,540-181,435kg)**
Cruising speed	**Mach 0.8**
	equal at initial 34,100ft (10,394m) to 532mph (857km/h)
Design range	**6,289-6,760 miles (10,121-10,880km)**

DATA FOR 767-400ER:

Span	**170ft 7in (51.99m)**
Length	**201ft 4in (61.37m)**
Wing area	*not published.*
Operating weight empty	*about* **238,000lb (108 tonnes)**
Maximum takeoff weight	**450,000lb (204,120kg)**
Cruising speed	**Mach 0.8**
Range	*about* **6,470 miles (10,412km)** *with 305 passengers*

TWINJET, TWINJET, MEGASTAR

The genesis of the "Triple-7" is complex. One account says "studies went back to late 1986", but in fact the designation was allotted to a study programme on 18 February 1978, along with the numbers 757 and 767. At that time the 777-100 (medium-range) and 777-200 (long-range) were simply heavier stretched versions of 767, retaining the narrow 198in body diameter but with an even larger wing.

Boeing had so many customers that it was often hard-pressed to keep up with market demand. It had little need to ponder over the magnitude of the gap between the 767's 198in and the 256in of the 747. However, by the 1980s the Airbus wide-bodies were at last offering serious competition, with their carefully optimised figure of 222in (5.64m). By 1985 Boeing returned to consider what might be a better twin-aisle fuselage, not only to fight Airbus in the near term but also to meet airline requirements into the next century. Super-stretched 767Xs

failed to excite possible customers, and in 1988 Boeing even asked for opinions on a grotesque humpbacked 767X with a full-length double deck!

At Christmas 1988 Boeing decided that the 777 would not be any kind of 767X but an all-new twin-engined design, with a body diameter greater than that of the Airbus rivals.

Though this aircraft was going to demand engines with takeoff thrust from 72,000lb (32,660kg) upwards, there was an instant response by all three big engine manufacturers. Pratt launched a new family of PW4000 engines with a 112in (2,845mm) fan, Rolls launched the Trent 800 series with a 110in (2,794mm) fan and GE launched the biggest engine in the world, the GE90, with a 123in (3,124mm) fan. Subsequently Pratt and GE both said: "Never again will all three scramble for one airplane!"

The go-ahead came on 15 October 1990, when United ordered 34 plus 34 options (it simultaneously added another 60 747s, powered like the 777s by Pratt). By this time Boeing had assembled an unprecedented force of over 200 all-

That's not a plastic kit model of the 247D - today Boeing builds 'em bigger.

digital design teams. As the estimated cost of development was $4 billion (actually an under-estimate) it also signed up an international group of risk-bearing airframe constructors. These include Mitsubishi, Kawasaki and Fuji (who together make most of the fuselage). The 777 Division moved from Renton to Everett, where the world's largest building was extended by a further 50 per cent, and also added a completely new plant south of Tacoma to build 777 tails.

Boeing had defined aircraft for what it called the A Market (US domestic, 353 passengers, range 5,297 miles), B Market (intercontinental, 280 passengers, 7,600 miles) and an even heavier C Market version for very long thin routes. These ideas resulted in following versions:

777-200

Designed to seat from 305 to 440 passengers, fuselage diameter is 244in (6.2m), and cabin length 161ft 1in (49.1m). Underfloor holds can accept standard LD3 containers, total volume being 5,656 cu ft (160.2m^3)

Like that of the 767, the wing was deliberately made overlarge. It was also exceptionally thick and without winglets, and with ±-chord sweepback of 31.6°. Wing movables follow traditional practice, with two differences: Boeing at last adopted full fly-by-wire flight controls, and when the flaps are lowered the small inboard all-speed ailerons droop by displacing their neutral setting. As before, selecting flaps also unlocks narrow-chord outboard ailerons. As on the 767, the inboard flaps, at 90°

to the fuselage, are double-slotted (not triple), and the large outboard flaps are only single-slotted.

Concerned over congestion at airport gates, Boeing offer a unique feature: folding wings. From the outset the 777 has been offered with the ability to unlatch eight pins and rotate the outer 21ft 3in (6.48m) of each wing vertically upwards by a hydraulic motor. So far no customer has requested either this option or structural provision for fitting it later.

The tail comprises trimming tailplanes, each with a one-piece elevator, a fixed fin and a one-piece rudder with a tab. CFRP skins are used throughout, and the movable surfaces have honeycomb interiors. .

The heaviest engine is the GE90, weighing 16,664lb (7,559kg). The PW4084 weighs 14,920lb (6,768kg), and the PW4090 15,585lb (7,069kg). The R-R Trent 800 series all weigh about 13,133lb (5,957kg). All these engines are available with takeoff thrust up to 92,000lb (41,731kg).

Centre, main and reserve integral tanks are all inboard of the outer ailerons (the intended wing-fold line), the standard capacity being 25,813gal (117,348lit). Each engine drives a 120kVA constant-speed alternator, with back-up alternators driven by the specially designed high-power GTCP331 APU in the tailcone and a drop-down ram-air turbine. The main hydraulic pumps are not engine-mounted but located in the rear part of the composite wing/body

fairing, where they are driven by engine bleed-air turbines. This is a remarkable throwback to B-52 philosophy. Boeing's ARINC 629 data-bus, using twisted pairs of wires, has provided what amounts to dual-triplex flight-control redundancy – dramatically reducing the numbers and weights of wires and connectors. The cockpit resembles that of the 747-400, with a single row of five Honeywell 18in (203mm) displays.

The first aircraft, N7771, was rolled out in Boeing livery on 9 April 1994. Powered by PW4084 engines, it began flight testing on 12 June 1994. Certification of the troubled GE90 engine was finally granted on 2 February 1995. The Pratt-engined 777 was FAA/JAA-certificated on 19 April 1995; the first delivery, to United, was made on 15 May 1995, with revenue service starting on 7 June.The GE aircraft was certificated on 9 November 1995, followed by the Trent-777 on 3 April 1996. On 2 April 1997 a Trent-powered 777 landed at Boeing Field having set a record of 41h 59min for the eastbound circumnavigation, with a single refuelling stop at Kuala Lumpur; this flight also set a great-circle distance record at 11,815 miles (19,014km) non-stop.

777-200IGW

The Increased Gross Weight version has a greatly enlarged centre tank holding an additional 11,407gal (51,860lit). With other minor changes, fuel capacity is 37,653gal

(171,176lit). The first, for BA, flew on 7 October 1996, and the first with the Trent 892, for Emirates, on 21 November 1996. The 777-200IGW+ has a further increase in fuel capacity.

777-200X

Engines in the 100,000lb (45,360kg) category make possible this ultra-long-haul version, with a fuel tank in the aft cargo hold.

777-300

Authorised on 26 June 1995, this could become the preferred variant. It features a 17ft 6in (5.33m) plug ahead of the wing and a 15ft 9in (4.80m) plug behind, making it the longest airliner (apart from airships) in history. Capacity varies from 368

up to 550 all-tourist. Features include a strengthened landing gear and inboard wing, a tailskid to protect the rear fuselage, and cameras on the tailplanes and wing/body fairing to assist manoeuvring round airports. The first 777-300, a Trent-engined aircraft for Cathay Pacific, first flew on 16 October 1997. Boeing say "Compared with a 747-100 the 777-300 carries almost the same payload further, for two-thirds of the fuel and with maintenance costs reduced by 40 per cent".

777-300X

Combines the fuel capacity of the Dash-200X with the fuselage of the 777-300, together with reinforced tail surfaces and further-strengthened wings with extended tips.

DATA FOR 777-200:	
Span	**199ft 11in (60.93m)**
Length	**209ft 1in (63.73m)**
Wing area	**4,605 sq ft (427.8m²)**
Weight empty	**306,500-306,800lb (139,025-139,160kg)**
Maximum takeoff weight	**506,000-545,000lb (229,520-247,210kg)**
Cruising speed	**Mach 0.84**
	equal at all optimum heights to 554mph (892km/h)
Range	**4,154-5,472 miles (6,685-8,806km)**
	with 375 two-class passengers

DATA FOR 777-200IGW:	
Dimensions as 777-200	
Weight empty	**314,000-315,300lb (142,430-143,015kg)**
Maximum takeoff weight	**580,000-590,000lb (263,085-267,620kg)**
Cruising speed	**Mach 0.84**
Range	**6,663-6,968 miles (10,723-11,213km)**
	with 305 three-class passengers

Curtained cabin divider
First-class passenger seating, six-abreast, 30-seats
Cabin window panels
Fuselage frame and stringer structure
Pressure relief outflow valves
Forward underfloor cargo hold
LD3 baggage containers, 24 in forward hold
Outward opening cargo door
Cabin wall trim panelling
ATC antenna
Forward cabin conditioned-air distribution ducting
Mid cabin dividing bulkhead
Anti-collision beacon (red)
VHF antenna
Central galley unit, Business-class
Sidewall toilet compartment, port and starboard
Forward cabin door/emergency exit
Wing/nacelle inspection light
Conditioned-air riser ducts to overhead distribution
Business-class passenger seating, seven-abreast, 84-seats
44 Forward fuselage 17ft 6in (5.13m) stretch section, ten-frames longer than series -200 aircraft

45 Cabin wall insulation blankets
46 Carbon-fibre composite floor beams
47 Conditioned-air distribution manifold
48 Forward wing spar to fuselage attachment main frame
49 Wing centre section carry-through structure
50 Centre section integral fuel tankage
51 Mid cabin doorway/emergency exit, additional to -200
52 Machined floor beams above wing centre section
53 Centre fuselage frame and stringer structure
54 SATCOM No 1 high gain antenna
55 Starboard wing integral fuel tank
56 Nacelle pylon rear mounting strut
57 Pylon mounted hydraulic reservoir; triple system
58 Inboard leading edge slat segment
59 Gap sealing Krueger flap
60 Thrust reverser cascades, open

61 Starboard engine nacelle
62 Nacelle pylon, 'short' version for GE and P & W engines
63 Wing tank dry bay
64 Wing stringers
65 Skin panelling
66 Fuel venting channels
67 Vent surge tank
68 Leading edge slat drive shaft and gearboxes
69 Roller mounted slat guide rails with geared arc track
70 Outboard six-segment leading edge slats
71 Starboard navigation (green) and strobe (white) lights
72 Rear position light (white)
73 Starboard aileron
74 Aileron dual hydraulic power units
75 Fuel jettison
76 Starboard outer spoiler panels
77 Flap hinge control linkage, screw-jack operated
78 Outboard single-slotted flap
79 No 11 (and No 4 port) spoiler panels limited travel

80 Inboard drooping aileron (flaperon)
81 Flap drive torque shaft
82 Screw-jack right-angle gearbox
83 Inboard flap hinge control linkage
84 Inboard spoiler panels
85 Inboard double-slotted flap segment
86 ADF antennas
87 Rear wing spar to fuselage attachment main frame
88 Pressure floor above wheel bay
89 Main wheel bay door hydraulic jack
90 Port main undercarriage wheel bay
91 Flap drive motor
92 Central hydraulic reservoir
93 Engine fire suppression bottles
94 Tourist-class nine-abreast passenger seating, 135-seats in mid cabin
95 ATC mode antenna
96 Rear fuselage 15ft 9in (4.7m) stretch section, eight frames longer than -200 aircraft
97 Overhead baggage lockers
98 Cabin wall trim/lighting panels
99 Passenger service units
100 Rear cabin conditioned-air distribution ducting
101 Tourist-class cabin divider and toilet compartments
102 Optional No 2 SATCOM high-gain antenna
103 Rear cargo door
104 Rear underfloor cargo hold
105 LD3 baggage containers, 20 in rear hold
106 Rear tourist-class cabin seating, 118 passengers

107 Fuselage skin panelling
108 Fin root fillet
109 Aluminium alloy leading edge skin
110 Glass-fibre leading edge structure
111 Toughened carbon-fibre reinforced plastic (CFRP) two-spar fin torsion box structure
112 HF antenna coupler
113 Starboard trimming tailplane
114 Starboard elevator
115 TV low-band antenna
116 TV high band antenna
117 Glass-fibre fin tip fairing
118 VOR localiser antenna
119 Static dischargers
120 Rudder
121 CFRP rudder structure
122 Rudder triple hydraulic actuators
123 Rudder trim tab
124 Auxiliary Power Unit (APU) air intake, open

125 AlliedSignal GTCP331-500 APU
126 Rear strobe light (white)
127 APU exhaust
128 Port elevator
129 Elevator CFRP structure
130 Static dischargers
131 Port trimming tailplane
132 CFRP two-spar tailplane torsion box structure
133 Optional fin 'logo' lights
134 Glass-fibre reinforced plastic (GFRP) leading edge structure with aluminium alloy leading edge skin
135 Tailplane pivot mountings
136 Hinge aperture sealing plate
137 Spar box centreline joint
138 Tailplane trim screw jack and hydraulic motor
139 Rear pressure dome
140 Rear cabin galley unit
141 Cockpit voice and flight recorder stowage
142 Central and sidewall toilet compartments
143 Rear cabin doorway/emergency exit, port and starboard
144 Rear fuselage pressurization outflow valve
145 Underfloor potable and waste water tanks
146 Rear bulk cargo hold
147 Rear cabin window panels
148 Tourist-class section mid-cabin door/emergency exit, port and starboard
149 Composite wing root trailing edge fillet
150 Hydraulic system air driven auxiliary pumps
151 Port inboard double-slotted flap
152 Inboard spoiler panels (2)
153 Flap inboard guide rail
154 Titanium main undercarriage support beam

155 Pre-closing mainwheel bay doors
156 Main undercarriage leg pivot mounting
157 Spoiler hydraulic jacks
158 Port flaperon
159 Flap CFRP structure
160 Port outboard spoiler panels (5)
161 Flap hinge fairings
162 Outboard single-slotted flap
163 Port fuel jettison
164 Aileron CFRP structure
165 Port outboard aileron
166 Static dischargers
167 Rear position light (white)
168 Wing tip fairing
169 Port strobe light (white)
170 Port navigation light (red)
171 Port leading edge slat segments
172 Leading edge slat rib structure
173 Wing panel access manholes
174 Bottom wing skin/stringer panel
175 Two-spar wing torsion box structure
176 Wing ribs
177 Port wing integral fuel tankage
178 Leading edge slat guide rail mounting ribs
179 Pressure refuelling/defuelling connections, starboard fitting optional
180 Slat de-icing air duct
181 Six-wheel main undercarriage bogie
182 Steerable rear pair of wheels
183 Main under-carriage leg strut
184 Hydraulic retraction jack
185 Side breaker strut
186 Ventral air conditioning pack, port and starboard
187 Engine bleed air ducting to air conditioning system
188 Landing and runway turn-off lights
189 Composite wing leading edge root fairing
190 Conditioning system heat exchanger air intake
191 Leading edge slat drive motor

192 Inboard leading edge slat segment
193 Nacelle pylon attachment fitting
194 Port nacelle pylon 'long' version for RR Trent engine
195 Nacelle strake
196 CFRP engine cowlings
197 Intake lip bleed air de-icing
198 Rolls-Royce Trent 800 turbofan engine
199 Accessory equipment gearbox
200 Fan casing
201 FADEC controller
202 Forward engine mounting
203 Engine bleed air pre-cooler
204 Thrust strut
205 Engine turbine section
206 Rear engine mounting
207 Core engine (hot stream) exhaust nozzle
208 Fan air (cold stream) exhaust duct
209 Thrust reverser cascades and blocker doors
210 Oil cooler
211 Hinged side cowling panels
212 Pratt & Whitney PW 4098 alternative engine
213 Core engine mounted accessory equipment gearbox and oil tank
214 General Electric GE90-100B alternative engine
215 Engine mounting pad and thrust struts

Bell/Boeing V-22 Osprey

1 Three-bladed main rotor/propeller
2 Glassfibre spinner
3 Engine air intake
4 Wing/pylon actuator fairing
5 Blade root cuff/hinge fairing
6 Graphite/ glassfibre composite blade construction
7 Honeycomb core trailing edge
8 Leading-edge anti-erosion sheath
9 Starboard two-segment elevons
10 Elevon carbonfibre composite rib construction
11 Elevon sealing vane cam linkage
12 Starboard engine IR suppression exhaust duct
13 Hinged elevon vane/sealing panel
14 Starboard rotor interconnecting drive shaft
15 Elevon hydraulic power units, two per elevon
16 Graphite/epoxy wing rib and spar construction
17 Starboard wing auxiliary fuel tanks (four), 500lb (227kg) capacity each
18 Leading-edge panel honeycomb core construction
19 Leading-edge pneumatic de-icing boot
20 Fuel feed tank, port and starboard, 675lb (306kg) capacity each

21 Starboard engine pylon support bearing
22 Pylon actuating screw jack
23 Screw jack hydraulic motor and support bearing
24 Screw jack housing
25 Starboard main proprotor blades, folded position
26 Door-mounted rescue hoist/winch
27 Cockpit roof glazing
28 Titanium windscreen framing
29 Windscreen panel electrically de-iced
30 Windscreen wipers
31 Pitot heads (three)
32 Composite nose compartment construction
33 Sloping front bulkhead
34 Flight refuelling probe
35 Hughes AN/AA-16 Forward Looking Infra-Red (FLIR) turret
36 FLIR turret swivelling mounting
37 Radome
38 Texas Instruments AN/APQ-174 terrain-following multifunction radar
39 Radar equipment pack
40 Nose undercarriage pivot fixing
41 Taxiing lamp
42 Menasco Canada steerable nose undercarriage leg

43 Twin nosewheels, aft retracting
44 Nosewheel doors
45 Forward radar warning antennas
46 Static port
47 Downward vision window
48 Rudder pedals
49 Control column/ cyclic control lever
50 Thrust/power control lever (collective)
51 Multifunction glass-panel cockpit displays
52 Instrument console
53 Instrument panel shroud
54 Pilot's seat
55 ILS glideslope antenna
56 Starboard avionics equipment rack
57 Co-pilot's seat
58 Adjustable, energy absorbing, seat mountings
59 Direct vision side window panel
60 Cockpit floor level
61 Underfloor control linkages
62 Window hatch emergency release
63 Jettisonable side window hatch
64 Sloping cockpit bulkhead
65 Tie-down shackle
66 Port avionics equipment racks
67 Fuselage top longeron
68 Composite fuselage frame construction
69 IFF antenna
70 TACAN antenna
71 Starboard side two-segment entry door and airstairs

72 Maintenance walkway
73 Wing/fuselage forward fairing
74 Electrical equipment compartment
75 Wing rotating screw jack
76 Wing fold latching point
77 Rotary carousel wing mounting ring frame
78 Wing mounting fuselage top deck
79 Cabin emergency exit hatch
80 Composite main cabin floor panels

81 Avionics cooling air intake grille
82 Air outlet vent
83 Forward external load hook
84 Port sponson fairing

85 Sponson fuel tank, 3,155lb (1,431kg) capacity, port and starboard
86 Fuel tank access panel
87 Fuel filler cap

88 Rear external load hook
89 Composite floor beam construction
90 Fold-away roller conveyor track
91 Cabin section main longeron
92 Cargo loading floor

93 Tie-down, energy absorbing load attachments
94 Cabin window panel
95 Folding troop seats, 12 per side
96 Wing front spar/carousel attachment joint

97 Machined wing mounting sub-frame and bracing struts
98 Rotary hydraulic and electrical services hub
99 Wing root rib
100 Rear spar/carousel attachment joint
101 Gearbox mounting beam
102 Gearbox mechanical lock and rotor brake

103 Generators, port and starboard
104 APU exhaust
105 Auxiliary power unit (APU)
106 Hinged gearbox fairing/access doors
107 Centre wing combining/trans-fer gearbox
108 Compressor
109 Oil cooler
110 Port engine interconnecting drive shaft
111 Compressor air intake
112 Oil cooler exhaust
113 Elevon external hinge
114 Rear cabin escape hatch
115 Rear fairing rotary guide rail
116 Wing/fuselage tail fairing
117 Cabin wall soundproofing lining
118 Ramp hydraulic actuator

119 VHF/UHF antenna
120 HF/SSB ant. rail
121 Ramp area roof escape hatch
122 Troop commander's communications antenna
123 Composite tail pylon construction
124 Starboard tailplane
125 Maintenance walkway
126 Starboard composite tailfin
127 Fin leading-edge pneumatic de-icing boot
128 Rudder horn balance
129 Static dischargers
130 Starboard rudder
131 One-piece elevator
132 Elevator hydraulic actuators (three)
133 Fin leading-edge rib construction
134 Port tailfin graphite/epoxy composite construction
135 Anti-collison light
136 Port rudder
137 Rudder hydraulic actuator
138 Rear radar warning antenna
139 Fin/tailplane attachment joints
140 Graphite/epoxy three-spar tailplane construction
141 Tailplane control system equipment
142 Ramp latch
143 Ramp aperture longeron
144 Cargo loading ramp
145 Port sponson tail fairing
146 Tie-down shackle
147 Port ramp hydraulic actuator

148 Air condit____ system equipmen____ 2,040lb (____ fuel tank ____ starboard
149 Elevon hy____ actuator
150 Elevon sh____ panel
151 Port outbo____ elevon
152 Port engin____ pylon supp____ bearing
153 Tilt axis ge____
154 Generator
155 Infra-Red (I____ suppressio____ exhaust air____
156 Exhaust du____ door actuat____
157 Variable geometry exhaust du____
158 Exhaust du____ doors
159 Cooling/mix____ air inlet
160 Engine fire ____ extinguisher
161 Engine turbi____ section
162 Allison T406____ 400 turbosh____ engine
163 Engine accessory equipment
164 Full Authority Digital Engine____ Control (FAD____
165 Intake particl____ separator
166 Tilt axis gear____ drive shaft
167 Gearbox oil c____
168 Pylon suppor____ bearing/gearb____ curvic couplin____
169 Swashplate hydraulic actuator (thre____
170 Oil cooler
171 Port navigatio____ light
172 Engine compressor intake
173 Engine power output shaft

Mike Badrocke

GO SELL IT TO THE MARINES

In several ways unique, this is the first tilt-rotor aircraft to go into production. The concept is not new; indeed one early tilt-rotor research aircraft, the Vertol 76, or VZ-2, became the Boeing Vertol 76 in 1960, when Boeing purchased the Vertol company. This aircraft had a turboprop, driving a huge propeller, under each of its rectangular wings, which were arranged to pivot 90° upwards for VTOL (vertical takeoff and landing). In 1955 Bell had flown the XV-3 with tilting rotors on the tips of fixed wings, and this layout was chosen for the Bell XV-15 research aircraft, first flown in May 1977.

The XV-15 demonstrated how a tilt-rotor can hover like a helicopter and also fly at over 300mph (483km/h) and manoeuvre impressively. In 1982 the Department of Defense authorised a JVX (Joint Services Vertical Lift Aircraft) programme, with the prospect of variants meeting the requirements of all the US

armed forces. This became the V-22.

Though the missions to be flown are diverse, all V-22 variants so far use the same basic airframe. From the outset, the JVX was seen as basically a transport, with a fuselage able to carry people or cargo, and with an installed power of about 12,000hp. The aircraft divides naturally into a fuselage/tail, for which Boeing Helicopters is responsible, and a superimposed wing/engine group, for which Bell Helicopter Textron is responsible.

The wing has a constant aerofoil profile, slight forward sweep and slight dihedral. The

The No 4 prototype, first flown at Wilmington, Delaware, on 21 December 1989, was the first to undertake operational type missions (in USMC markings).

trailing edge is fitted with two-section flaperons, which operate as both flaps and ailerons. On each tip is a 6,150shp Allison T406-400 turboshaft engine. Each drives a front gearbox coupled to a unique "proprotor" with three enormous blades made of composite materials, with a diameter twice as great as any normal propeller. At the back of the gearbox a shaft carried

back across the engine drives another gearbox connected to shafts passing through the wing linking both engines. Thus, failure of either engine still enables the remaining engine to drive both proprotors, but with reduced power.

In cruising flight the engine nacelles are horizontal and the proprotors act as propellers. The fly-by-wire flight controls drive the fully powered flaperons, elevators and two rudders in the usual way. At the destination the pilot can command the engine nacelles to rotate upwards through an angle up to 97.5°. This slows the V-22 to a hover, by which time the pilot's flight controls have automatically been transferred to the proprotors. Special swashplate controls enable the pilot to vary the pitch of the blades in three ways. By applying variation in cyclic pitch of both rotors together the fuselage can be tilted nose-up or nose-down. By varying cyclic pitch differentially the nose can be swung left or right. By varying collective pitch differentially the V-22 can be rolled to left or right.

For shipboard operations the V-22 can be folded into a compact space hardly bigger than the fuselage. Having arrived in the helicopter mode, the proprotors are power-folded so that the blades all point towards each other above the wing. Second, the nacelles are rotated to the horizontal position, so that the blades are in front of the leading edge. Third, the wing is rotated clockwise through 90° to lie fore-and-aft above the fuselage.

The rest of the V-22 is conventional. The fuselage, made like other parts partly of composites and partly of light alloys, has the side-by-side cockpit in the nose, and a

main cabin about 6ft (1.83m) square in cross-section, with a full-width rear ramp door and another door at the front on the right. The main units of the twin-wheel landing gears retract into large side sponson fairings which also house the crash-resistant fuel tanks with a total capacity of 1,022gal (4,647lit). Capacity can be brought up to a total of 1,678gal (7,627lit) using tanks in the wing.

Typical payloads include 24 combat-equipped troops facing inwards, plus two gunners, or 12 litter casualties plus medics, or a cargo load of 20,000lb (9,072kg). Cargo tiedowns are designed to absorb energy, and all seats are stressed to be called "crashworthy". The

flight crew, typically three, have armour. The whole machine is equipped for sustained independent operations in all weathers. Comprehensive navaids are backed up by multifunction radar with terrain-following or terrain-avoidance capability, a FLIR (forward-looking infra-red) and laser ranger, rescue hoist and flight-refuelling probe. Various weapon fits have been studied, but so far no customer has specified any.

The main customer is the Marine Corps, which is to receive up to 425 MV-22A Ospreys starting in June 1999. The MV-22A will replace helicopters in the assault transport mission. Next, in 2003, the Air Force will begin to receive 50

CV-22A long-range special-missions aircraft. Third, from 2010, the Navy is to receive 48 HV-22A Ospreys configured for CSAR (combat search and rescue), special warfare and fleet logistics. The Navy has also studied how an ASW (anti-submarine warfare) SV-22A could replace the S-3B Viking, but without taking a decision. The Army is not at present due to receive Ospreys, but its requirement for medevac, special operations and combat assault support remains.

Few aircraft have ever been subjected to so many "reviews". The five prototypes, first flown between 19 March 1989 and June 1991, have done everything required of them. Despite this, political opponents have repeatedly tried to get the programme scaled down or abandoned. In many cases critics have ignored the colossal difference in speed, altitude, range and payload capability between the V-22 and conventional helicopters. By early 1998 the programme was at last on track for deliveries of the MV-22A and CV-22A. Once fully established, export sales are virtually certain.

DATA FOR MV-22A:

Span over proprotors	**83ft 10in (25.55m)**
Proprotor diameter	**38ft 0in (11.58m)**
Length	**57ft 4in (17.47m)** excluding flight-refuelling probe
Combined area of proprotors	**2,268.2sq ft (210.72m²)**
Weight empty	**32,628lb (14,800kg)** basic MV-22A
Maximum takeoff weight	**47,500lb (21,546kg)** VTO
	60,500lb (27,442kg) STO
Maximum cruising speed	**397mph (638km/h)**
Range	**1,382 miles (2,224km)**
	VTO with 12,000lb (5,443kg) payload
	2,073 miles (3,336km) short takeoff, max payload

ANOTHER BOEING 717

In the Introduction it was stated that Boeing purchased McDonnell Douglas mainly because of the latter's valuable defence and space business. However, the Douglas commercial jets were no small acquisition. After an exhaustive analysis of the Douglas products, markets and costs, the new management decided to terminate the MD-80/ MD-90, but to continue to offer the MD-11F freighter, and to pursue aggressive marketing of the MD-95. Instead of competing with established Boeing products, this aircraft extends the range downwards. Boeing have renamed it the 717, despite the active existence of many hundreds of 717s of an earlier generation.

Powered by two BMW Rolls-Royce BR715 turbofans, flexibly rated at from 18,500-21,000lb (8,392-9,526kg), the 717 is the ultimate development of the aft-engined jets which began with the DC-9 in 1963. Features include a fuselage of almost circular section

with a diameter of 142in (3.61m), a wing swept at 24.5° at the ¼-chord line with full-span slats and double-slotted flaps, manually operated ailerons and spoiler/airbrakes, a T-tail with manual elevators but a powered rudder, very short twin-wheel landing gears, integral tanks between the spars for 3,056gal (13,892lit), and a two-pilot cockpit with a single row of 8 x 8in (203 x 203mm) displays.

Douglas offered the standard MD-95-30, an MD-95-30ER with 3,997gal (18,170lit) of fuel (reducing underfloor hold volume from 945 cu ft, 26.8m³, to 689 cu ft, 19.5m³), and a stretched MD-95-50 to seat 130. Boeing consider that the latter would compete against the 737-600, and have modified the programme:

717-200

This is the baseline aircraft, previously the MD-95-30. Typical two-class seating is 106. Production at Long Beach is supported by many international suppliers. The original order for 50 plus 50 options was signed by ValuJet (subsequently restarted as AirTran).

Formerly Douglas, Long Beach is the Boeing facility from where the first 717 emerged in May 1998.

A second order, for six, came from Bavaria. Boeing will keep production at Long Beach, and hope to offer this aircraft at $18 million. The first was rolled out on 19 May 1998,

and is scheduled to be certificated in June 1999. Data below are for this version.

717-100

Boeing are investigating the market for this 70/80-seat version, possibly to be priced as low as $16 million. Boeing estimate the total 717 market at 2,500 by 2020.

DATA FOR 717-200:	
Span	**93ft 3.5in (28.44m)**
Length	**124ft 0.5in (37.81m)**
Wing area	**1,000.7 sq ft (92.97m²)**
Weight empty	**67,870lb (30,786kg)**
Maximum takeoff weight	**114,000lb (51,710kg).**
Cruising speed	**Mach 0.76**
	equal at typical heights to 504mph (811km/h)
Design range	**1,780 miles (2,865km)** *with 106 passengers*

BOEING SIKORSKY RAH-66 COMANCHE

THEY BUILT THE COMPUTER GAME

In 1981 the US Army decided the time was right to invite industry to propose concepts for an LHX (Light Helicopter Experimental). It was envisaged that 5,000, in several versions, would be required to replace the UH-1, AH-1, OH-6 and OH-58. To compete for this glittering prize, in 1985 Boeing Helicopters formed a joint team with Sikorsky Aircraft, later named the First Team. However, in 1987 the requirement was reduced to 2,096 for the scout/attack mission only, further cut to 1,292 in 1990. In April 1991 the First Team was selected, to build four prototypes, reduced to three in 1992 and to two in 1994.

After several changes of plan, which at one time delayed development indefinitely, a programme was eventually devised in 1995. This features only two prototypes, followed by six EOC (Early Operational Capability) machines for reconnaissance only. The production phase would probably restore the planned armament fits.

The basic RAH-66 helicopter is almost as large as an AH-64 Apache, but much lighter. It has two specially designed LHTEC T800 engines, each rated at 1,432shp, driving a five-blade "flex-beam" bearingless main rotor, and an eight-blade tail rotor mounted inside the fin as in the French Fenestron. The blades, fuselage and fixed T-tail are made mainly of composites. The fuselage comprises a central box beam surrounded by

equipment and the retractable main landing gears, all accessed by hinged doors. The cockpit seats the WSO (Weapon Systems Officer) behind and above the pilot. The MEP (Mission Equipment Package) has maximum commonality with the F-22A Raptor.

Inbuilt armament comprises a French Giat chin turret with a Lockheed Martin three-barrel 20mm gun, and a weapon bay on each side of the fuselage with a rapid-opening door carrying three Hellfire or six Stinger missiles, or other weapons. Stub wings can be added, under which can be hung four Hellfires, eight Stingers, rocket launchers or four fuel tanks for long-range self-deployment.

Sikorsky are responsible for the front fuselage and final assembly, and Boeing for the rest. The first prototype, 94-0327, flew at Sikorsky's West Palm Beach flight-test centre on 4 January 1996. Despite problems, development is proceeding, with the No 2 machine due to fly in September 1998. Production was to be ordered in 2003; this slipped to 2004, but Congress now wants the programme accelerated. The US Army's first unit is planned to form in 2007.

DATA FOR RAH-66	
Main-rotor diameter	**39ft 0.5in (11.9m)**
Length	**46ft 10.25in (14.28m)** *including rotor*
Length of fuselage	**43ft 3½in (13.2m)** *excluding gun*
Weight empty	**7,765lb (3,522kg)**
Maximum takeoff weight	**12,829lb (5,819kg)** *alternative mission*
	17,408lb (7,896kg) *self-deployment ferry*
Maximum speed	**201mph (324km/h)**
Endurance	**1,450 miles (2,333km)** *standard fuel 2½h*

**RAH-66
Comanche**

1 Pilot's night vision sensor
2 Rotating sensor turret
3 FLIR targeting system
4 Lockheed Martin/ Giat three-barrel

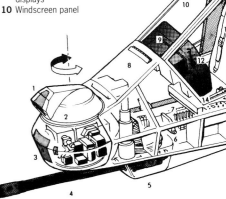

20mm cannon
5 Swivelling cannon mounting
6 Yaw control rudder pedals
7 Ammunition feed chute
8 Windscreen rain dispersal air duct
9 Shrouded instrument console, dual multi-function displays
10 Windscreen panel

11 Pilot's seat
12 Sidestick controller on right for dual triplex fly-by-wire system
13 Seat armour
14 Port side entry hatch

15 Collective pitch lever
16 Weapon Systems Officer's instrument console
17 Forward avionics equipment bay, port and starboard
18 Ammunition magazine,

normal load 320 rounds, maximum 500 rounds
19 Mainwheel door
20 Mainwheel, rebound position
21 Port mainwheel, undercarriage can be 'kneeled' for air transportation
22 Mainwheel bay

23 Hydraulic retraction jack/ shock absorber strut
24 WSO's seat
25 WSO's port side entry hatch
26 Starboard stub wing

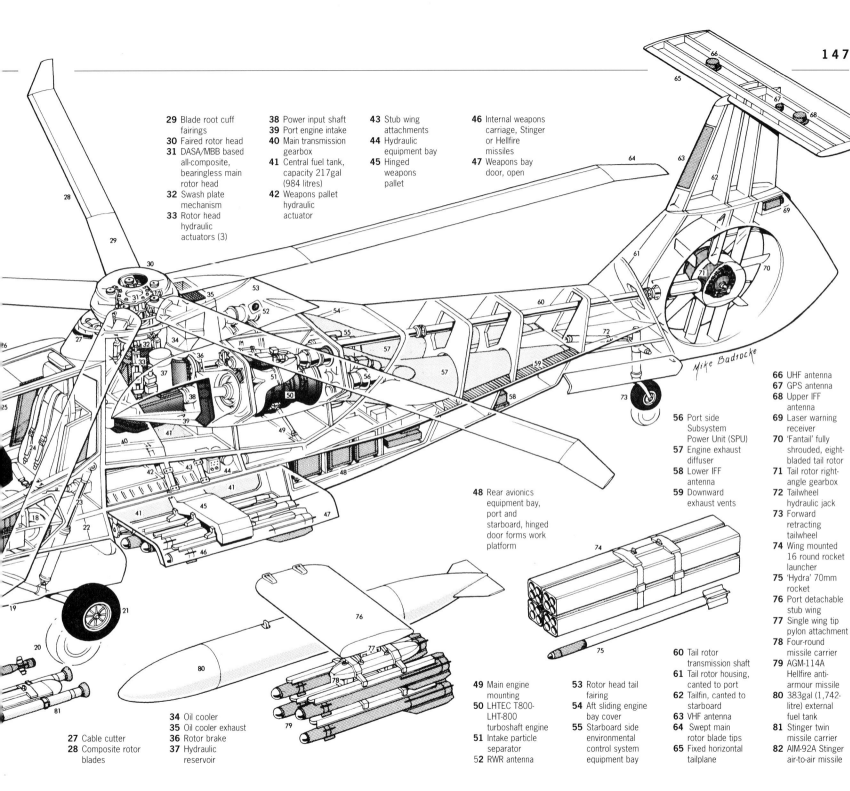

29 Blade root cuff fairings
30 Faired rotor head
31 DASA/MBB based all-composite, bearingless main rotor head
32 Swash plate mechanism
33 Rotor head hydraulic actuators (3)

38 Power input shaft
39 Port engine intake
40 Main transmission gearbox
41 Central fuel tank, capacity 217gal (984 litres)
42 Weapons pallet hydraulic actuator

43 Stub wing attachments
44 Hydraulic equipment bay
45 Hinged weapons pallet

46 Internal weapons carriage, Stinger or Hellfire missiles
47 Weapons bay door, open

48 Rear avionics equipment bay, port and starboard, hinged door forms work platform

56 Port side Subsystem Power Unit (SPU)
57 Engine exhaust diffuser
58 Lower IFF antenna
59 Downward exhaust vents

66 UHF antenna
67 GPS antenna
68 Upper IFF antenna
69 Laser warning receiver
70 'Fantail' fully shrouded, eight-bladed tail rotor
71 Tail rotor right-angle gearbox
72 Tailwheel hydraulic jack
73 Forward retracting tailwheel
74 Wing mounted 16 round rocket launcher
75 'Hydra' 70mm rocket
76 Port detachable stub wing
77 Single wing tip pylon attachment
78 Four-round missile carrier
79 AGM-114A Hellfire anti-armour missile
80 383gal (1,742-litre) external fuel tank
81 Stinger twin missile carrier
82 AIM-92A Stinger air-to-air missile

60 Tail rotor transmission shaft
61 Tail rotor housing, canted to port
62 Tailfin, canted to starboard
63 VHF antenna
64 Swept main rotor blade tips
65 Fixed horizontal tailplane

49 Main engine mounting
50 LHTEC T800-LHT-800 turboshaft engine
51 Intake particle separator
52 RWR antenna

53 Rotor head tail fairing
54 Aft sliding engine bay cover
55 Starboard side environmental control system equipment bay

34 Oil cooler
35 Oil cooler exhaust
36 Rotor brake
37 Hydraulic reservoir

27 Cable cutter
28 Composite rotor blades

BOEING SIKORSKY RAH-66 COMANCHE

X-32 JOINT STRIKE FIGHTER

FIGHTER FOR THE WORLD

Having – except for the Marine Corps – for 30 years sneered at the idea of a jet-lift STOVL (Short Take Off, Vertical Landing) combat aircraft, the US military establishment got round to serious consideration of it in late 1992. Boeing was one of five contenders in the Advanced Research Project Agency's CALF (Common Affordable Lightweight Fighter) competition, teamed with Pratt & Whitney for the engine (derived from the F119) and Rolls-Royce for the direct-lift system. This was realigned as the SSF (STOVL/CTOL Strike Fighter), which in November 1994 was merged by Congress into the JAST (Joint Advanced Strike Technology) programme. In late 1995 this was renamed JSF (Joint Strike Fighter). On 16 November 1996 Boeing Military Airplanes was named one of the two finalists, the other being Lockheed Martin.

The JSF programme is potentially the world's largest for a combat aircraft. Managed by the US Naval Air Systems Command, it was launched on the basis of a requirement for 3,218 aircraft, since reduced to 3,038. Of these, 2,036 would replace the F-16 in the Air Force, 300 would replace the A-6 and F-14 in the Navy, 642 would replace the AV-8B and F/A-18 in the Marine Corps, and 60 would replace the Sea Harrier in the Royal Navy.

Each contractor will build two prototypes, one CTOL (Conventional Take Off and Landing) and one STOVL. Thus, Boeing is now building two X-32 aircraft. Having been awarded two $32 million contracts during the CALF programme, Boeing is now working under a 51-month Concept Demonstration Program priced at $661.8 million.

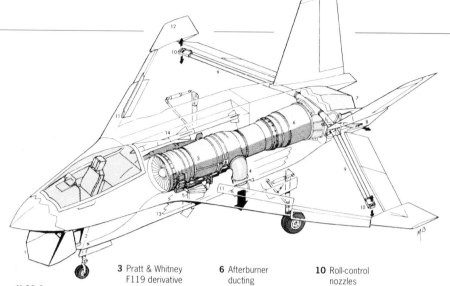

X-32 Concept Demonstrator

1 Translating cowl air intake, open position
2 Auxiliary intake slot
3 Pratt & Whitney F119 derivative engine
4 Rotating direct lift nozzles, STOL variants
5 Jet screen duct, anti-recirculation shield, STOL variant
6 Afterburner ducting
7 Two-dimensional pitch-vectoring propulsion nozzle
8 Yaw control nozzles, port and starboard
9 Roll-control bleed-air ducting
10 Roll-control nozzles
11 Vortex flaps, naval aircraft
12 Extended wing tip, USAF and US Navy aircraft
13 Lateral weapons bay, port and starboard

The basic X-32 is a compact blended-delta with no separate horizontal tail. The wing has inboard and outboard movable surfaces on both the leading and trailing edges. There is no fuselage above the wing. Above the trailing edge are two canted fins and rudders. The

long-stroke Messier-Dowty main landing gears retract backwards into underwing fairings. Armament of the CTOL versions include an internal gun and internal bays for two AIM-120A missiles and two 2,000lb Joint Direct Attack Munitions (1,000lb in the STOVL aircraft). All versions incorporate low-observable "stealth" features, and have an airframe made about 36 per cent from composites. Boeing estimate commonality between the different versions at 87 to 95 per cent.

The USAF requires an uncompromised CTOL version for operation from runways. At least in the first version, this

DATA FOR THE USAF VERSION:

Span	about **35ft (10.67m)**
Length	about **46ft (14m)**
Wing area	about **580 sq ft (53.9m²)**
Weight empty	about **23,000lb (10,433kg)**
Maximum takeoff weight	about **56,000lb (25,402kg)**
Maximum speed	about **Mach 1.6** equivalent at high altitude to about 1,050mph (1,690km/h)
Range/weapon load	highly variable depending on variant and mission but "2½ times that of the F-16 and F-18"

will be powered by a Pratt & Whitney augmented turbofan derived from the F119 but with a larger fan, raising takeoff thrust to about 40,000lb (18,144kg). General Electric's alternate (alternative) engine is the YF120-X, possibly able to reach 50,000lb (22,680kg). This engine features an LO-Axi (low-observable axisymmetric) nozzle claimed to be lighter and cheaper than previous variable-area nozzles. The GE engine could be fitted from the 72nd production aircraft.

The Navy requires a CTOL version for operation from carriers. This will be structurally strengthened for catapult launch and arrested landings. The wings would have upper-surface vortex flaps inboard of a mid-span hinge for the folding outer sections. There would be differences in the high-lift surfaces and flight controls.

The Marine Corps and Royal Navy will operate the STOVL version. This will be based on the USAF aircraft, but Pratt's SE614 engine will have three large integrally bladed rotors raising dry thrust to over 35,000lb (15,876kg). For jet lift the unaugmented jetpipe will

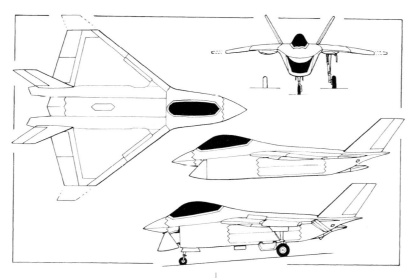

Boeing JSF: lower side-view shows the aircraft in STOVL configuration.

be closed, and the efflux ducted to twin retractable nozzles under the aircraft centre of gravity able to vector through about 100°. Rolls-Royce is contractor for the lift-nozzle module, and also for a jet screen to reduce hot-gas ingestion, and an auxiliary reaction-jet flight control system for use during STOVL operation. In 1997 the Air Force announced that it was considering switching 200-300 of its buy to this version for use in an air-expeditionary role. This would be valuable in reducing the unit price of this version.

In June 1995, at Tulalip near Seattle, Boeing began testing a 94-per-cent scale JSF powered by a YF119 engine. The results verified previous model testing. To assemble and

test the X-32 Boeing is setting up a JSF Center at Palmdale in the former B-1B plant. Both Boeing's X-32s will be STOVL-capable, but the first is expected to fly as a CTOL in late 1999, with the STOVL X-32 following in mid-2000.

It is expected that the EMD (Engineering and Manufacturing Development) phase will begin in the second quarter of 2001. The first EMD aircraft is likely to fly in 2004, followed by the start of operational testing in 2008. The LRIP (Low-Rate Initial Production) plan specifies 12 aircraft delivered in 2007, 24 delivered from late

the same year, 36 from 2008, 60 from 2009 and 110 from 2010.

The UK's involvement is almost certain to increase, as the RAF discovers that there is no other option for replacing the Jaguar and, later, the Tornado GR.4. By 1998 nine other countries had signified their interest in participating, starting with Australia, the Netherlands, Denmark and Norway. Involvement of foreign industrial partners is being discussed. British Aerospace, originally the partner of McDonnell Douglas, threw in its lot with Lockheed Martin. Perhaps it should have waited for McDonnell Douglas to become a Boeing company.

For the more distant future Boeing has studied a UTA (Unmanned Tactical Aircraft) derived from its CTOL JSF design. This appears likely to have a unit cost not much more than half the $30 million, which is the target for the USAF manned version. Another advantage would be that the manoeuvre envelope could be expanded from 9g to a sustained 20g or more. This version has a target operational service date of 2020-25.

INDEX